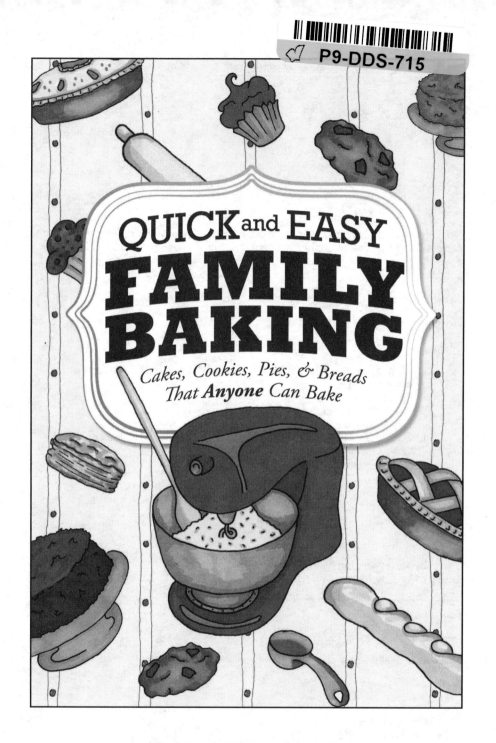

QUICK and EASY
FAMILY
BAKING

Cakes, Cookies, Pies, & Breads
*That **Anyone** Can Bake*

Cookbook Resources, LLC
Highland Village, Texas

Quick and Easy Family Baking
*Cakes, Cookies, Pies & Breads That **Anyone** Can Make*

Printed June 2012

International Standard Book Number: 978-1-59769-109-3

Library of Congress Control Number: 2011033041

Library of Congress Cataloging-in-Publication Data:

    Quick and easy family baking : cakes, cookies, pies & breads that anyone can make.
      p. cm.
   Includes bibliographical references and index.
   ISBN 978-1-59769-109-3 (alk. paper)
   1. Baking. 2. Quick and easy cooking. I. Cookbook Resources, LLC.
   TX765.Q53 2011
   641.81'5--dc23

                  2011033041

Cover by Rasor Design
Illustrations by Nancy Griffith

Edited, Designed, Published and Manufactured in the United States of America
Cookbook Resources, LLC
541 Doubletree Drive
Highland Village, Texas 75077

Toll free 866-229-2665

www.cookbookresources.com

Bringing Family and Friends to the Table

Quick and Easy Family Baking

There really is magic in every cookie jar no matter its size, color or shape. The magic jumps out of the jar and into the hands of kids (young or old), then straight into mouths that remember all the smells and flavors rolled into a few wonderful bites.

Baking is special, but it doesn't have to be a hassle. We've included some of the quickest, easiest dessert recipes in this quick and easy cookbook to help you with your own special kind of magic.

Breads, Brunches, Bars, Cookies, Cakes, Pies and Desserts fill these pages so you can enjoy choosing your favorites. There are also lots of ideas for quick and easy desserts so you don't have to bake all day.

Enjoy yourself and give your families the magic of the sights, smells and tastes right from your oven.

There's magic in that cookie jar...
your magic...
your homemade goodness.

Contents

Dedication

Cookbook Resources' mission is

Bringing Family and Friends to the Table.

We recognize the importance of shared meals as a means of building family bonds with memories and traditions that will last a lifetime. At mealtimes we share more than food. We share ourselves.

This cookbook is dedicated with gratitude and respect to all those who show their love by making home-cooked meals and bringing family and friends to the table.

Great memories begin with great food.

Baking Tips

❖ Always read recipes and ingredients before starting.

❖ Set out all the ingredients so that you can work quickly. Ingredients should be at room temperature unless the recipe states otherwise.

❖ Baking recipes are based on the use of large eggs.

❖ Leavening agents such as baking powder and baking soda activate as soon as they are moistened. Do not let cake and muffin batters or biscuit dough stand, but bake as soon as possible.

Continued next page...

Continued from previous page...

❖ Pastry bags and tips are wonderful when you have the time to make a cake or cupcake really special. You can make your own pastry bag with a medium-size plastic bag. Cut small hole in one of the bottom corners and use just like a regular pastry bag, squeezing from the top down. You don't have to have special tips unless you want pretty swirls and designs.

❖ Cookies are the easiest baked goods to make. They're great for the beginner.

❖ Check on doneness a few minutes before the time called for in the recipe.

❖ Insert a toothpick in the center of cakes, muffins or cupcakes to test for doneness. When the toothpick comes out clean, they're done. Keep in mind that the smaller the cupcake, the quicker it cooks. The longer it cooks, the drier it will be.

 The cake mix icon indicates recipes made with cake, muffin, brownie mixes, etc., for extra convenience.

Breakfast and Brunch

Gigantic German Pancake

½ cup flour	60 g
3 eggs, slightly beaten	
½ cup milk	125 ml
2 tablespoons butter, melted	30 g
Powdered sugar	
Maple syrup	

Preheat oven to 425° (220° C).

Beat flour and eggs in bowl. Stir in remaining ingredients and ¼ teaspoon salt.

Pour into sprayed 9-inch (23 cm) pie pan. Bake for 20 minutes. Pancake will puff into big bubbles while baking.

Cut into wedges and dust with powdered sugar. Serve with melted butter and maple syrup. Serves 3 to 4.

Family meals help children learn the basics of good nutrition and how to take care of themselves. Family meals don't have to big deals, but can be simple meals with basic nutrition. Children learn how to strive for good health and how they are responsible for themselves. Family meals provide a time for family traditions and family memories to grow.

Applesauce-Spice Muffins

Don't be scared by the number of ingredients. This is easy.

1 cup (2 sticks) butter, softened	225 g
1 cup packed brown sugar	220 g
1 cup sugar	200 g
2 eggs	
1¾ cups applesauce	445 g
2 teaspoons ground cinnamon	10 ml
1 teaspoon ground allspice	5 ml
½ teaspoon ground cloves	2 ml
2 teaspoons baking soda	10 ml
3½ cups flour	420 g
1½ cups chopped pecans	165 g

Preheat oven to 375° (190° C).

Cream butter, brown sugar and sugar in bowl.

Add eggs, applesauce, cinnamon, allspice, cloves, ½ teaspoon (2 ml) salt, baking soda and flour and mix well. Add pecans and stir well.

Pour into 28 sprayed or paper-lined muffin cups. Bake for 16 minutes. Makes 28 muffins.

In recent years, Gala apples, whose origin is New Zealand, were first introduced in 1965 and have become popular because of their sweet, sharp flavor. They are great for snacks, salad ingredients, pies or applesauce. Their pinkish-orange contrast with a yellow background.

Apricot-Pineapple Muffins

This is a winner!

⅓ cup finely cut dried apricots	50 g
½ cup (1 stick) butter, softened	115 g
1 cup sugar	200 g
1 egg	
1 (8 ounce) can crushed pineapple with juice	225 g
1¼ cups flour	150 g
½ teaspoon baking soda	2 ml
½ cup quick-cooking oats	40 g

 Preheat oven to 350° (175° C).

Cut apricots with kitchen shears and set aside.

Cream butter and sugar in bowl until smooth. Add egg and pineapple and beat well. Add flour, baking soda, oats and ½ teaspoon (2 ml) and mix well. Fold in apricots.

Spoon into sprayed muffin cups or use paper liners and bake for 20 minutes. Makes 12 muffins.

Muffin cups should be filled ⅔ to ¾ full. If you want "bakery style" muffins with a large mushroom shape, fill the muffin cups full.

Banana-Bran Muffins

1 cup Bran Flakes®	30 g
1 cup milk	250 ml
2 medium bananas, mashed	
⅓ cup canola oil	75 ml
1 cup flour	120 g
4 teaspoons baking powder	20 ml
¼ teaspoon baking soda	1 ml
⅔ cup sugar	135 g
1 egg	

 Preheat oven to 400° (205° C).

 Combine Bran Flakes®, milk, bananas and oil in bowl and mix and soften for 5 minutes.

 In separate bowl, sift flour, baking powder, baking soda and ½ teaspoon (2 ml) salt and add to banana mixture. Add sugar and egg and mix only until all combines.

Fill 12 sprayed, large-size muffin cups and bake for 16 to 20 minutes. Makes 12 muffins.

Always use the freshest ingredients available to get the best results. Be sure to check expiration dates, particularly leavening agents such as yeast, baking soda and baking powder. Be sure dairy and other perishable products are fresh.

Fresh Blueberry Muffins

1¼ cups sugar	250 g
2 cups flour	240 g
1½ teaspoons baking powder	7 ml
½ cup (1 stick) butter, softened	115 g
1 egg, beaten	
1 cup milk	250 ml
1½ cups fresh blueberries	225 g
½ cup chopped pecans	55 g

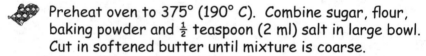

Preheat oven to 375° (190° C). Combine sugar, flour, baking powder and ½ teaspoon (2 ml) salt in large bowl. Cut in softened butter until mixture is coarse.

Stir in egg and milk and beat well. Gently fold in blueberries and pecans, but do not beat.

Spoon into muffin cups and bake for 35 minutes or until light brown. Makes 12 muffins.

Work quickly when preparing baking recipes. Many ingredients begin to work together immediately. Baking powder, for example, begins its leavening action as soon as it is moist. Make sure your pans and other equipment are ready, your ingredients are ready (at room temperature for most recipes), and your oven is preheating to the right temperature. Pre-measuring your ingredients will also help you work quickly.

 # Blueberry-Orange Muffins

1 (16 ounce) package blueberry muffin
   mix with blueberries, separated   455 g
2 egg whites
½ cup orange juice   125 ml
Orange marmalade

 Preheat oven to 375° (190° C). Combine muffin mix, egg whites and orange juice in bowl and break up any lumps.

 Drain and rinse blueberries; gently fold blueberries into batter. Pour into 8 muffin cups (with paper liners) about half full.

 Bake for 18 to 20 minutes or until toothpick inserted in center comes out clean. Spoon orange marmalade over top of hot muffins. Serves 8.

 # Gingerbread Muffins

1 (18 ounce) box gingerbread mix   510 g
1 egg
2 (1.5 ounce) boxes seedless raisins 2 (45 g)

 Preheat oven to 350° (175° C). Combine gingerbread mix, 1¼ cups (310 ml) lukewarm water and egg in bowl and mix well.

 Stir in raisins and pour into sprayed muffin cups half full. Bake for 20 minutes or until toothpick inserted in center comes out clean. Makes 12 to 14 muffins.

Ginger Muffins

¾ cup (1½ sticks) butter, softened	170 g
¾ cup sugar	150 g
¼ cup corn syrup	60 ml
¼ cup sorghum molasses	60 ml
2 eggs	
1 teaspoon baking soda	5 ml
½ cup buttermilk*	125 ml
2 cups flour	240 g
1 teaspoon ground ginger	5 ml
¼ teaspoon ground cinnamon	1 ml
¼ cup raisins	40 g
½ cup chopped pecans	55 g

Preheat oven to 350° (175° C). Combine butter, sugar, corn syrup and molasses in bowl and mix well. Add eggs and beat well.

In separate bowl, combine baking soda into buttermilk, add to butter-sugar mixture and beat. Add flour, pinch of salt, ginger and cinnamon and beat. Stir in raisins and pecans and mix well.

Pour into 20 to 24 sprayed muffin cups and bake for 16 to 18 minutes or more depending on size of muffins. Makes 20 to 24 muffins.

*TIP: To make buttermilk, mix 1 cup (250 ml) milk with 1 tablespoon (15 ml) lemon juice or vinegar and let stand for about 10 minutes.

Mayo Muffins

1 ¼ cups self-rising flour	155 g
3 tablespoons mayonnaise	45 g
1 cup milk	250 ml

 Preheat oven to 375° (190° C). Mix all ingredients in bowl and spoon into sprayed muffin cups.

 Bake for 20 minutes or until light brown. Serves 6.

Salad Muffins

⅓ cup sugar	70 g
⅓ cup oil	75 ml
¾ cup milk	175 ml
2 eggs	
2 cups biscuit mix	240 g

 Preheat oven to 400° (205° C). Combine sugar, oil and milk in bowl. Beat in eggs and biscuit mix.

 Mix well; mixture will be a little lumpy. Pour into sprayed muffin cups two-thirds full.

 Bake for about 10 minutes or until light brown. Serves 8.

Baked goods began with simple breads. Muffins, cakes, cookies, pastries, biscuits all owe their beginning to bread.

Hidden Secret Muffins

When people taste these muffins, someone always says,
"Yum. These are so good. What's in them?" And you'll say,
"It's a secret."

Filling:

1 (8 ounce) package cream cheese, softened	225 g
1 egg	
⅓ cup sugar	70 g
1 tablespoon grated orange peel	15 ml

 Preheat oven to 375° (190° C). Beat cream cheese, eggs, sugar and orange peel in bowl and set aside.

Batter:

1 cup (2 sticks) butter, softened	115 g
1¾ cups sugar	350 g
3 eggs	
3 cups flour	360 g
2 teaspoons baking powder	10 ml
1 cup milk	250 ml
1 teaspoon almond extract	5 ml
1 cup chopped almonds, toasted	190 g

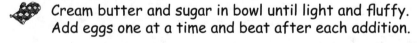 Cream butter and sugar in bowl until light and fluffy. Add eggs one at a time and beat after each addition.

Continued next page...

Continued from previous page...

 In separate bowl, combine flour and baking powder and add alternately with milk to butter-sugar mixture. Begin and end with flour. Add almond extract and fold in almonds.

 Fill 26 lightly sprayed muffin cups half full with batter. Spoon 1 heaping tablespoon (15 ml) filling in each muffin cup and top with muffin batter.

 Bake muffins for 20 to 25 minutes or until muffin bounces back when pressed or until they are light brown. Makes 26 muffins.

Familiar Mom-isms

Are you deaf?

Am I talking to a brick wall?

You will eat it... and you will like it.

*You're going to put out
an eye with that thing.*

A little birdy told me.

Apricot Coffee Cake

1 cup (2 sticks) butter, softened	225 g
1 (3 ounce) package cream cheese, softened	85 g
1½ cups sugar	300 g
2 eggs	
1 teaspoon vanilla	5 ml
1½ teaspoons baking powder	7 ml
2¼ cups flour	270 g
1 (20 ounce) can apricot pie filling	565 g

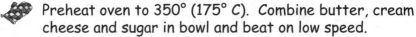 Preheat oven to 350° (175° C). Combine butter, cream cheese and sugar in bowl and beat on low speed.

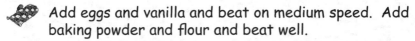 Add eggs and vanilla and beat on medium speed. Add baking powder and flour and beat well.

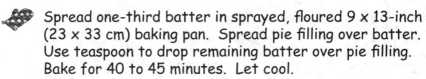 Spread one-third batter in sprayed, floured 9 x 13-inch (23 x 33 cm) baking pan. Spread pie filling over batter. Use teaspoon to drop remaining batter over pie filling. Bake for 40 to 45 minutes. Let cool.

Icing:

1½ cups powdered sugar	180 g
2 tablespoons milk	30 ml
2 tablespoons butter, melted	30 g
½ teaspoon almond extract	2 ml

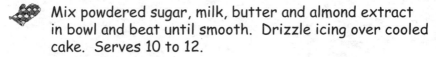 Mix powdered sugar, milk, butter and almond extract in bowl and beat until smooth. Drizzle icing over cooled cake. Serves 10 to 12.

TIP: This is great with other pie fillings as well.

Breakfast Cinnamon Cake

⅔ cup packed brown sugar	145 g
1 tablespoon grated orange peel	15 ml
2 (12 ounce) packages refrigerated cinnamon rolls	2 (340 g)

 Preheat oven to 375° (190° C).

 Combine brown sugar and orange peel in small bowl. Open cans of rolls (save frosting), cut each in quarters and coat each with cooking spray.

 Dip in sugar-orange mixture and arrange evenly in sprayed, floured 10-inch (25 cm) bundt pan. Gently press down on each. Bake for 35 minutes until light brown and about double in size.

 Cool slightly in pan. Invert serving plate on top of pan, hold plate and pan together with oven mitts and invert. Remove pan. Spread frosting unevenly over top of cake and serve warm. Serves 6.

The ancient Egyptians, Greeks, Romans, Chinese, Indians all made preserves and confections. Sugar was used as a preservative for fruit. These were primarily treats for the well-to-do. The availability of sugar for everyone is a relatively recent development in the last two centuries. By the Middle Ages, physicians had discovered that sugar made bad-tasting medicines easier to take — a practice that still exists with drugs today.

Cherry-Nut Breakfast Cake

1 (8 ounce) package cream cheese, softened	225 g
1 cup (2 sticks) butter, softened	225 g
1½ cups sugar	300 g
1½ teaspoons vanilla	7 ml
3 eggs	
2¼ cups flour	270 g
1½ teaspoons baking powder	7 ml
1 (10 ounce) jar maraschino cherries, drained	280 g
½ cup chopped pecans	55 g

 Preheat oven to 350° (175° C).

 Combine cream cheese, butter, sugar, vanilla and eggs in bowl and beat for 3 minutes. Add flour and baking powder and beat well.

 Cut each cherry into 3 or 4 pieces; then fold in cherries and pecans. Pour batter into sprayed, floured 9 x 13-inch (23 x 33 cm) baking pan and bake for 40 minutes.

Continued next page...

Family meals help children learn financial responsibility. They see how a family must live within their means and provide nutritional meals to avoid health problems like diabetes and heart disease. Eating out is more expensive, the food has more calories and the family time is lost. Eating out is for special occasions.

Continued from previous page...

Glaze:

1 ½ cups powdered sugar	180 g
2 ½ tablespoons milk	35 ml
2 tablespoons butter, melted	30 g
½ teaspoon almond extract	2 ml
½ cup chopped pecans	55 g

Just before cake is done, combine powdered sugar, milk, butter and almond extract in bowl. Glaze while cake is still warm and top with pecans. Serves 10 to 12.

The idea of sweets for breakfast wasn't a new one to the Europeans who settled in America. They brought recipes for sweet breads and sweet cakes and served them with coffee, a tradition they continued in their new lives.

German, Dutch and Scandinavian settlers often served coffee with cake and Scandinavian settlers kept coffee brewing on the stove throughout the day. This tradition was probably the origin of the coffee break and continues today.

Coffee Lover's Coffee Cake

2 cups flour	240 g
2 teaspoons instant coffee granules	10 ml
2 cups packed brown sugar	440 g
1 teaspoon ground cinnamon	5 ml
½ cup (1 stick) butter	115 g
1 (8 ounce) carton sour cream	225 g
1 teaspoon baking soda	5 ml
1 egg	
¾ cup chopped pecans	55 g

Preheat oven to 350° (175° C). Combine flour, instant coffee, brown sugar, ½ teaspoon salt and cinnamon in bowl and stir well.

Cut in butter until crumbly. Press half of mixture into sprayed 9-inch (23 cm) square pan.

In separate bowl, combine sour cream, baking soda and egg and mix well. Add to remaining crumb mixture and stir until dry ingredients are moist.

Pour mixture over crumb crust in pan. Sprinkle with pecans. Bake for 45 to 60 minutes. Serves 16.

Cakes should be cooled in pans for about 10 to 15 minutes before turning out on a wire rack to cool. Put a couple of paper towels on the rack to keep the wires from leaving an imprint on the cake or breaking the top of the cake.

 # Cranberry Coffee Cake

2 eggs
1 cup mayonnaise   225 g
1 (18 ounce) box spice cake mix   510 g
1 (16 ounce) can whole cranberry sauce   455 g
Powdered sugar

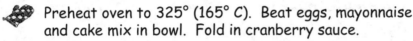

Preheat oven to 325° (165° C). Beat eggs, mayonnaise
and cake mix in bowl. Fold in cranberry sauce.

Pour into sprayed, floured 9 x 13-inch (23 x 33 cm)
baking pan. Bake for 45 minutes. Cake is done when
toothpick inserted in center comes out clean.

After cake cools, dust with sifted powdered sugar.
(If you would rather have icing than powdered sugar,
use prepared icing.) Serves 18.

French Apple Coffee Cake

This is an excellent cake to have on hand for Sunday morning or when you have out-of-town company. It is rich and moist and just needs a cup of steaming hot coffee to go with it.

¾ cup sugar	150 g
1 cup packed light brown sugar	220 g
⅔ cup buttermilk*	150 ml
2 eggs	
2½ cups flour	300 g
2 teaspoons baking soda	10 ml
2 teaspoons ground cinnamon	10 ml
1 (20 ounce) can apple pie filling**	565 g
¼ cup white raisins	40 g

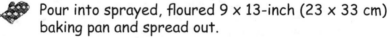 Preheat oven to 350° (175° C). Combine sugar, brown sugar, buttermilk and eggs in bowl and mix with spoon.

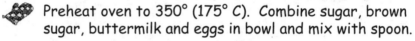 Add flour, baking soda, cinnamon and ½ teaspoon (2 ml) salt and mix well. Fold in pie filling and raisins

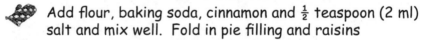 Pour into sprayed, floured 9 x 13-inch (23 x 33 cm) baking pan and spread out.

Continued next page...

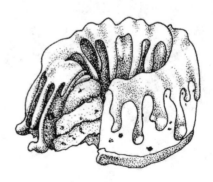

Continued from previous page...

Toping:

1 teaspoon ground cinnamon	*5 ml*
¼ cup sugar	*50 g*
⅓ cup packed light brown sugar	*75 g*
⅔ cup chopped walnuts	*85 g*
½ cup (1 stick) butter melted	*115 g*

Combine cinnamon, sugar, brown sugar and walnuts in bowl and sprinkle over top of cake. Bake for 45 minutes.

When cake is done, drizzle butter over top of cake. Makes 12 big squares.

*TIP: To make buttermilk, mix 1 cup (250 ml) milk with 1 tablespoon (15 ml) lemon juice or vinegar and let stand for about 10 minutes.

**TIP: If you like apple slices to be smaller, empty the can of pie filling onto a plate and cut each slice in half.

 # Graham-Streusel Coffee Cake

2 cups graham cracker crumbs	210 g
¾ cup chopped pecans	85 g
¾ cup firmly packed brown sugar	165 g
1½ teaspoons ground cinnamon	7 ml
¾ cup (1½ sticks) butter	170 g
1 (18 ounce) box yellow cake mix	510 g
½ cup canola oil	125 ml
3 eggs	

 Preheat oven to 350° (175° C). Mix graham cracker crumbs, pecans, brown sugar, cinnamon and butter in bowl and set aside.

 In separate bowl, blend cake mix, 1 cup (250 ml) water, oil and eggs on medium speed for 3 minutes.

 Pour half batter in sprayed, floured 9 x 13-inch (23 x 33 cm) baking pan. Sprinkle with half crumb mixture.

 Spread remaining batter evenly over crumb mixture. Sprinkle remaining crumb mixture over top. Bake for 45 to 50 minutes.

Glaze:

1½ cups powdered sugar	180 g

 Mix powdered sugar and 2 tablespoons (30 ml) water in bowl and drizzle over cake while still hot. Serves 8 to 10.

 # Pineapple Coffee Cake

1 (18 ounce) box butter cake mix	510 g
½ cup canola oil	125 ml
4 eggs, slightly beaten	
1 (20 ounce) can pineapple pie filling	565 g

Preheat oven to 350° (175° C). Combine mix, oil and eggs in bowl and beat well.

Pour batter into sprayed, floured 9 x 13-inch (23 x 33 cm) baking pan. Bake for 45 to 50 minutes. Cake is done when toothpick inserted in center comes out clean.

Punch holes in cake about 2 inches (5 cm) apart with knife. Spread pineapple pie filling over cake while it is still hot. Serves 12 to 14.

 # Short-Cut Blueberry Coffee Cake

1 (16 ounce) package blueberry muffin
    mix with blueberries, separated   455 g
⅓ cup sour cream   80 g
1 egg
⅔ cup powdered sugar   80 g

Preheat oven to 400° (205° C). Combine muffin mix, sour cream, egg and ½ cup water in bowl.

Drain and rinse blueberries from muffin mix and gently fold into batter. Pour into sprayed, floured 7 x 11-inch (18 x 28 cm) baking dish.

Bake for about 25 minutes and cool.

Mix powdered sugar and 1 tablespoon water in bowl and drizzle over coffee cake. Serves 12.

Blueberries are one of the few fruits that early settlers found growing in North America. Over the years, blueberries along with the leaves and roots have been used for a number of medicinal purposes. During the Civil War, soldiers drank a blueberry concoction for its health benefits.

Blueberries are cultivated from Florida to Canada and are available all year round. Michigan is the largest producer of cultivated blueberries in the world followed by Canada's British Columbia. North America accounts for 90% of the world's cultivated blueberry crop.

Apricot Bake

4 (15 ounce) cans apricot halves, drained, divided	4 (425 g)
1 (16 ounce) box light brown sugar, divided	455 g
2 cups round, buttery cracker crumbs, divided	120 g
½ cup (1 stick) butter, sliced, divided	115 g

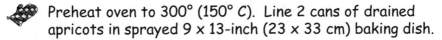

Preheat oven to 300° (150° C). Line 2 cans of drained apricots in sprayed 9 x 13-inch (23 x 33 cm) baking dish.

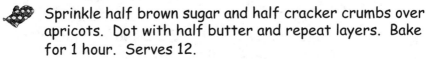

Sprinkle half brown sugar and half cracker crumbs over apricots. Dot with half butter and repeat layers. Bake for 1 hour. Serves 12.

Apricots are native to central Asia and are members of the same plant family as the roses we grow in our gardens. Today apricots are grown commercially in Turkey, Iran, Italy, Pakistan and Greece as well as other nations in the Mediterranean area and Asia. They are also grown in southern Australia. California produces 95% of the apricots grown in the United States.

Apple Bake

1 (8 ounce) can refrigerated crescent dinner rolls	225 g
3 tablespoons plus ½ cup sugar, divided	40 g / 100 g
2 teaspoons ground cinnamon, divided	10 ml
1 apple, peeled, cored	
½ cup whipping cream	125 ml
1 tablespoon almond extract	15 ml
1 egg, beaten	
½ cup sliced almonds	95 g

Preheat oven to 375° (190° C). Separate crescent dinner rolls and place on sprayed baking sheet. Flatten each roll into 8 triangles, but do not let them touch.

Mix 3 tablespoons (40 g) sugar and 1 teaspoon (5 ml) cinnamon in small bowl. Sprinkle mixture over each triangle and pat into dough.

Cut apple into 8 slices and place each slice on wide end of triangle. Wrap sides on left and right over apple and roll starting with wide end. Press and seal seams.

Place each triangle seam-side down around 9-inch (23 cm) round baking dish with 1 in middle. Bake for 15 to 20 minutes.

Continued next page...

Continued from previous page...

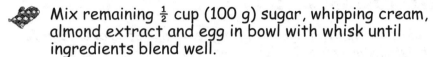

Mix remaining ½ cup (100 g) sugar, whipping cream, almond extract and egg in bowl with whisk until ingredients blend well.

Drizzle mixture evenly over partially cooked rolls. Sprinkle almonds and remaining 1 teaspoon cinnamon over top.

Bake for additional 14 to 15 minutes or until cake is golden brown. If necessary, cover pan with foil during last 5 minutes of baking time to prevent excessive browning. Serve warm. Serves 8.

Christmas Breakfast

12 - 14 eggs, slightly beaten	
1 pound sausage, cooked, drained, crumbled	455 g
2 cups whole milk	500 ml
1½ cups shredded cheddar cheese	175 g
1 (5 ounce) box seasoned croutons	145 g

Preheat oven to 350° (175° C). Mix all ingredients in bowl and pour into sprayed, floured 9 x 13-inch (23 x 33 cm) baking dish.

Bake for 40 minutes. Let stand for about 10 minutes before serving. Serves 10.

Breakfast Bake

This is a favorite for overnight guests and special enough for Christmas morning.

1 pound hot sausage, cooked, crumbled	455 g
1 cup shredded cheddar cheese	115 g
1 cup biscuit mix	120 g
5 eggs, slightly beaten	
2 cups milk	500 ml

Preheat oven to 350° (175° C). Place cooked, crumbled sausage in sprayed 9 x 13-inch (23 x 33 cm) baking dish and sprinkle with cheese.

Combine biscuit mix, a little salt and eggs in bowl and beat well. Add milk and stir until fairly smooth. Pour over sausage mixture.

Bake for 35 minutes. (You can mix this up night before and refrigerate. To cook next morning, add 5 minutes to cooking time.) Serves 8.

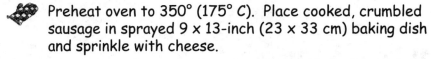

Familiar Mom-isms

I'm going to skin you alive.

Some day your face will freeze that way.

Shut your mouth and eat.

This hurts me more than it does you.

What part of NO do you not understand?

Who do you think you are?

Chiffon Cheese Souffle

Wow! Is this ever good! It is light and fluffy, but still very rich. The Old English cheese gives it that special cheese flavor.

12 slices white bread, crusts trimmed
2 (5 ounce) jars sharp processed
   cheese spread, softened   2 (145 g)
6 eggs, beaten
3 cups milk   750 ml
¾ cup (1½ sticks) butter, melted   170 g

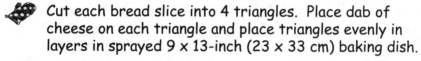

Cut each bread slice into 4 triangles. Place dab of cheese on each triangle and place triangles evenly in layers in sprayed 9 x 13-inch (23 x 33 cm) baking dish.

Combine eggs, milk, butter and a little salt and pepper in bowl. Pour over layers. Cover and refrigerate for 8 hours.

Remove from refrigerator 10 to 15 minutes before baking.

When ready to bake, preheat oven to 350° (175° C). Bake for 1 hour. Serves 12.

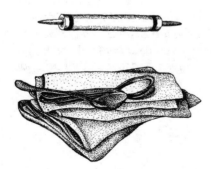

Corned Beef Hash Bake

2 (15 ounce) cans corned beef hash,
    slightly warmed   2 (425 g)
Butter
6 - 8 eggs
⅓ cup half-and-half cream   105 g

Preheat oven to 350° (175° C). Spread corned beef
hash in sprayed 9 x 13-inch (23 x 33 cm) pan.

Pat down with back of spoon and make 6 to 8 deep
hollows in hash large enough for egg to fit. Fill hollows
with tiny dab of butter.

Pour eggs into each hollow and cover with about
1 tablespoon (15 ml) or so of half-and-half cream.

Bake for 15 to 20 minutes or until eggs set as desired.
Divide into squares to serve. Serves 6.

*Before the days of modern food storage,
twice-baked biscuits (hardtack or ship's
biscuit) were used as a portable food, particularly
for ocean voyages because they had a long storage
life and could keep for months or even years.*

Green Chili Puff

This recipe is so versatile! Cut it in little squares and serve warm as an appetizer, for a brunch or for lunch. It would also go well with a Mexican meal – morning, noon or night!

10 eggs	
½ cup flour	60 g
1 teaspoon baking powder	5 ml
1 (16 ounce) carton small curd	
cottage cheese	455 g
1 (8 ounce) package shredded	
mozzarella cheese	225 g
1 bunch green onions with tops,	
chopped	
1 (8 ounce) package shredded	
cheddar cheese	225 g
½ cup (1 stick) butter, melted	115 g
1 (7 ounce) can diced green chilies	200 g
Salsa	

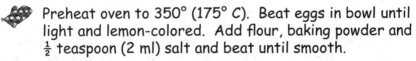 Preheat oven to 350° (175° C). Beat eggs in bowl until light and lemon-colored. Add flour, baking powder and ½ teaspoon (2 ml) salt and beat until smooth.

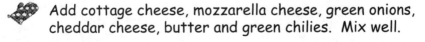 Add cottage cheese, mozzarella cheese, green onions, cheddar cheese, butter and green chilies. Mix well.

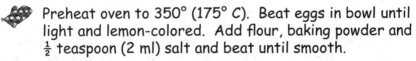 Pour mixture into sprayed 9 x 13-inch (23 x 33 cm) baking pan and bake for 40 minutes or until top is brown around edges and center appears firm.

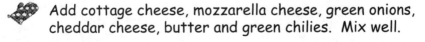 Serve immediately with salsa. Serves 10 to 12,

Ham and Cheese Bars

These are good made for a brunch or lunch, using as bread.

2 cups biscuit mix	240 g
1 heaping cup cooked, finely chopped ham	140 g
4 ounces shredded cheddar cheese	115 g
½ onion, finely chopped	
½ cup grated parmesan cheese	50 g
¼ cup sour cream	60 g
1 teaspoon garlic powder	5 ml
1 cup milk	250 ml
1 egg	

 Preheat oven to 350° (175° C).

 Combine biscuit mix, ham, cheese, onion, parmesan cheese, sour cream, garlic powder, milk, egg ½ teaspoon (2 ml) in bowl and mix with spoon.

 Spread in sprayed 9 x 13-inch (23 x 33 cm) baking pan and bake for 30 minutes or until light brown. Cut in rectangles, about 2 x 1-inch (5 x 2.5 cm). Serves 10 to 12.

TIP: Cook and store in refrigerator. Reheat to serve. Heat at 325° (165° C) for 20 minutes and they will be good and crispy heated a second time.

Grandmas are moms with lots of frosting.
—Author Unknown

Pineapple-Cheese Casserole

This would be good served at a brunch or luncheon or as a side dish to sandwiches or ham. It's also great served at a morning bridge club along with coffee cake or delicious strawberry spread.

2 (20 ounce) cans pineapple chunks, drained	2 (565 g)
1 cup sugar	200 g
5 tablespoons flour	45 g
1½ cups shredded cheddar cheese	175 g
1 stack round, buttery crackers, crushed	
½ cup (1 stick) butter, melted	115 g

 Preheat oven to 350° (175° C).

 Spray 9 x 13-inch (23 x 33 cm) baking dish and layer ingredients as follows: pineapple, sugar-flour, cheese, cracker crumbs and butter drizzled over casserole.

 Bake for 25 minutes or until bubbly. Serves 8 to 10.

Many people prefer to bake pies in glass pie pans because they can check the browning of the crust on the bottom. Most recommend that the oven temperature be reduced by 25° (15° C) when using glass.

Quesadilla Pie

1 (4 ounce) can chopped green chilies, drained	115 g
½ pound sausage, cooked	225 g
1 (16 ounce) package shredded cheddar cheese	455 g
3 eggs, well beaten	
1½ cups milk	375 ml
¾ cup biscuit mix	90 g
Hot salsa	

Preheat oven to 350° (175° C). Sprinkle green chilies, sausage and cheddar cheese in sprayed 9-inch (23 cm) pie pan.

Combine eggs, milk and biscuit mix in bowl. Pour mixture over green chilies-sausage mixture and bake for 30 to 40 minutes. Serve with salsa. Serves 8 to 10.

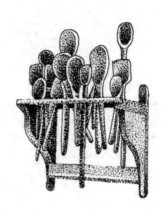

Crabmeat Quiche

3 eggs, beaten
1 (8 ounce) carton sour cream   225 g
1 (6 ounce) can crabmeat, rinsed   170 g
½ cup shredded Swiss cheese   60 g
Garlic salt
1 (9 inch) piecrust   23 cm

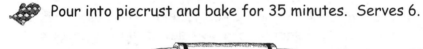 Preheat oven to 350° (175° C). Combine eggs and sour cream in bowl. Blend in crabmeat and cheese and add a little garlic salt and pepper.

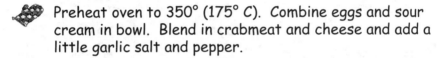 Pour into piecrust and bake for 35 minutes. Serves 6.

Asparagus Quiche

1 (9 inch) refrigerated piecrust	23 cm
¼ cup (½ stick) butter	55 g
3 tablespoons flour	40 g
1½ cups milk	375 ml
4 eggs	
1 pound fresh asparagus, trimmed, chopped	455 g
½ cup shredded Swiss cheese	55 g
¼ cup breadcrumbs	30 g

Preheat oven to 450° (220° C). Place piecrust in pie pan. Place several sheets of heavy-duty foil in piecrust and over edge. Bake for about 5 minutes.

Remove from oven, discard foil and bake for additional 5 minutes.

Melt butter in saucepan and stir in flour and a little salt. Stir to dissolve all lumps. Cook over medium heat and gradually pour in milk. Continue to stir until mixture thickens.

Add remaining ingredients except breadcrumbs and beat. Pour into piecrust and sprinkle breadcrumbs over quiche.

Bake for about 30 minutes or until knife inserted in center comes out clean. Cool slightly, slice into wedges and serve warm. Serves 6.

An excellent health tip: Forgive Everyone for Everything.

Quick Quiche

½ cup (1 stick) butter, melted	115 g
1½ cups half-and-half cream	375 ml
3 green onions with tops, chopped	
½ cup biscuit mix	60 g
1 cup shredded Swiss cheese	115 g
¾ cup cooked, chopped ham	105 g
4 eggs, beaten	

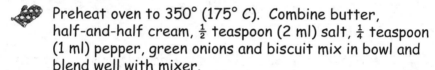 Preheat oven to 350° (175° C). Combine butter, half-and-half cream, ½ teaspoon (2 ml) salt, ¼ teaspoon (1 ml) pepper, green onions and biscuit mix in bowl and blend well with mixer.

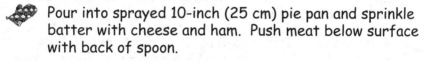 Pour into sprayed 10-inch (25 cm) pie pan and sprinkle batter with cheese and ham. Push meat below surface with back of spoon.

Beat eggs in same bowl and pour over ham and cheese. Bake for 4 minutes. Let stand at room temperature for about 10 minutes before slicing. Serves 6 to 8.

> Quiche is a French dish with a pastry crust and a mixture of eggs and milk with vegetables and/or meats. Quiche Lorraine is one of the most popular and well-known quiches. It is a blend of egg and cream custard in a piecrust. The French version of Quiche Lorraine does not use cheese. Bacon, spinach, broccoli, mushrooms, onions, ham or seafood are common additions to the basic egg and cream or milk mixture.

Sausage and Chilies Quiche

1 (9 inch) refrigerated piecrust	23 cm
1 (7 ounce) can whole green chilies, drained	200 g
1 pound hot sausage, cooked, crumbled, drained	455 g
4 eggs, slightly beaten	
2 cups half-and-half cream	500 ml
½ cup grated parmesan cheese	50 g
¾ cup shredded Swiss cheese	80 g

Preheat oven to 350° (175° C). Place piecrust in pie pan. Line bottom of piecrust with green chilies. Sprinkle sausage over chilies.

Combine eggs, half-and-half cream, cheeses, ½ teaspoon (2 ml) salt and ¼ teaspoon (1 ml) pepper in bowl and pour over sausage.

Cover edge of pastry with foil to prevent excessive browning.

Bake for 35 minutes or until top is golden brown. Let quiche stand for about 5 minutes before serving. Serves 4 to 6.

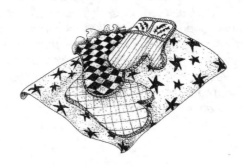

Biscuits and Breads

Angel Biscuits

5 cups flour	600 g
¼ cup sugar	50 g
1 tablespoon baking powder	15 ml
1 teaspoon baking soda	5 ml
⅔ cup shortening	160 g
1½ packages dry yeast	
2 cups buttermilk*	500 ml
Canola oil	

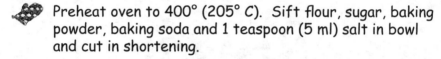

Preheat oven to 400° (205° C). Sift flour, sugar, baking powder, baking soda and 1 teaspoon (5 ml) salt in bowl and cut in shortening.

In separate bowl, dissolve yeast in ¼ cup (60 ml) warm water and add with buttermilk to dry ingredients. Mix well, but only until dough moistens well. Place in covered bowl and refrigerate to use as needed.

To bake biscuits, remove amount desired, roll out on floured board to ½ inch (1.2 cm) thickness and cut with biscuit cutter.

Place on oiled baking pan and turn once to grease both sides. Bake for 12 to 15 minutes or until nicely brown.

Remaining dough will keep in refrigerator for 2 weeks. Makes about 2 to 3 dozen.

*TIP: To make buttermilk , mix 1 cup (250 ml) milk with 1 tablespoon (15 ml) lemon juice or vinegar and let milk stand for about 10 minutes.

Cream Biscuits

2 cups flour	240 g
1 tablespoon baking powder	15 ml
1 (8 ounce) carton whipping cream	250 ml

Preheat oven to 175° (290° C). Combine flour, baking powder and ½ teaspoon (2 ml) salt in bowl.

In separate bowl, beat whipping cream only until it holds shape. Combine flour mixture and cream and mix with fork.

Put dough on lightly floured board and knead it for about 1 minute. Pat dough to ¾ inch (1.8 cm) thickness. Cut out biscuits with small biscuit cutter.

Place on sprayed baking sheet and bake for about 12 minutes or until light brown. Serves 6 to 8.

Use a fork to gently mix dry and liquid ingredients for biscuits. Knead the dough gently only until it holds together well enough to be rolled out. Too much mixing and handling will make biscuits tough.

Cream Cheese Biscuits

1 (3 ounce) package cream cheese, softened	85 g
½ cup (1 stick) butter, softened	115 g
1 cup self-rising flour	125 g

 Preheat oven to 350° (175° C). Beat cream cheese and butter in bowl. Add flour and mix well.

Roll out to ½-inch (1.2 cm) thickness and cut with small biscuit cutter. Place on sprayed baking sheet and bake for 20 minutes or until light brown. Serves 6.

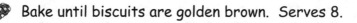

Lickety-Split Biscuits

2 cups flour	240 g
¼ cup mayonnaise	60 g
1 cup milk	250 ml

 Preheat oven to 425° (220° C). Mix all ingredients in bowl and drop spoonfuls of dough onto sprayed baking sheet.

Bake until biscuits are golden brown. Serves 8.

Maple Syrup Biscuits

2¼ cups biscuit mix	270 g
⅔ cup milk	150 ml
1½ cups maple syrup	375 ml

 Preheat oven to 425° (220° C). Combine baking mix and milk. Stir just until moist. On floured surface, roll dough into ½-inch (1.2 cm) thickness. Cut with 2-inch (5 cm) biscuit cutter.

Pour syrup into 7 x 11-inch (18 x 28 cm) baking dish. Place biscuits on top of syrup. Bake for 13 to 15 minutes or until biscuits are golden brown. Serves 6 to 8.

Hot Cheese Biscuits

1 (5 ounce) jar Old English cheese spread	145 g
¼ cup (½ stick) butter, softened	60 g
½ cup flour	60 g

Combine cheese spread and butter in bowl and mix well. Add flour and a little salt. Mix well. Roll into small balls and refrigerate for 1 hour.

When ready to bake, preheat oven to 400° (205° C). Place balls onto baking sheet.

Bake for 10 minutes. Balls will flatten as they cook. Serve hot. Serves 4.

Sausage-Cheese Biscuits

1 (8 ounce) package shredded cheddar cheese	225 g
1 pound hot bulk pork sausage	455 g
2 cups biscuit mix	240 g
¾ cup milk	175 ml

 Preheat oven to 400° (205° C). Combine cheese, sausage and biscuit mix in bowl.

Drop tablespoonfuls of dough onto baking sheet. Bake until light brown. Serve hot. Serves 8.

French Onion Biscuits

2 cups biscuit mix	240 g
¼ cup milk	60 ml
1 (8 ounce) container French onion dip	225 g
2 tablespoons finely minced green onion	20 g

 Preheat oven to 400° (205° C). Combine all ingredients in bowl until soft dough forms.

Drop tablespoonfuls of dough onto sprayed baking sheet. Bake for 10 minutes or until light golden brown. Serves 6 to 8.

Date Biscuits

1 cup chopped dates	150 g
2 cups biscuit mix	240 g
½ cup shredded American cheese	60 g
¾ cup milk	175 ml

Preheat oven to 400° (205° C). Combine dates, biscuit mix and cheese in bowl.

Add milk and stir well to moderately soft dough. Drop spoonfuls of dough onto sprayed baking sheet. Bake for 12 to 15 minutes. Serve hot. Serves 8.

Old South Sweet Potato Biscuits

1 (15 ounce) can sweet potatoes, drained	425 g
1 tablespoon sugar	15 ml
¼ cup milk	60 ml
1½ cups biscuit mix	180 g

Preheat oven to 450° (230° C). Mash sweet potatoes in bowl, add sugar and milk and beat until creamy.

Stir in biscuit mix with fork until most lumps dissolve. Pour mixture onto floured, wax paper and knead 5 to 6 times.

Press down to about ½-inch (1.2 cm) thick and cut out biscuits with biscuit cutter or small glass. Bake for 10 to 12 minutes onto baking sheet. Serves 8.

Sourdough Bullets

Biscuits were very important on cattle drives in the Old West. The mood of the wranglers often depended on good biscuits from the chuck wagon cook.

1 cup flour	120 g
2 teaspoons sugar	10 ml
1 teaspoon baking powder	5 ml
¼ cup (3 tablespoons) bacon grease or butter	60 g
1 cup Cattle-Drive Sourdough Starter (recipe follows)	250 ml
Butter	
Honey	

 Combine flour, sugar, baking powder and ½ teaspoon (2 ml) salt in large bowl and mix well. Pour in a little bacon grease at a time and stir to mix well.

 Form well in center of dough and pour in sourdough starter. Stir well to mix.

 Lay out wax paper on counter and sprinkle flour over paper. Flour your hands and knead dough on wax paper just until smooth.

 Press dough out to make large piece about ½ inch (1.2 cm) thick. Use small, thin-brimmed glass and cut out biscuits.

 Pour a little bacon grease in 9 x 13-inch (23 x 33 cm) baking pan and coat bottom of pan. Place each biscuit in pan, turn them over so both sides have a little bacon grease on them.

Continued next page...

Continued from previous page...

 Cover with cup towel or wax paper and place in warm area for about 30 minutes.

 When ready to bake, preheat oven to 400° (205° C).

 Bake for about 25 minutes or until biscuits are light brown. Serve hot with lots of butter and honey. Serves 8.

Cattle Trail Sourdough Starter:

1 package dry yeast
2 cups flour   *240 g*
2 cups warm water   *500 ml*

 Combine ingredients in large plastic, glass or ceramic bowl (not metal) and mix well.

 Cover loosely with cheesecloth or old dish towel and put in warm place for 48 hours. Stir several times each day to mix ingredients.

 Starter will increase in volume a little, but not the way bread rises. Store starter in refrigerator.

 When ready to make bread or biscuits, stir well and remove amount needed. Replenish starter with 1 cup (120 g) flour and 1 cup (250 ml) water, mix well and store in refrigerator.

OPTIONAL: Another way to replenish sourdough starter calls for 1 cup (120 g) flour, 1 cup (250 ml) milk and ¼ cup (50 g) sugar. Since cowboys did not put milk in their biscuits, we stuck with the real chuckwagon-cowboy version.

Popovers

2 cups flour   *240 g*
6 eggs, beaten
2 cups milk   *500 ml*
Butter

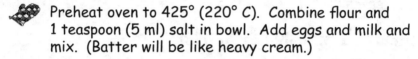 Preheat oven to 425° (220° C). Combine flour and
1 teaspoon (5 ml) salt in bowl. Add eggs and milk and
mix. (Batter will be like heavy cream.)

Coat popover pans with butter and heat in oven. Fill
each cup half full.

Bake for 20 minutes. Reduce heat to 375° (190° C) and
bake for additional 25 minutes. Serve immediately.
Serves 8.

Butter Rolls

2 cups biscuit mix   *240 g*
1 (8 ounce) carton sour cream   *225 g*
½ cup (1 stick) butter, melted   *115 g*

Preheat oven to 400° (205° C). Combine all ingredients
in bowl and mix well.

Spoon into sprayed muffin cups and fill only half full.
Bake for 12 to 14 minutes or light brown. Serves 6 to 8.

Cheddar Cheese Loaf

3¾ cups biscuit mix	450 g
¾ cup shredded sharp cheddar cheese	85 g
1½ cups milk	375 ml
2 small eggs	
⅛ teaspoon ground red pepper	.5 ml

- Preheat oven to 350° (175° C).

- Combine biscuit mix and cheese in bowl. Add milk, eggs and pepper and stir for 2 minutes or until they blend well.

- Spoon into sprayed 9 x 5-inch (23 x 13 cm) loaf pan. Bake for 45 minutes.

- Cool before slicing. Serves 8 to 10.

While chuck wagon cooks were making sour dough bread at every stop along the trail from Texas and Oklahoma to markets in Kansas, Gold Rush prospectors or "49'ers" were making the same sour dough bread daily. San Francisco is famous for sour dough bread today primarily because it continues with this culinary tradition traced back to the Gold Rush days in 1849. Getting started with sour dough takes about three days, but from then on, all you have to do is replenish your "starter" as you use it. If you find someone who already has sour dough starter, you can get a "start" from them and save yourself three days.

Mincemeat Bread

1¾ cups flour	210 g
1¼ cups sugar	250 g
2½ teaspoons baking powder	12 ml
2 eggs, beaten	
1 teaspoon vanilla	5 ml
1½ cups mincemeat	455 g
¾ cups chopped pecans	85 g
⅓ cup shortening, melted	65 g

Preheat oven to 350° (175° C). Combine flour, sugar, baking powder and ½ teaspoon (2 ml) salt in large bowl.

In separate bowl, combine eggs, vanilla, mincemeat and pecans and mix well. Stir in shortening and mix quickly. Batter will be stiff.

Pour egg mixture into dry ingredients and stir only enough to moisten flour.

Spoon batter into sprayed, floured loaf pan and bake for 1 hour or until toothpick inserted in center comes out clean. Cool for 15 minutes and remove from pan to cool completely.

Continued next page...

Mincemeat is a mixture of chopped dried fruits, spices and spirits. Originally a mixture of minced beef and fruits used for meat pies in medieval and renaissance times, the fruits and spices acted as a preservative for the meat. Mincemeat pies became sweeter over the years and meat is no longer a common ingredient. It's now a dessert rather than a savory dinner dish.

Continued from previous page...

Glaze:

1 cup powdered sugar	*120 g*
1 tablespoon milk	*15 ml*
¼ cup finely chopped pecans	*30 g*

Combine powdered sugar and milk in bowl and stir until smooth. Stir in pecans and spread over loaf. Slice bread and spread a little butter on each slice and toast. Serves 8 to 10.

TIP: *This bread is well worth the cost of the prepared mincemeat. It usually comes in a large jar so you will have enough left to make the mincemeat cookies. They are delicious.*

Glazes are thin coats of sweet mixture that makes the end product look shiny and taste sweeter. A basic glaze uses 2 cups (240 g) powdered sugar, ¼ cup (55 g) melted butter and 2 tablespoons (30 ml) milk. Several drops of vanilla or almond flavoring are a nice addition to the mixture.

Substitute orange juice for milk and add a little orange zest to give the glaze a citrus flavor. Half-and-half cream or whipping cream instead of milk will produce a thicker, richer glaze.

Drizzle glazes over cooled cakes, muffins or breads. Or, use a toothpick or fork to make holes in the top of a cake while it's still hot. Drizzle glaze over hot cake so glaze soaks in.

Apple-Banana Tree Bread

3 apples, peeled, grated	
3 bananas, mashed	
2 teaspoons lemon juice	10 ml
½ cup (1 stick) butter, softened	115 g
2 cups sugar	400 g
2 eggs	
3 cups flour	360 g
1½ teaspoons baking powder	7 ml
1½ teaspoons baking soda	7 ml
1 teaspoon vanilla	5 ml

Preheat oven to 350° (175° C). Sprinkle apples and bananas with lemon juice in bowl.

In separate bowl, cream butter, sugar and eggs and beat well. Stir in fruit. Add flour, baking powder, baking soda, vanilla and ¼ teaspoon (1 ml) salt and stir.

Pour into 2 sprayed, floured loaf pans and bake for 50 to 55 minutes or until golden brown. Bread is done when toothpick inserted in center comes out clean. Serves 14 to 16.

Why are bananas never lonely?

Because they hang aroung in bunches.

Applesauce-Pecan Bread

1 cup sugar
1 cup applesauce
⅓ cup canola oil
2 eggs
2 tablespoons milk
1 teaspoon almond extract
2 cups flour
1 teaspoon baking soda
½ teaspoon baking powder
¾ teaspoon ground cinnamon
¼ teaspoon ground nutmeg
¾ cup chopped pecans

Preheat oven to 350° (175° C). Combine sugar, applesauce, oil, eggs, milk and almond extract in bowl and mix well.

Combine all dry ingredients and ¼ teaspoon salt; add to sugar mixture and mix well. Fold in pecans. Pour into sprayed, floured loaf pan.

Topping:

½ cup chopped pecans
½ teaspoon ground cinnamon
½ cup packed brown sugar

Combine pecans, cinnamon and brown sugar in bowl. Sprinkle over batter. Bake for 1 hour 5 minutes.

Bread is done when toothpick inserted in center comes out clean. Cool on rack. Serves 12.

Apricot Bread Extraordinaire

This is "it" for apricot lovers!

3 cups flour	360 g
1 ½ teaspoons baking soda	7 ml
2 cups sugar	400 g
1 ½ cups canola oil	375 ml
4 eggs	
1 teaspoon vanilla	5 ml
1 (5 ounce) can evaporated milk	145 g
Apricot butter (recipe follows)	
1 ¼ cups chopped pecans	145 g

 Preheat oven to 350° (175° C). Combine flour, baking soda and ½ teaspoon (2 ml) salt in bowl.

 Add sugar, oil, eggs, vanilla and evaporated milk. Mix thoroughly. Add apricot butter and pecans and blend.

 Pour into 2 sprayed, floured loaf pans and bake for 1 hour 10 minutes or until toothpick inserted in center comes out clean. Serves 14 to 16.

Apricot Butter:

1 ¼ cups peeled, diced apricots	205 g
1 cup sugar	200 g

 Cover apricots with water in bowl and soak overnight. Combine apricots and sugar in saucepan and simmer for 10 minutes or until soft. Cool completely before adding to recipe.

Banana-Pineapple Loaf

This is wonderful sliced, buttered and toasted for breakfast.

1 cup (2 sticks) butter, softened	225 g
1 cup sugar	200 g
4 eggs	
1 cup mashed ripe bananas	
4 cups flour	480 g
2 teaspoons baking powder	10 ml
1 teaspoon baking soda	5 ml
1 (15 ounce) can crushed	
pineapple with liquid	425 g
1 (7 ounce) can flaked coconut	200 g
1 cup chopped pecans	110 g

Preheat oven to 350° (175° C). Cream butter and sugar in bowl, add eggs and mix well. Stir in bananas.

In separate bowl, sift flour, baking powder, baking soda and ½ teaspoon salt and add to butter mixture. Fold in pineapple, coconut and pecans.

Pour into 2 sprayed, floured 9 x 5-inch (23 x 13 cm) loaf pans. Bake for 1 hour 10 minutes. Bread is done when toothpick inserted in center comes out clean. Serves 12 to 16.

TIP: *For lunch or brunch, spread cream cheese on slices of banana-pineapple bread, cut into thirds and serve as finger sandwiches. (Remove crusts for ladies.)*

Coconut Bread

This recipe makes a pretty plate of red and white sandwiches.

1 ¼ cups shredded coconut	105 g
2 ⅔ cups flour	320 g
1 ¼ cups sugar	250 g
4 teaspoons baking powder	20 ml
1 ½ cups milk	375 ml
1 egg	
2 tablespoons canola oil	30 ml
1 ¼ teaspoons coconut extract	6 ml
Strawberry Butter (recipe follows)	

Preheat oven to 300° (150° C). Place coconut on baking sheet and bake for 15 minutes. Shake pan and stir 2 times so that it will toast evenly.

Remove from oven and cool. Turn oven temperature up to 350° (175° C).

Sift flour, sugar, baking powder and 1 teaspoon (5 ml) salt in bowl and stir in coconut.

In separate bowl, combine milk, egg, oil and coconut extract. Beat a little to blend egg into milk. Add liquid mixture to dry ingredients all at once and mix well, but do not over mix.

Pour batter into sprayed 9 x 5-inch (23 x 13 cm) loaf pan and bake for 1 hour 5 minutes. Bread is done when toothpick inserted in center comes out clean. Cool.

Continued next page...

Continued from previous page...

 To serve, cut in thin slices and spread with Strawberry
Butter. Place another slice on top. Cut in 3 strips.
Serves 6 to 8.

Strawberry Butter:

1 ¼ cups powdered sugar	150 g
1 (10 ounce) package frozen strawberries, thawed, drained	285 g
1 cup (2 sticks) unsalted butter, softened	230 g

Place all ingredients in food processor and process until
well blended.

Refrigerate and spread on bread. (This is good served
on biscuits and muffins, too.)

---

*Flavored butters make any meat or vegetable
more exciting. Butter is simply mixed with
flavorful ingredients such as minced onions, crushed
nuts, spices, herbs or citrus zests, just to mention
a few.*

*One-half cup (115 g) butter with about ½ cup
(125 ml) flavorful ingredients will yield about ¾ cup
(175 ml) of flavored butter. Try ½ cup (115 g) butter
with ⅓ cup (20 g) chopped parsley, ½ teaspoon
(2 ml) cracked black pepper, 1 to 2 teaspoons (5 to
10 ml) lemon zest and 1 tablespoon (15 ml) lemon
juice. Use this wonderful mixture on meats, seafood
and vegetables.*

Glazed Lemon Bread

½ cup shortening	95 g
1 cup sugar	200 g
2 eggs	
1½ cups flour	180 g
1 teaspoon baking powder	5 ml
½ cup milk	125 ml
1 teaspoon lemon extract	5 ml
Peel of 2 lemons, grated	
½ cup chopped pecans	55 g

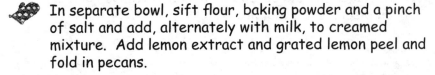 Preheat oven to 325° (165° C). Cream shortening and sugar in large bowl. Add eggs and beat thoroughly.

In separate bowl, sift flour, baking powder and a pinch of salt and add, alternately with milk, to creamed mixture. Add lemon extract and grated lemon peel and fold in pecans.

Pour in sprayed, floured, 9 x 5-inch (23 x 13 cm) loaf pan and bake for 60 to 65 minutes. Bread is done when toothpick inserted in center comes out clean.

Glaze:

Juice of 2 lemons	
¼ cup sugar	50 g

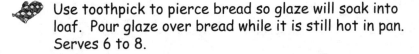 Combine lemon juice and sugar in saucepan and bring to a boil.

Use toothpick to pierce bread so glaze will soak into loaf. Pour glaze over bread while it is still hot in pan. Serves 6 to 8.

Island Mango Bread

This is wonderful, moist and delicious bread — great toasted for breakfast.

2 cups flour	240 g
1 teaspoon baking soda	5 ml
1 teaspoon ground cinnamon	5 ml
1 cup sugar	200 g
3 eggs, beaten	
¾ cup plus 1 tablespoon canola oil	175 ml/15 ml
2 cups peeled, seeded and finely diced mangoes (2 ripe mangoes)	310 g
1 teaspoon lemon juice	5 ml
⅓ cup shredded coconut	30 g
⅔ cup chopped pecans	85 g

Preheat oven to 350° (175° C). Combine flour, baking soda, cinnamon, ¼ teaspoon (1 ml) salt and sugar in large bowl and mix well.

In separate bowl, combine eggs, oil, mangoes and lemon juice. Pour into flour mixture and mix well with spoon.

Stir in coconut and pecans and pour into 2 sprayed, floured 8 x 4-inch (20 x 10 cm) loaf pans.

Bake for 40 to 45 minutes. Bread is done when toothpick inserted in center comes out clean. Serves 8 to 10.

Old Pioneer Pumpkin Bread

This is fabulous served with lots of butter or for sandwiches with cream cheese filling.

1 cup canola oil	250 ml
3 cups sugar	600 g
4 eggs	
1 teaspoon vanilla	5 ml
1 (15 ounce) can pumpkin	425 g
2 teaspoons baking soda	10 ml
2 teaspoons ground cinnamon	10 ml
¼ teaspoon ground allspice	1 ml
3 cups flour	360 g
1 cup chopped dates	150 g
1½ - 2 cups chopped pecans	165 - 220 g

Preheat oven to 350° (175° C). Combine oil and sugar in bowl; add eggs one at a time and beat well after each addition. Add vanilla and pumpkin and mix well.

In separate bowl, sift 1 teaspoon salt, baking soda, cinnamon, allspice and flour. Add to sugar-pumpkin mixture and beat well. Stir in dates and pecans.

Pour into 2 large sprayed, floured 9 x 5-inch (23 x 13 cm) loaf pans.

Bake for 1 hour 10 minutes to 1 hour 15 minutes. Bread is done when toothpick inserted in center comes out clean. Serves 12 to 16.

 # Quick Pumpkin Bread

1 (16 ounce) package pound cake mix	455 g
1 cup canned pumpkin	245 g
2 eggs	
1/3 cup milk	75 ml
1 teaspoon allspice	5 ml

Preheat oven to 350° (175° C). Beat all ingredients in bowl and blend well. Pour into sprayed, floured 9 x 5-inch (23 x 13 cm) loaf pan.

Bake for 1 hour. Bread is done when toothpick inserted in center comes out clean.

Cool and turn out onto cooling rack. Serves 15.

Pumpkins were a primary food source for Native American Indians. They introduced pumpkins to the Pilgrims who served them at the second Thanksgiving. Native Americans used complementary crops by growing squash and pumpkins, beans and corn together.

The bean stalks grew up the corn stalks using them much like a trellis while the bean stalks made the corn stalks sturdier in high winds. Pumpkin plants covered the shallow roots of the corn protecting them from extreme conditions.

Very Berry Strawberry Bread

This is extra delicious!

3 cups sifted flour	360 g
2 cups sugar	400 g
1 teaspoon baking soda	5 ml
1 tablespoon ground cinnamon	15 ml
3 large eggs, beaten	
1 cup canola oil	250 ml
1¼ cups pecans, chopped	140 g
2 (10 ounce) packages frozen sweetened strawberries with juice, thawed	2 (280 g)
1 (8 ounce) package light cream cheese, softened	225 g

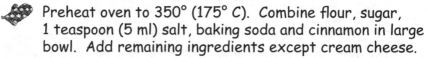 Preheat oven to 350° (175° C). Combine flour, sugar, 1 teaspoon (5 ml) salt, baking soda and cinnamon in large bowl. Add remaining ingredients except cream cheese.

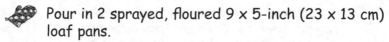 Pour in 2 sprayed, floured 9 x 5-inch (23 x 13 cm) loaf pans.

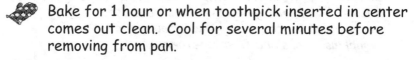 Bake for 1 hour or when toothpick inserted in center comes out clean. Cool for several minutes before removing from pan.

 To serve, slice bread and spread cream cheese between 2 slices. For finger sandwiches, cut in smaller pieces. Serves 12 to 16.

Zucchini-Pineapple Bread

3 eggs, beaten
2 cups sugar   400 g
1 cup canola oil   250 ml
2 teaspoons vanilla   10 ml
2 cups grated zucchini
3 cups flour   360 g
1 teaspoon baking soda   5 ml
1 tablespoon ground cinnamon   15 ml
½ teaspoon baking powder   2 ml
1 cup chopped pecans   110 g
1 (8 ounce) can crushed
    pineapple, drained   225 g
1 (8 ounce) carton cream cheese,
    softened   225 g

Preheat oven to 325° (165° C). Mix eggs, sugar, oil and vanilla in bowl and mix well.

Add remaining ingredients except cream cheese. Add 1 teaspoon salt, mix well and pour in 2 sprayed, floured 9 x 5-inch (23 x 13 cm) loaf pans.

Bake for 60 minutes or until toothpick inserted in center comes out clean. Cool for several minutes.

To serve, slice and spread with cream cheese. Serves 12 to 16.

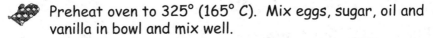

An excellent health tip: Take a 10 to 30-Minute Walk Every Day and Smile While Doing It.

Texas Beer Bread

3 cups self-rising flour	375 g
¼ cup sugar	50 g
1 (12 ounce) can beer, room temperature	355 ml
1 egg, beaten	
2 tablespoons butter, melted	30 g

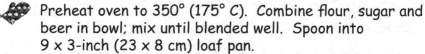 Preheat oven to 350° (175° C). Combine flour, sugar and beer in bowl; mix until blended well. Spoon into 9 x 3-inch (23 x 8 cm) loaf pan.

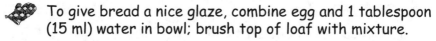 To give bread a nice glaze, combine egg and 1 tablespoon (15 ml) water in bowl; brush top of loaf with mixture.

Bake for 40 to 45 minutes; when removing loaf from oven, brush top with melted butter. Serves 8.

Poppy Seed Bread

3¾ cups biscuit mix	450 g
1½ cups shredded cheddar cheese	175 g
1 tablespoon poppy seeds	15 ml
1 egg, beaten	
1½ cups milk	375 ml

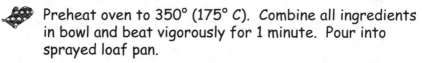 Preheat oven to 350° (175° C). Combine all ingredients in bowl and beat vigorously for 1 minute. Pour into sprayed loaf pan.

Bake for 50 to 60 minutes. Bread is done when toothpick inserted in center comes out clean. Remove from pan and cool before slicing. Serves 10.

Just Plain Ol' Cornbread

1 cup flour	120 g
1 cup yellow cornmeal	160 g
¼ cup sugar	50 g
4 teaspoons baking powder	20 ml
2 eggs	
1 cup milk	250 ml
¼ cup canola oil	60 ml

 Preheat oven to 375° (190° C). Combine all ingredients plus ¾ teaspoon (4 ml) salt in bowl and mix well.

 Pour mixture into sprayed 9 x 13-inch (23 x 33 cm) baking pan and bake for 30 minutes or until light brown. Serves 12 to 16.

Corn Sticks

2 cups biscuit mix	240 g
2 tablespoons minced green onions	10 g
1 (8 ounce) can cream-style corn	225 g
Melted butter	

 Preheat oven to 400° (205° C). Combine biscuit mix, green onions and cream-style corn in bowl.

 Place dough on floured surface and cut into 3 x 1-inch (8 x 2.5 cm) strips. Roll in melted butter. Bake for 15 to 16 minutes. Serves 8.

Tex-Mex Cornbread

This is a meal by itself! Add crumbled bacon and it's a feast!

2 eggs, beaten	
1 cup sour cream	240 g
1 (15 ounce) can cream-style corn	425 g
½ cup canola oil	125 ml
1 (8 ounce) package shredded	
cheddar cheese	225 g
1 (4 ounce) can diced green chilies	115 g
3 tablespoons chopped onion	30 g
3 tablespoons chopped bell pepper	30 g
1½ cups cornmeal	240 g
2½ teaspoons baking powder	12 ml

Preheat oven to 350° (175° C). Mix eggs, sour cream, creamed corn, oil, cheese, green chilies, onion and bell pepper in bowl.

In separate bowl, mix cornmeal, baking powder and 1 teaspoon (5 ml) salt and quickly add to sour cream mixture.

Pour in sprayed 9 x 13-inch (23 x 33 cm) baking pan and bake for 45 minutes. Serves 8.

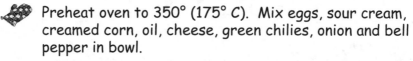
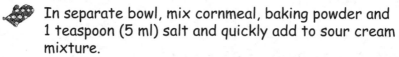

Hot Water Cornbread

Grandma made cornbread this way...

1 ½ cups cornmeal	*240 g*
1 egg, beaten	
¼ cup (½ stick) butter, melted	*60 ml*
Canola oil	
Butter	

 Pour 1¼ cups (310 ml) boiling water over cornmeal and 1 teaspoon (5 ml) salt in bowl, stir very well and cool.

 Stir in egg and butter. Drop tablespoonfuls of mixture into skillet with a little oil and form into small patty shapes with spoon.

 Brown on both sides and drain on paper towels. Serve hot with butter. Serves 6.

You cannot help the poor by destroying the rich. You cannot strengthen the weak by weakening the strong. You cannot bring about prosperity by discouraging thrift. You cannot lift the wage earner up by pulling the wage payer down. You cannot further the brotherhood of man by inciting class hatred. You cannot build character and courage by taking away people's initiative and independence. You cannot help people permanently by doing for them, what they could and should do for themselves.

—Abraham Lincoln

A Different Hot Water Cornbread

2 cups cornmeal	320 g
½ teaspoon baking soda	2 ml
3 tablespoons butter	45 g
2 eggs, separated	

Preheat oven to 350° (175° C). Pour 1½ cups (375 ml) boiling water over cornmeal, 1 teaspoon (5 ml) salt, baking soda and butter in bowl and stir vigorously to remove lumps. (Mixture will be thick.)

Cool slightly and stir in beaten egg yolks. Fold in stiffly beaten egg whites and drop tablespoonfuls of mixture onto sprayed baking sheet.

Bake for about 7 to 8 minutes or until light brown. Serves 8.

Cheddar Cornbread

2 (8.5 ounce) packages cornbread-muffin mix	2 (225 g)
2 eggs, beaten	
1 cup plain yogurt	225 g
1 (14 ounce) can cream-style corn	395 g
½ cup shredded cheddar cheese	60 g

Preheat oven to 400° (205° C). Combine cornbread mix, eggs and yogurt in bowl and blend well. Stir in corn and cheese.

Pour into sprayed 9 x 13-inch (23 x 33 cm) baking dish. Bake for 18 to 20 minutes or until slightly brown. Serves 8 to 10.

Mexican Cornbread

This is almost a meal by itself. It's great.

1 cup flour	120 g
1 cup cornmeal	160 g
4 teaspoons baking powder	20 ml
1 egg	
1 cup milk	250 ml
1 (15 ounce) can cream-style corn	425 g
¼ cup canola oil	60 ml
1 jalapeno, chopped	
1 (8 ounce) package shredded 4-cheese blend, divided	225 g

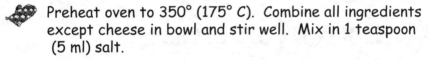 Preheat oven to 350° (175° C). Combine all ingredients except cheese in bowl and stir well. Mix in 1 teaspoon (5 ml) salt.

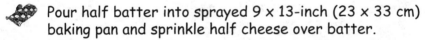 Pour half batter into sprayed 9 x 13-inch (23 x 33 cm) baking pan and sprinkle half cheese over batter.

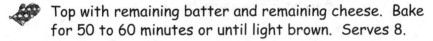 Top with remaining batter and remaining cheese. Bake for 50 to 60 minutes or until light brown. Serves 8.

Cornbread dates back to as long ago as corn was first harvested. By drying the corn and grinding it down to a meal or flour, Native American Indians made bread with cornmeal. It was very simple, similar to hot water cornbread, but provided a good source of food.

Spicy Cornbread Twists

3 tablespoons butter	45 g
½ cup cornmeal	80 g
¼ teaspoon cayenne pepper	1 ml
1 (11 ounce) can refrigerated soft breadsticks	310 g

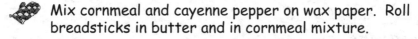 Preheat oven to 350° (175° C). Melt butter in pie pan in oven. Remove from oven as soon as butter melts.

Mix cornmeal and cayenne pepper on wax paper. Roll breadsticks in butter and in cornmeal mixture.

Twist breadsticks according to label directions and place on large baking sheet. Bake for 15 to 18 minutes. Serves 6.

Broccoli Cornbread

1 (10 ounce) package frozen hopped broccoli, thawed	280 g
2 (6 ounce) boxes cornbread muffin mix	2 (170 g)
¾ cup (1½ sticks) butter, melted	170 g
1 medium onion, chopped	
4 eggs, slightly beaten	
1 cup small curd cottage cheese	225 g

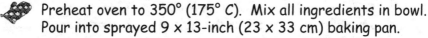 Preheat oven to 350° (175° C). Mix all ingredients in bowl. Pour into sprayed 9 x 13-inch (23 x 33 cm) baking pan.

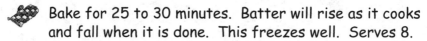 Bake for 25 to 30 minutes. Batter will rise as it cooks and fall when it is done. This freezes well. Serves 8.

Mexican Spoon Bread

1 cup yellow cornmeal	160 g
1 tablespoon sugar	15 ml
½ teaspoon baking soda	2 ml
¾ cup milk	175 ml
⅓ cup canola oil	75 ml
2 eggs, beaten	
1 (16 ounce) can cream-style corn	455 g
1 (4 ounce) can diced green chilies, divided	115 g
2 cups shredded cheddar cheese, divided	225 g

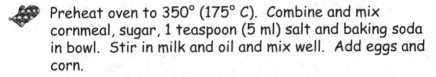
Preheat oven to 350° (175° C). Combine and mix cornmeal, sugar, 1 teaspoon (5 ml) salt and baking soda in bowl. Stir in milk and oil and mix well. Add eggs and corn.

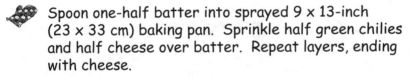
Spoon one-half batter into sprayed 9 x 13-inch (23 x 33 cm) baking pan. Sprinkle half green chilies and half cheese over batter. Repeat layers, ending with cheese.

Bake for 45 minutes or until light brown. To serve, spoon from pan. Serves 8 to 10.

TIP: This will serve as a substitute for potatoes or rice.

Kids' Corn Dog Muffins

2 (6 ounce) packages cornbread muffin mix	2 (170 g)
2 tablespoons brown sugar	30 g
2 eggs	
1 cup milk	250 ml
1 (8 ounce) can whole kernel corn, drained	225 g
5 hot dogs, chopped	

Preheat oven to 400° (205° C). Combine cornbread mix and brown sugar in bowl.

In separate bowl, combine eggs and milk and stir into dry ingredients. Stir in corn and hot dogs. (Batter will be thin.)

Fill sprayed muffin cups three-fourths full. Bake for 16 to 18 minutes or until golden brown. Serves 8.

Bars
and
Brownies

Coconut-Cherry Squares

This is not only pretty — it is good, good, good!

Pastry:

1⅓ cups flour	160 g
⅔ cup (1¼ sticks) butter, softened	150 g
1½ cups powdered sugar	180 g

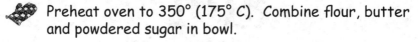

Preheat oven to 350° (175° C). Combine flour, butter and powdered sugar in bowl.

Press into 9 x 13-inch (23 x 33 cm) baking pan. Bake for 20 minutes or until golden and set aside.

Filling:

3 eggs, beaten	
1½ cups sugar	300 g
¾ cup flour	90 g
¾ teaspoon baking powder	4 ml
1 teaspoon vanilla	5 ml
¾ cup chopped pecans	85 g
¾ cup flaked coconut	65 g
¾ cup maraschino cherries, drained, chopped	180 g

Use same bowl, combine ½ teaspoon (2 ml) salt and remaining filling ingredients and mix well.

Spread over crust. Bake for 25 minutes or until golden brown. Cool and cut into squares. Makes 20 to 30 bars.

TIP: *You could give this an even more holiday look by using half green and half red maraschino cherries.*

Apricot Bars

1 ¼ cups flour	150 g
¾ cup packed brown sugar	165 g
6 tablespoons (¾ stick) butter	90 g
¾ cup apricot preserves	240 g

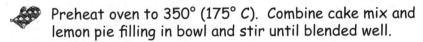 Preheat oven to 350° (175° C). Combine flour, brown sugar and butter in bowl and mix well. Place half mixture in 9-inch (23 cm) square baking pan. Spread apricot preserves over top of mixture.

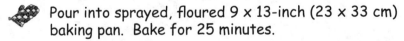 Add remaining flour mixture over top. Bake for 30 minutes. Cut into squares. Makes 9 bars.

Lemon Angel Bars

1 (16 ounce) package one-step angel food cake mix	455 g
1 (20 ounce) can lemon pie filling	565 g
⅓ cup butter, softened	75 g
2 cups powdered sugar	240 g
2 tablespoons lemon juice	30 ml

Preheat oven to 350° (175° C). Combine cake mix and lemon pie filling in bowl and stir until blended well.

Pour into sprayed, floured 9 x 13-inch (23 x 33 cm) baking pan. Bake for 25 minutes.

Just before cake is done, mix butter, powdered sugar and lemon juice in bowl and spread over hot cake.

When cool, cut into bars. Store in refrigerator. Makes 20 bars.

Lemon Bars

1 cup (2 sticks) butter	225 g
2 cups flour	240 g
½ cup powdered sugar	60 g
2 cups sugar	400 g
6 tablespoons flour	45 g
4 eggs, lightly beaten	
6 tablespoons lemon juice	90 ml
½ teaspoon grated lemon peel	2 ml
Powdered sugar	

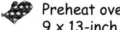 Preheat oven to 350° (175° C). Melt butter in
9 x 13-inch (23 x 33 cm) baking pan in oven.

 Add 2 cups (240 g) flour and powdered sugar, stir into
melted butter in pan and mix well. Press down evenly
and firmly and bake for 15 minutes.

 For filling, combine sugar, 6 tablespoons (90 ml) flour,
eggs, lemon juice and lemon peel in bowl. Mix and pour
over crust.

 Bake for 20 minutes more. Cool and dust with powdered
sugar. To serve, cut into squares. Makes about 2 to
3 dozen bars.

 *Two cannibals are eating a clown. One says to
the other, "Does this taste funny to you?"*

Iced Pineapple Squares

1½ cups sugar	300 g
2 cups flour	240 g
1½ teaspoons baking soda	7 ml
1 (16 ounce) can crushed	
pineapple with juice	455 g
2 eggs	

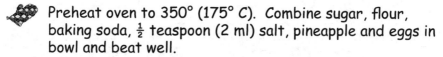

Preheat oven to 350° (175° C). Combine sugar, flour, baking soda, ½ teaspoon (2 ml) salt, pineapple and eggs in bowl and beat well.

Pour into sprayed 9 x 13-inch (23 x 33 cm) baking pan and bake for 35 minutes.

Frosting:

1½ cups sugar	300 g
½ cup (1 stick) butter	115 g
1 (5 ounce) can evaporated milk	145 g
1 cup chopped pecans	110 g
1 (3 ounce) can flaked coconut	85 g
1 teaspoon vanilla	5 ml

Prepare frosting as squares bake. Combine sugar, butter and evaporated milk in saucepan and boil for 4 minutes. Stir constantly.

Remove from heat and add pecans, coconut and vanilla; spread over hot squares. Makes 20 to 24 squares.

Creamy Strawberry Bars

1 (18 ounce) box strawberry cake mix	510 g
½ cup (1 stick) butter	115 g
3 eggs, divided	
1 (8 ounce) package cream cheese, softened	225 g
2 cups powdered sugar	240 g

Preheat oven to 325° (165° C). In large bowl, combine cake mix, butter and 1 egg and blend well.

Press mixture into bottom of sprayed, 9 x 13-inch (23 x 33 cm) baking pan.

In medium bowl, mix cream cheese, 2 eggs and powdered sugar until mixture is smooth. Pour mixture over cake batter.

Bake for 30 to 35 minutes or until light brown. Makes about 20 to 30 bars.

> Brownies and bars are much easier to remove from the pan if you line the pan with foil. Here's an easy method. Turn the pan upside down and cover it with a big enough piece to cover the sides as well as the bottom of the pan. Be sure to place the foil shiny side down. Press the foil around the pan, carefully remove it and turn the pan over. Fit the shaped foil, shiny side up, in the pan. Use a paper towel to smooth it down.

Almond-Coconut Squares

2 cups graham cracker crumbs	210 g
3 tablespoons brown sugar	40 g
½ cup (1 stick) butter, melted	115 g
1 (14 ounce) can sweetened condensed milk	395 g
1 (7 ounce) package shredded coconut	200 g
1 teaspoon vanilla	5 ml

 Preheat oven to 325° (165° C). Combine graham cracker crumbs, brown sugar and butter in bowl and mix well.

 Pat mixture evenly into sprayed 9 x 13-inch baking pan and bake for 10 minutes. Cool.

 Combine sweetened condensed milk, coconut and vanilla in bowl and pour over baked crust. Bake for additional 25 minutes. Cool.

Topping:

1 (6 ounce) package chocolate chips	170 g
1 (6 ounce) package butterscotch chips	170 g
¼ cup (½ stick) butter	55 g
6 tablespoons crunchy peanut butter	110 g
½ cup slivered almonds	85 g

 Melt all topping ingredients in double boiler and spread mixture over baked ingredients. Cool and cut into squares. Makes 20 squares.

Buttery Walnut Squares

1 cup (2 sticks) butter, softened	*225 g*
1¾ cups packed brown sugar	*365 g*
1¾ cups flour	*210 g*

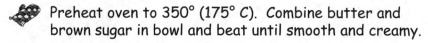 Preheat oven to 350° (175° C). Combine butter and brown sugar in bowl and beat until smooth and creamy.

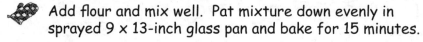 Add flour and mix well. Pat mixture down evenly in sprayed 9 x 13-inch glass pan and bake for 15 minutes.

Topping:

1 cup packed brown sugar	*220 g*
4 eggs, lightly beaten	
2 tablespoons flour	*30 ml*
2 cups chopped walnuts	*260 g*
1 cup flaked coconut	*85 g*

Combine sugar and eggs in medium bowl. Add flour and mix well. Fold in walnuts and coconut and pour over crust.

Bake for 20 to 25 minutes or until set in center. Cool in pan and cut into squares. Makes 20 squares.

TIP: *Serve these delicious squares with a scoop of ice cream for a great dessert.*

 Make peace with your past so it won't ruin your present.

Pecan Squares

2 cups flour	240 g
½ cup powdered sugar	60 g
1 cup (2 sticks) butter, cut up	225 g
1 (14 ounce) can sweetened condensed milk	395 g
2 eggs	
1 teaspoon vanilla	5 ml
1 (7.5 ounce) package almond toffee chips	210 g
1 cup chopped pecans	110 g

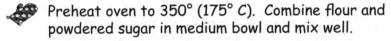 Preheat oven to 350° (175° C). Combine flour and powdered sugar in medium bowl and mix well.

Cut in butter with pastry blender or fork until crumbly. Press mixture evenly into sprayed 9 x 13-inch (23 x 33 cm) baking pan and bake for 15 minutes.

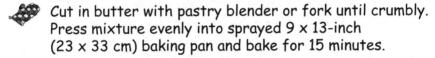 Combine sweetened condensed milk, eggs, vanilla, almond toffee chips and pecans in bowl and pour over prepared crust.

Bake for 25 minutes or until golden brown. Cool and cut into squares. Makes about 3 dozen squares.

 # Pecan Cream Cheese Squares

1 (18 ounce) box yellow cake mix	510 g
3 eggs, divided	
½ cup (1 stick) butter, softened	115 g
2 cups chopped pecans	220 g
1 (8 ounce) package cream cheese, softened	225 g
3⅔ cups powdered sugar	440 g

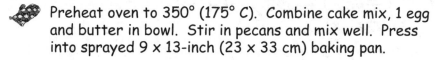

Preheat oven to 350° (175° C). Combine cake mix, 1 egg and butter in bowl. Stir in pecans and mix well. Press into sprayed 9 x 13-inch (23 x 33 cm) baking pan.

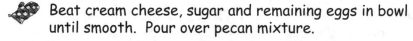

Beat cream cheese, sugar and remaining eggs in bowl until smooth. Pour over pecan mixture.

Bake for 55 minutes or until golden brown. Cool and cut into squares. Makes 20 squares.

Easy Nutty Bars

4 eggs	
1 (16 ounce) box brown sugar	455 g
2 tablespoons butter	30 g
2 cups self-rising flour	250 g
1 cup nuts	170 g

 Preheat oven to 350° (175° C). Beat eggs and add brown sugar and butter. Place in medium saucepan over low heat and cook until sugar and butter melt.

 Remove from heat and add flour and nuts. Place in sprayed 9 x 13-inch (23 x 33 cm) baking pan. Bake for 25 to 30 minutes. Cool and cut into bars. Makes 20 to 30 bars.

Cinnamon Pecans

Here's a no-brainer for something sweet.

1 pound pecan halves	455 g
1 egg white, slightly beaten	
2 tablespoons ground cinnamon	30 ml
¾ cup sugar	150 g

Preheat oven to 325° (165° C). Combine pecan halves with egg white and mix well. Sprinkle with mixture of cinnamon and sugar and stir until cinnamon-sugar coats pecans. Spread on baking sheet and bake for about 20 minutes. Cool. Store in covered container.

Macadamia Bars

Crust:

1 cup (2 sticks) butter, softened	225 g
2/3 cup sugar	135 g
2 cups flour	240 g

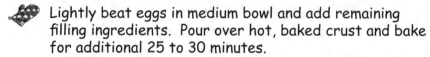

Preheat oven to 350° (175° C). Cream butter, sugar and flour in bowl. Press into sprayed 9 x 13-inch baking dish and bake for 20 minutes.

Filling:

4 eggs	
1 cup flaked coconut	85 g
3 cups packed light brown sugar	660 g
2 (3.2 ounce) jars macadamia nuts, chopped	2 (90 g)
1/4 cup flour	30 g
1 tablespoon vanilla	15 ml
1 teaspoon baking powder	5 ml

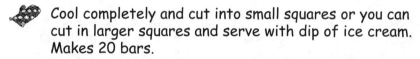

Lightly beat eggs in medium bowl and add remaining filling ingredients. Pour over hot, baked crust and bake for additional 25 to 30 minutes.

Cool completely and cut into small squares or you can cut in larger squares and serve with dip of ice cream. Makes 20 bars.

TIP: You could substitute 1½ cups (195 g) chopped walnuts for macadamia nuts. Either way, these bars are moist, chewy and absolutely sinful.

Walnut Bars

1⅔ cups graham cracker crumbs	175 g
1½ cups coarsely chopped walnuts	195 g
1 (14 ounce) can sweetened condensed milk	395 g
¼ cup flaked coconut, optional	20 g

Preheat oven to 350° (175° C).

Place graham cracker crumbs and walnuts in bowl. Slowly add sweetened condensed milk, coconut and pinch of salt. Mixture will be very thick.

Pack into sprayed 9-inch (23 cm) square pan. Pack mixture down with back of spoon.

Bake for 35 minutes. When cool cut into squares. Makes 9 to 12 bars.

 # Yummy Chess Squares

1 (18 ounce) box butter cake mix	510 g
4 eggs, divided	
½ cup (1 stick) butter, melted	115 g
2 teaspoons vanilla, divided	10 ml
1 (8 ounce) package cream cheese, softened	225 g
1 (16 ounce) box powdered sugar	455 g

Preheat oven to 300° (150° C). Combine cake mix, 1 egg, butter and 1 teaspoon (5 ml) vanilla in bowl and mix well. Batter will be very thick.

Spread in sprayed, floured 9 x 13-inch (23 x 33 cm) baking dish. Combine remaining 3 eggs, 1 teaspoon (5 ml) vanilla, cream cheese and powdered sugar in bowl and beat well.

Spread over cake mixture. Bake for 1 hour. Refrigerate and serve. Makes 12 to 14 squares.

Very Chocolate Streusel Bars

1¾ cups flour	210 g
1½ cups powdered sugar	180 g
½ cup cocoa	40 g
1 cup (2 sticks) butter, softened	225 g
1 (8 ounce) package cream cheese, softened	225 g
1 (14 ounce) can sweetened condensed milk	395 g
1 egg	
2 teaspoons vanilla	10 ml
½ cup chopped pecans	55 g

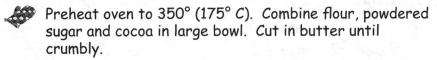

Preheat oven to 350° (175° C). Combine flour, powdered sugar and cocoa in large bowl. Cut in butter until crumbly.

Set aside 1 cup crumb mixture and press remaining dough firmly in sprayed, floured 9 x 13-inch baking pan. Bake for 15 minutes.

Beat cream cheese in large bowl until fluffy. Gradually beat in sweetened condensed milk until smooth. Add egg and vanilla and mix well. Pour over prepared crust.

Combine pecans with reserved crumb mixture and sprinkle over cream cheese mixture. Bake for 25 minutes or until bubbly.

Cool and refrigerate. Cut into bars and store in covered container. Makes 12 to 14 bars.

 # Chocolate-Cherry Bars

1 (18 ounce) box devil's food cake mix   510 g
1 (20 ounce) can cherry pie filling   565 g
2 eggs
1 cup milk chocolate chips   170 g

Preheat oven to 350° (175° C). Mix all ingredients in large bowl with spoon and blend well.

Pour batter into sprayed, floured 9 x 13-inch (23 x 33 cm) baking dish.

Bake for 25 to 30 minutes or until toothpick inserted in center comes out clean. Cool and frost.

Frosting:

3 (1 ounce) squares semi-sweet
    chocolate, melted   3 (30 g)
1 (3 ounce) package cream cheese,
    softened   85 g
½ teaspoon vanilla   2 ml
1½ cups powdered sugar   180 g

Beat chocolate, cream cheese and vanilla in medium bowl until smooth. Gradually beat in powdered sugar.

Pour over chocolate-cherry bars. Makes 20 bars.

Everything comes to him who hustles while he waits.
                                    —Thomas A. Edison

Chocolate Chip Cheese Bars

1 (18 ounce) tube refrigerated chocolate chip cookie dough	510 g
1 (8 ounce) package cream cheese, softened	225 g
½ cup sugar	100 g
1 egg	

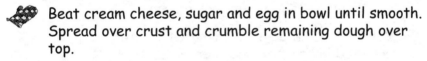 Preheat oven to 350° (175° C). Cut cookie dough in half. For crust, press half dough onto bottom of sprayed 9-inch (23 cm) square baking pan or 7 x 11-inch (18 x 28 cm) baking pan.

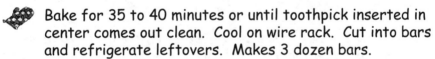 Beat cream cheese, sugar and egg in bowl until smooth. Spread over crust and crumble remaining dough over top.

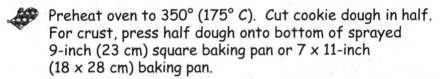 Bake for 35 to 40 minutes or until toothpick inserted in center comes out clean. Cool on wire rack. Cut into bars and refrigerate leftovers. Makes 3 dozen bars.

 # Caramel-Chocolate Chip Bars

1 (18 ounce) box caramel cake mix	510 g
2 eggs	
⅓ cup packed light brown sugar	75 g
¼ cup (½ stick) butter, softened	60 g
1 cup semi-sweet chocolate chips	170 g

Preheat oven to 350° (175° C). Combine cake mix, eggs, ¼ cup (60 ml) water, brown sugar and butter in large bowl. Stir until it blends thoroughly. (Mixture will be thick.)

Stir in chocolate chips. Spread in sprayed, floured 9 x 13-inch (23 x 33 cm) baking pan.

Bake for about 25 to 30 minutes or until toothpick inserted in center comes out clean. Cool. Makes 20 bars.

TIP: These bars are especially good when frosted with a prepared caramel icing.

 A smile is the best thing you can wear.
—Grandma Mullins

Carmelitas

Crust:

1 cup flour	120 g
¾ cup packed brown sugar	165 g
1 cup quick-cooking oats	80 g
½ teaspoon baking soda	2 ml
¾ cup (1½ sticks) butter, melted	170 g

Preheat oven to 350° (175° C). Combine flour, brown sugar, ⅛ teaspoon (.5 ml) salt, oats, baking soda and butter in bowl and blend well enough to form crumbs.

Pat down two-thirds crumb mixture into sprayed 9 x 13-inch (23 x 33 cm) baking pan and bake for 10 minutes.

Filling:

1 (6 ounce) package chocolate chips	170 g
¾ cup chopped pecans	85 g
1 (12 ounce) jar caramel ice cream topping	340 g
3 tablespoons flour	45 g

Remove from oven and sprinkle with chocolate chips and pecans. Blend caramel topping with flour in bowl and spread over chips and pecans.

Sprinkle with remaining crumb mixture and bake for 20 minutes or until golden brown. Refrigerate for 2 hours before cutting into squares. Makes about 2 to 3 dozen.

Gooey Turtle Bars

½ cup (1 stick) butter, melted	115 g
2 cups vanilla wafer crumbs	320 g
1 (12 ounce) semi-sweet chocolate chips	340 g
1 cup pecan pieces	110 g
1 (12 ounce) jar caramel topping	340 g

Preheat oven to 350° (175° C). Combine butter and wafer crumbs in 9 x 13-inch (23 x 33 cm) baking pan and press into bottom of pan. Sprinkle with chocolate chips and pecans.

Remove lid from caramel topping and microwave on HIGH for 30 seconds or until hot. Drizzle over pecans.

Bake for about 15 minutes or until chips melt. Cool in pan.

Refrigerate for at least 30 minutes before cutting into squares. Makes 20 bars.

TIP: Watch bars closely – you want the chips to melt, but you don't want the crumbs to burn.

Hello Dollies

1½ cups graham cracker crumbs	155 g
1 (6 ounce) package chocolate chips	170 g
1 cup flaked coconut	85 g
1¼ cups chopped pecans	140 g
1 (14 ounce) can sweetened condensed milk	395 g

Preheat oven to 350° (175° C). Sprinkle cracker crumbs in 9-inch (23 cm) square pan. Layer chocolate chips, coconut and pecans.

Pour sweetened condensed milk over top of layered ingredients. Bake for 25 to 30 minutes. Cool and cut into squares. Makes 16 squares.

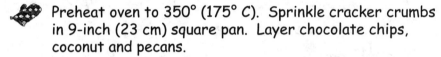

Believe it or not, you can bake peanut butter cookies with no flour and they are terrific. Preheat the oven to 350° (175° C). Mix 2 cups (575 g) creamy or crunchy peanut butter with 2 cups (500 ml) Splenda® (or sweetener to equal 2 cups (400 g) sugar), 2 eggs and 2 teaspoons (10 ml) vanilla. Mix well and drop on cookie sheet. Don't forget to make the criss-cross sign on top with a fork.

Peanut butter has been around as long as peanuts have been grown. Peanuts spread from South America to Africa, Europe and finally to the colonies. The first peanut crop was grown in Virginia in the mid 1840's.

Million-Dollar Bars

½ cup (1 stick) butter	115 g
2 cups graham cracker crumbs	210 g
1 (6 ounce) package chocolate chips	170 g
1 (6 ounce) package butterscotch chips	170 g
1 cup chopped pecans	110 g
1 (7 ounce) can flaked coconut	200 g
1 (14 ounce) can sweetened condensed milk	395 g

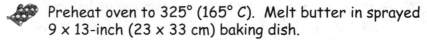

Preheat oven to 325° (165° C). Melt butter in sprayed 9 x 13-inch (23 x 33 cm) baking dish.

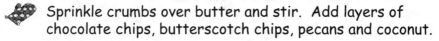

Sprinkle crumbs over butter and stir. Add layers of chocolate chips, butterscotch chips, pecans and coconut.

Pour sweetened condensed milk over top and bake for about 30 minutes. Cool in pan and cut bars. Makes 12 to 14 bars.

Baking is a method of applying dry heat to food in an enclosed space — like an oven.

Rainbow Cookie Bars

½ cup (1 stick) butter	115 g
2 cups graham cracker crumbs	210 g
1 (14 ounce) can sweetened	
condensed milk	395 g
⅔ cup flaked coconut	60 g
1 cup chopped pecans	110 g
1 cup M&M's® plain chocolate	
candies	170 g

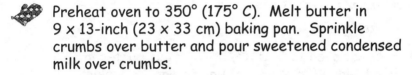 Preheat oven to 350° (175° C). Melt butter in 9 x 13-inch (23 x 33 cm) baking pan. Sprinkle crumbs over butter and pour sweetened condensed milk over crumbs.

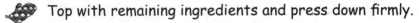 Top with remaining ingredients and press down firmly.

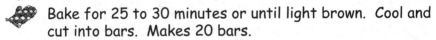 Bake for 25 to 30 minutes or until light brown. Cool and cut into bars. Makes 20 bars.

TIP: If you don't have M&M's®, white chocolate bits work but you won't have the "rainbow".

Pre-measure ingredients. Everything will be ready to mix and distractions like the phone or the kids are less likely to cause you to leave something out. Use custard cups or ramekins or, for dry ingredients, waxed paper.

Seven-Layer Bars

½ cup (1 stick) butter	115 g
1 cup crushed graham crackers	105 g
1 (6 ounce) package semi-sweet chocolate chips	170 g
1 (6 ounce) package butterscotch chips	170 g
1 (3.5 ounce) can flaked coconut	100 g
1 (14 ounce) can sweetened condensed milk	395 g
1 cup chopped pecans	110 g

 Preheat oven to 350° (175° C). Melt butter in 9 x 13-inch (23 x 33 cm) baking pan. Sprinkle remaining ingredients in order listed. Do not stir or mix.

Bake for 30 minutes. Allow to cool before cutting. Makes about 4 dozen bars.

Prepare your baking pans ahead of time so they will be ready to use when the mixture is placed in them. Be sure to prepare the pans according to the directions in the recipe.

Toffee Bars

1½ cups (3 sticks) butter, softened	340 g
1¾ cups packed light brown sugar	385 g
2 teaspoons vanilla	10 ml
3 cups flour	360 g
1 (8 ounce) package chocolate chips	225 g

Preheat oven to 350° (175° C). In mixing bowl, combine butter, brown sugar and vanilla and beat on medium speed for 3 minutes.

Add flour, mix until completely blended and stir in chocolate chips. Place dough on sprayed 9 x 13-inch (23 x 33 cm) baking pan.

Bake for 25 minutes or until light brown. Cool slightly and cut into bars. Makes 4 to 5 dozen bars.

Butter should be just below room temperature (65° to 67°/18° to 19° C) for most recipes. Set it out 15 to 30 minutes before use. However, if the recipe calls for cold butter, leave it in the refrigerator until you are ready to add it or you may not get the desired results, especially with piecrust and other pastry. It's often helpful to slice the butter ahead of time and put it back into the refrigerator so it chills well.

Cheerleader Brownies

⅔ cup canola oil	150 ml
2 cups sugar	400 g
⅓ cup corn syrup	75 ml
4 eggs, beaten	
½ cup cocoa	40 g
1½ cups flour	180 g
1 teaspoon baking powder	5 ml
2 teaspoons vanilla	10 ml
1 cup chopped pecans	110 g

Preheat oven to 350° (175° C). Beat oil, sugar, corn syrup and eggs in bowl. Add cocoa, flour, ½ teaspoon (2 ml) salt, baking powder and vanilla. Beat well and add pecans.

Pour in sprayed, floured 9 x 13-inch (23 x 33 cm) baking pan and bake for 45 minutes. Makes 9 to 12 brownies.

Eggs work much better at room temperature.
If you forget to take the eggs out of the refrigerator, put the eggs in bowl of warm, not hot, water for 2 minutes only. Stir them so they do not begin to cook. If they are still cold, repeat for another 2 minutes. Dry the eggs with a towel before cracking them.

If separating eggs, separate while they are still cold. Then let the separated yolks and whites come to room temperature.

Everyday Special Brownies

1 cup (2 sticks) butter	*225 g*
1½ cups dark chocolate pieces	*255 g*
3 eggs	
1¼ cups sugar	*250 g*
1 cup flour	*120 g*

 Preheat oven to 350° (175° C). Melt butter and chocolate in double boiler over low heat. Cool to room temperature.

Beat eggs in medium bowl until foamy. Stir in sugar and beat at medium speed for 2 to 3 minutes.

Reduce speed and slowly pour in chocolate-butter mixture. Slowly beat in flour in several additions.

Pour into sprayed, floured 9 x 13-inch baking pan. Bake for 35 to 40 minutes or until brownies are done in middle. Cool and cut into squares. Makes 12 to 18 brownies.

Your kitchen chores become easier if you clean up as you go.

 # German Chocolate Brownie Bars

1 (14 ounce) package caramels	395 g
1 (12 ounce) can evaporated milk, divided	355 ml
1 (18 ounce) box chocolate cake mix	510 g
1 cup chopped pecans	110 g
1 cup semi-sweet chocolate chips	340 g

Preheat oven to 350° (175° C). Combine caramels with
⅓ cup (75 ml) evaporated milk in top of double boiler set
over simmering water.

Stir until caramels melt and mixture is smooth. Remove
from heat and set aside.

In large bowl, combine cake mix with pecans and
remaining evaporated milk. Spread half of batter in
sprayed 9 x 13-inch (23 x 33 cm) baking pan. Bake for
6 minutes.

Remove from oven, sprinkle with chocolate chips and
drizzle caramel mixture evenly over top. Drop remaining
half of batter by spoonfuls over caramel mixture.

Bake additional 15 to 20 minutes. Remove from oven and
cool before cutting. Makes 12 bars.

*Use pure extracts, not imitation. It really
does make a difference.*

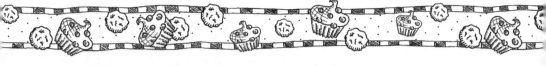

 # Snickers Brownies

1 (18 ounce) box German chocolate cake mix	510 g
¾ cup (1½ sticks) butter, melted	170 g
½ cup evaporated milk	125 ml
4 (3 ounce) Snickers® candy bars, cut in ⅛-inch (3 mm) slices	4 (85 g)

Preheat oven to 350° (175° C). Combine cake mix, butter and evaporated milk in large bowl. Beat on low speed until mixture blends well.

Add half batter into sprayed, floured 9 x 13-inch (23 x 33 cm) baking pan. Bake for 10 minutes.

Remove from oven and place candy bar slices evenly over brownies. Drop spoonfuls of remaining batter over candy bars and spread as evenly as possible.

Place back in oven and bake for additional 20 minutes. When cool, cut into bars. Makes 16 to 20 brownies.

Frank and Ethel Mars, who created the Mars® chocolate bar and the Mars Company in the early 1920's, introduced Snickers® in 1930. This chocolate candy bar has become one of the most popular candy bars in world with more than 150 million Snickers® produced each day.

The candy bar got its name from Ethel Mars' favorite racehorse, Snickers, raised on the Milky Way Farm. Today Snickers® continues its association with athletes and sports for its promotions.

Chewy Caramel Brownies

1 (14 ounce) package caramels	395 g
1 (5 ounce) can evaporated milk, divided	150 ml
1 (18 ounce) box German chocolate cake mix	510 g
¾ cup (1½ sticks) butter, melted	170 g
1 cup chopped pecans	110 g
1 cup semi-sweet chocolate chips	170 g

Preheat oven to 350° (175° C). Melt caramels and $\frac{1}{3}$ cup (75 ml) evaporated milk in saucepan over low heat. Stir constantly.

Combine cake mix, butter and remaining milk in bowl. Spread half cake mixture into sprayed 9 x 13-inch (23 x 33 cm) baking pan and bake for 7 minutes.

Sprinkle with pecans and chocolate chips and spoon on melted caramels.

Drop spoonfuls of remaining cake mixture over top and lightly spread with back of spoon.

Bake for 18 to 20 minutes and cool completely before cutting into squares. Makes 24 brownies.

For most recipes, it is best that all ingredients be at or close to room temperature. (However, some recipes, such as piecrusts and other pastries, do call for cold ingredients.)

Easy Blonde Brownies

This is one of those recipes that seems too easy to be a real recipe, but it is and they are chewy and wonderful.

1 (16 ounce) box light brown sugar	455 g
4 eggs	
2 cups biscuit mix	240 g
2 cups chopped pecans	220 g

Preheat oven to 350° (175° C). Beat brown sugar, eggs and biscuit mix in bowl.

Stir in pecans and pour into sprayed 9 x 13-inch (23 x 33 cm) baking pan.

Bake for 35 minutes. Cool and cut into squares. Makes 12 to 15 brownies.

Glazed Butterscotch Brownies

3 cups packed brown sugar	660 g
1 cup (2 sticks) butter, softened	225 g
3 eggs	
3 cups flour	360 g
2 tablespoons baking powder	30 ml
1½ cups chopped pecans	165 g
1 cup flaked coconut	85 g

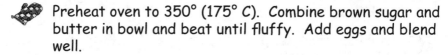 Preheat oven to 350° (175° C). Combine brown sugar and butter in bowl and beat until fluffy. Add eggs and blend well.

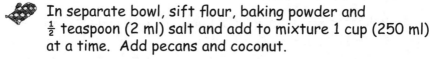 In separate bowl, sift flour, baking powder and ½ teaspoon (2 ml) salt and add to mixture 1 cup (250 ml) at a time. Add pecans and coconut.

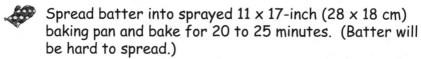 Spread batter into sprayed 11 x 17-inch (28 x 18 cm) baking pan and bake for 20 to 25 minutes. (Batter will be hard to spread.)

Continued next page...

Continued from previous page...

Glaze:

½ cup packed brown sugar	110 g
⅓ cup evaporated milk	75 ml
½ cup (1 stick) butter	115 g
2 tablespoons baking powder	30 ml
1 cup powdered sugar	120 g
½ teaspoon vanilla	2 ml

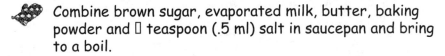 Combine brown sugar, evaporated milk, butter, baking powder and ☐ teaspoon (.5 ml) salt in saucepan and bring to a boil.

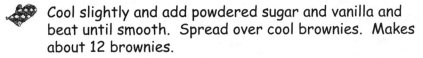 Cool slightly and add powdered sugar and vanilla and beat until smooth. Spread over cool brownies. Makes about 12 brownies.

 # Peanut Butter Brownies

1 (20 ounce) box brownie mix	*565 g*
1 cup peanut butter chips	*170 g*

 Preheat oven to 350° (175° C). Prepare brownie mix according to package directions and stir in peanut butter chips.

 Spoon mixture into sprayed 9 x 13-inch (23 x 33 cm) baking pan. Bake for 35 minutes. Cool and cut into squares. Makes 20 brownies.

Chocolate was a delicacy only the rich could afford. In 1780 the first chocolate factory opened and was financed by Dr. James Baker, namesake of Baker's Chocolate, a brand name now owned by General Mills Corporation.

By the early 1900's, chocolate was much easier and less expensive to get and chocolate cakes were not just for the rich.

One of the first brownie recipes appeared in Fannie Farmer's Boston Cooking School Cook Book in 1905. The brownies had less flour and no leavening so the texture was more dense and chewy than cake.

Cookies

Mmm-Mmm Sugar Cookies

½ cup (1 stick) butter, softened	115 g
1 cup sugar	100 g
1 egg	
1 tablespoon cream	15 ml
½ teaspoon vanilla	2 ml
2 cups flour	240 g
1 teaspoon baking powder	5 ml

Preheat oven to 375° (190° C). Cream butter in bowl and slowly add sugar. Beat until light and fluffy.

In separate bowl, combine egg, cream and vanilla; add to butter mixture and beat to mix.

In a separate bowl, combine flour, baking powder and ¼ teaspoon (1 ml) salt. Add flour mixture to butter mixture a little at a time and mix after each addition.

Drop spoonfuls of mixture onto sprayed cookie sheet. Bake for about 8 to 10 minutes. Makes about 5 dozen cookies.

Sugar cookies were once round and plain with an unassuming dusting of granulated sugar on top. Today these delicious cookies are a favorite of both professional and amateur bakers who cut them into various shapes and decorate them with frosting, cookie paints and candy. Sugar cookie bouquets are popular for showers, parties and other special occasions.

Snappy Almond-Sugar Cookies

1 cup (2 sticks) butter	*225 g*
1 cup plus 2 tablespoons sugar	*225 g*
½ teaspoon almond extract	*2 ml*
2 cups flour	*240 g*
1 cup chopped almonds	*170 g*

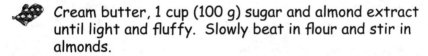

Cream butter, 1 cup (100 g) sugar and almond extract until light and fluffy. Slowly beat in flour and stir in almonds.

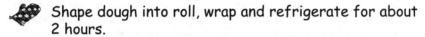

Shape dough into roll, wrap and refrigerate for about 2 hours.

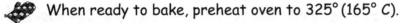

When ready to bake, preheat oven to 325° (165° C).

Slice roll into ¼-inch (6 mm) pieces and bake for 20 minutes. Sprinkle with remaining 2 tablespoons (25 g) sugar while still hot. Makes about 3 to 4 dozen cookies.

It is best to refrigerate cookie dough before using a cookie cutter or slicing the dough.

To keep cookie dough from sticking and getting stuck when rolling it out, sprinkle a mixture of flour and powdered sugar on the work surface.

When using cookie cutters, particularly plastic ones, dip the cutter in warm vegetable oil so the edges will cut cleanly.

Baylor Cookies

1 cup shortening	190 g
¼ cup packed brown sugar	55 g
1 cup sugar	200 g
1 egg	
1½ teaspoons vanilla	7 ml
2 cups flour	240 g
2 teaspoons baking powder	10 ml
1 cup chopped pecans	110 g

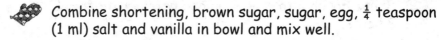

Combine shortening, brown sugar, sugar, egg, ¼ teaspoon (1 ml) salt and vanilla in bowl and mix well.

Add flour and baking powder and mix until it blends well. Add pecans and mix. Divide dough in half and roll out in long jellyroll shape on floured wax paper.

Place each rolled dough on a piece of wax paper and wrap in paper. Refrigerate for several hours.

When ready to bake, preheat oven to 350° (175° C).

Slice in ¼-inch (6 mm) slices. Place on cookie sheet and bake for 15 minutes or until slightly brown. Makes about 4 dozen cookies.

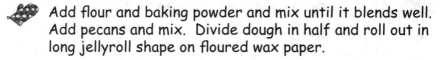

The best way to keep refrigerated cookie dough from getting flat on one side when you are slicing it is to roll it on the countertop after each slice. Another method is to roll it one-fourth of the way around after each slice.

Brown Sugar Cookies

¾ cup packed brown sugar	165 g
1 cup (2 sticks) butter, softened	225 g
1 egg yolk	
2 cups flour	240 g

Cream brown sugar and butter in bowl until light and fluffy. Mix in egg yolk. Blend in flour. Refrigerate dough for 1 hour.

When ready to bake, preheat oven to 325° (165° C).

Form dough into 1-inch (2.5 cm) balls, flatten and criss-cross with fork on lightly sprayed cookie sheet.

Bake for 10 to 12 minutes or until golden brown. Makes 2 dozen cookies.

Granulated sugar tends to make cookies crispy. Brown sugar tends to make cookies soft and chewy. The moisture in brown sugar creates the chewy quality.

Drop Cookies

1 cup (2 sticks) butter, softened	*225 g*
¾ cup cornstarch	*95 g*
⅓ cup powdered sugar	*40 g*
1 cup flour	*120 g*

 Preheat oven to 350° (175° C). Mix butter, cornstarch, sugar and flour in bowl and mix well.

 Drop onto cookie sheet in small balls and flatten slightly. Bake for about 15 minutes but do not brown. When cool, ice.

Icing:

1 (3 ounce) package cream cheese,	
softened	*85 g*
1 teaspoon vanilla	*5 ml*
1 cup powdered sugar	*120 g*

 Blend all ingredients in bowl and mix well. Ice cookies. Makes 2 dozen cookies.

Holiday Spritz Cookies

½ cup plus 2 tablespoons (1¼ sticks)
    butter, softened   140 g
1¼ cups sugar   250 g
1 egg, well beaten
1 teaspoon almond flavoring   5 ml
Food coloring
3 cups flour   360 g
1 teaspoon baking powder   5 ml

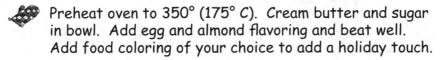

Preheat oven to 350° (175° C). Cream butter and sugar
in bowl. Add egg and almond flavoring and beat well.
Add food coloring of your choice to add a holiday touch.

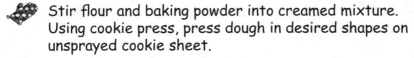

Stir flour and baking powder into creamed mixture.
Using cookie press, press dough in desired shapes on
unsprayed cookie sheet.

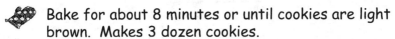

Bake for about 8 minutes or until cookies are light
brown. Makes 3 dozen cookies.

TIP: Use some of the decorative icings or sprinkles found in
     grocery stores to decorate cookies.

 # Butter Cookie Special

1 (18 ounce) box butter cake mix	510 g
1 (3.4 ounce) package butterscotch instant pudding mix	100 g
1 cup canola oil	250 ml
1 egg, beaten	
1¼ cups chopped pecans	140 g

Preheat oven to 350° (175° C). Combine cake mix, pudding mix, oil and egg in bowl and mix with spoon. Beat thoroughly.

Stir in pecans. Drop spoonfuls of dough onto cookie sheet about 2 inches (5 cm) apart.

Bake for about 8 minutes. Do not overcook. Makes 3 dozen cookies.

Butter Cookies

1 cup (2 sticks) butter, softened	225 g
1 (16 ounce) box powdered sugar	455 g
1 egg	
1 teaspoon almond extract	5 ml
1 teaspoon vanilla	5 ml
2½ cups plus 1 tablespoon flour	310 g
¾ teaspoon cream of tartar	4 ml
1 teaspoon baking soda	5 ml
Sugar	

 Cream butter, powdered sugar and add egg, almond extract and vanilla in bowl and mix well.

 In separate bowl, sift flour, cream of tartar and baking soda and add to creamed mixture. Cover and refrigerate for several hours.

 When ready to bake, preheat oven to 350° (175° C).

 Roll cookie dough into ¼ inch (6 mm) thickness and use cookie cutters to make desired shapes. Place on cookie sheet.

 Bake for 7 to 8 minutes, but do not brown. Sprinkle a little sugar over each cookie while still hot. Makes 2 dozen cookies.

Butter Pecan Cookies

1 cup (2 sticks) butter	225 g
½ cup packed light brown sugar	110 g
1 large egg	
2 cups flour	120 g
¾ cup chopped pecans, toasted	85 g

In medium bowl, beat butter and brown sugar until light and fluffy. Beat in egg. Add flour and beat until well blended. Stir in pecans.

Divide dough in half. Shape each half into 8 x 1½-inch (20 x 4 cm) log. Cover each log well in either wax paper or plastic wrap and freeze until firm, about 30 minutes or refrigerate for up to 2 days.

When ready to bake, preheat oven to 350° (175° C).

Slice dough into pieces ⅜-inch (1 cm) thick and place slices 2 inches (5 cm) apart on unsprayed cookie sheet.

Bake for 15 minutes or until cookies are light brown around edges. Remove from oven and transfer cookies to cooling rack. Makes 2 to 3 dozen cookies.

When eggs are called for in baking, use large eggs. Most recipes are based on large eggs.

Cheesecake Cookies

1 cup (2 sticks) butter, softened	*225 g*
2 (3 ounce) packages cream cheese, softened	*2 (85 g)*
2 cups sugar	*400 g*
2 cups flour	*240 g*

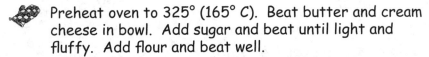

Preheat oven to 325° (165° C). Beat butter and cream cheese in bowl. Add sugar and beat until light and fluffy. Add flour and beat well.

Drop spoonfuls of dough onto cookie sheet and bake for 12 to 15 minutes or until edges are golden. Makes 3 dozen cookies.

TIP: These are even better if you add 1 cup (110 g) chopped pecans.

The first cookbook written by an American and published in the U.S. was American Cookery by Amelia Simmons. It included two recipes for cookies. Here is the one entitled "Christmas Cookey":

To three pound of flour, sprinkle a tea cup of fine powdered coriander seed, rub in one pound of butter, and one and half pound sugar, dissolve one tea spoonful of pearlash in a tea cup of milk, kneed all together well, roll three quarter of an inch thick, and cut or stamp into shape and size you please, bake slowly fifteen or twenty minutes; tho' hard and dry at first, if put in an earthern pot, and dry cellar, or damp room, they will be finer, softer and better when six months old.

Classic Gingersnaps

¾ cup packed brown sugar	165 g
¾ cup (1½ sticks) butter or shortening	170 g/140 g
¾ cup light molasses	175 ml
1 egg	
¾ cup flour	90 g
2 teaspoons baking soda	10 ml
1 teaspoon ground cinnamon	5 ml
1 teaspoon ground ginger	5 ml
½ teaspoon ground cloves	2 ml
¼ cup sugar	50 g

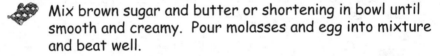

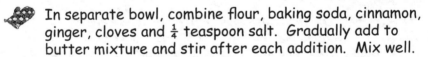

Mix brown sugar and butter or shortening in bowl until smooth and creamy. Pour molasses and egg into mixture and beat well.

In separate bowl, combine flour, baking soda, cinnamon, ginger, cloves and ¼ teaspoon salt. Gradually add to butter mixture and stir after each addition. Mix well.

Refrigerate overnight or for several hours.

When ready to bake, preheat oven to 350° (175° C).

Form dough in 1 to 2-inch (2.5 to 5 cm) balls and roll in sugar. Place 2 inches apart on sprayed cookie sheet. Bake for 10 to 12 minutes. Makes 3 dozen cookies.

 # Gingerbread Cookies

¾ cup (1½ sticks) butter, softened   170 g
2 egg yolks
1 (18 ounce) box spice cake mix   510 g
1 teaspoon ground ginger   5 ml

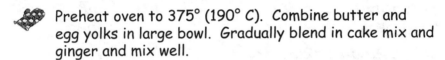 Preheat oven to 375° (190° C). Combine butter and egg yolks in large bowl. Gradually blend in cake mix and ginger and mix well.

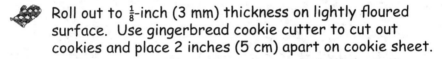 Roll out to ⅛-inch (3 mm) thickness on lightly floured surface. Use gingerbread cookie cutter to cut out cookies and place 2 inches (5 cm) apart on cookie sheet.

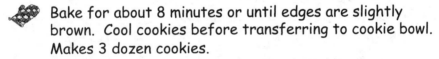 Bake for about 8 minutes or until edges are slightly brown. Cool cookies before transferring to cookie bowl. Makes 3 dozen cookies.

Ginger originated in Asia, but came to Europe through the Mediterranean, probably carried by crusaders. Throughout the ages ginger has been used as an ingredient in savory and sweet dishes. Many believe that ginger aids in digestion and many cultures think of it as medicine.

Today gingerbread means soft, moist cake or heavy cookies usually cut in familiar shapes, both made with ginger.

Grammy's Ginger-Oat Cookies

½ cup (1 stick) butter, softened	115 g
¾ cup sugar	150 g
¾ cup packed brown sugar	165 g
1 egg	
½ teaspoon vanilla	2 ml
1 cup flour	120 g
½ teaspoon baking soda	2 ml
½ cup finely chopped crystallized ginger	125 ml
1½ cups quick-cooking oats	120 g
1 (6 ounce) package chocolate chips	170 g
½ cup chopped pecans	55 g

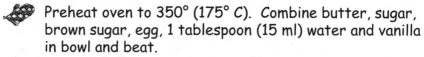 Preheat oven to 350° (175° C). Combine butter, sugar, brown sugar, egg, 1 tablespoon (15 ml) water and vanilla in bowl and beat.

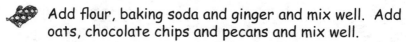 Add flour, baking soda and ginger and mix well. Add oats, chocolate chips and pecans and mix well.

 Drop spoonfuls of dough onto sprayed cookie sheet and bake for 12 to 15 minutes or until cookies brown. Makes 4 dozen cookies.

Hugs and Kisses Molasses Cookies

1 cup (2 sticks) butter, softened	225 g
1½ cups sugar	300 g
1 egg	
¾ cup molasses	175 ml
3 cups flour	360 g
1 teaspoon baking powder	5 ml
1 teaspoon ground ginger	5 ml
1 cup chopped nuts	160 g

Cream butter and sugar in large bowl. Add egg and molasses and continue to cream mixture.

In separate bowl, mix flour, baking powder and ginger and add to creamed mixture a little at a time. Add nuts and mix well.

Form into 3 rolls, wrap in plastic paper and refrigerate overnight.

When ready to bake, preheat oven to 350° (175° C).

Cut rolls into ¼-inch (1.3 cm) slices and bake for about 10 minutes or until light brown. Makes 4 dozen cookies.

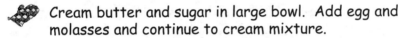
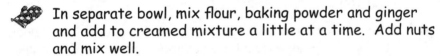

Molasses played a big role in trade in the American colonies and continued to be a primary sweetener until after World War I. Until that time, molasses was less expensive and more readily available than sugar and was often used to sweeten baked goods like pies, cakes, gingerbread, toffee candy, and cookies.

Yankee Doodle's Snickerdoodles

½ cup (1 stick) butter, softened	115 g
½ cup shortening	95 g
1¾ cups sugar, divided	350 g
2 eggs	
2¼ cups flour	270 g
2 teaspoons cream of tartar	10 ml
1 teaspoon baking soda	5 ml
2 teaspoons ground cinnamon	10 ml

Preheat oven to 350° (175° C). Mix butter, shortening, 1½ cups (300 g) sugar and eggs in medium bowl and beat well.

Stir in flour, cream of tartar, baking soda and ¼ teaspoon (1 ml) salt. Shape dough by rounded spoonfuls into balls.

Mix remaining ¼ cup (50 g) sugar and cinnamon in small bowl and roll balls in mixture to cover. Place balls 2 inches (5 cm) apart on unsprayed cookie sheet and use bottom of jar or glass to flatten cookies.

Bake 8 to 10 minutes or until edges just begin to brown. Makes 24 to 30 cookies.

The origin and name of snickerdoodles are unknown; some credit Dutch settlers and others Germans who came to colonial America. Whatever their origin, snickerdoodles have survived and changed little throughout America's history.

Hurly-Burly Oatmeal Cookies

1 cup packed brown sugar	220 g
1 cup sugar	200 g
1 cup shortening	190 g
2 eggs	
2 teaspoons vanilla	10 ml
1 teaspoon baking soda	5 ml
1½ cups flour	180 g
3 cups quick-cooking oats	240 g
1 cup chopped pecans	110 g

Preheat oven to 350° (175° C). Combine brown sugar, sugar, shortening, eggs, 2 tablespoons (30 ml) water and vanilla in bowl and beat well.

Add 1 teaspoon (5 ml) salt, baking soda and flour and mix well. Pour in oats and pecans and mix.

Drop spoonfuls of dough onto sprayed cookie sheet and bake for 14 to 15 minutes or until cookies brown. Makes 4 dozen cookies.

The Quaker Company is the largest producer of oats in America. The original package was square. The familiar cylinder shape was introduced in 1915.

 # Oatmeal-Chocolate Chip Cookies

1 (18 ounce) box yellow cake mix   510 g
1 cup quick-cooking oats   80 g
¾ cup (1½ sticks) butter, softened   170 g
2 eggs
1 cup semi-sweet chocolate chips   170 g

Preheat oven to 350° (175° C). Combine cake mix, oats, butter and eggs in bowl and beat until they blend well.

Stir in chocolate chips. Drop spoonfuls of dough onto unsprayed cookie sheet.

Bake for 10 to 12 minutes or until light brown.

Allow cookies to cool slightly, remove from cookie sheet and cool completely on wire rack. Makes 2 to 3 dozen cookies.

Established in 1877, Quaker Oats received the first trademark registered for a breakfast cereal. The logo had a man dressed in Quaker clothing. The Quaker Company was the first company to offer sample-size boxes of breakfast cereal.

In 1891 Quaker introduced premium products inside boxes of Quaker cereal. In the same year Quaker became the first company to put a recipe on the product box.

In 1908 the first oatmeal cookie recipe appeared on the Quaker cereal box.

Favorite Chocolate Chip Cookies

½ cup (1 stick) butter, softened	115 g
¾ cup sugar	150 g
¾ cup packed brown sugar	165 g
1 egg	
½ teaspoon vanilla	2 ml
1 cup flour	120 g
½ teaspoon baking soda	2 ml
1½ cups quick-cooking oats	120 g
1 (6 ounce) package chocolate chips	170 g
½ cup chopped pecans, optional	55 g

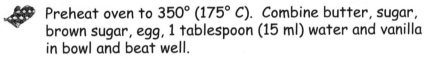 Preheat oven to 350° (175° C). Combine butter, sugar, brown sugar, egg, 1 tablespoon (15 ml) water and vanilla in bowl and beat well.

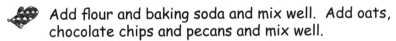 Add flour and baking soda and mix well. Add oats, chocolate chips and pecans and mix well.

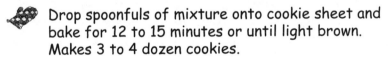 Drop spoonfuls of mixture onto cookie sheet and bake for 12 to 15 minutes or until light brown. Makes 3 to 4 dozen cookies.

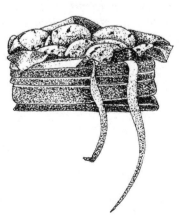

Chocolate Cookies

6 egg whites
3 cups powdered sugar   360 g
¼ cup cocoa   20 g
3½ cups finely chopped pecans   390 g

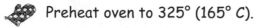

Preheat oven to 325° (165° C).

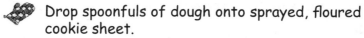

Beat egg whites in bowl until light and frothy. Fold powdered sugar and cocoa into egg whites and beat lightly. Fold in pecans.

Drop spoonfuls of dough onto sprayed, floured cookie sheet.

Bake for about 20 minutes. Do not over bake and cool completely before removing from cookie sheet. Makes 3 dozen cookies.

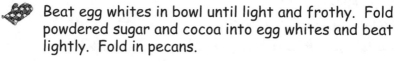

Cookie recipes expanded in variety with modern transportation. Railroads allowed the shipment of coconuts, oranges and other foods. When cornflakes were invented, this and other cereal products became ingredients.

Chocolate Kisses

2 egg whites, room temperature
⅔ cup sugar   135 g
1 teaspoon vanilla   5 ml
1¼ cups chopped pecans   140 g
1 (6 ounce) package chocolate
    chips   170 g

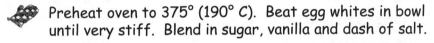 Preheat oven to 375° (190° C). Beat egg whites in bowl
until very stiff. Blend in sugar, vanilla and dash of salt.

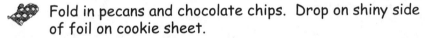 Fold in pecans and chocolate chips. Drop on shiny side
of foil on cookie sheet.

Put cookies in oven, TURN OVEN OFF and leave
overnight. If cookies are a little sticky, leave out in air
to dry. Makes 3 dozen cookies.

The Hershey Company introduced Hershey's®
Kisses in 1907. The small chocolate pieces
were given the name kisses when the machine making
them reminded someone of kisses.

Whoopie Pies

This Pennsylvania Dutch dessert or snack has cake-like rounds on the top and bottom with a creamy, yummy filling between them.

1 cup shortening, divided	190 g
1¼ cups sugar	250 g
2 eggs, separated	
1 cup milk	250 ml
2 teaspoons vanilla, divided	5 ml
2 cups flour	240 g
¼ cup cocoa	20 g
1 teaspoon baking powder	5 ml
1 teaspoon baking soda	5 ml
2 cups powdered sugar, divided	240 g

Preheat oven to 375° (190° C). Cream ½ cup (95 g) shortening and sugar in large bowl. Beat egg yolks until lightly colored and pour into sugar mixture; add milk and 1 teaspoon (2 ml) vanilla. Mix well and beat again.

In separate bowl, mix flour, cocoa, baking powder, baking soda and ½ teaspoon (2 ml) salt. Gradually pour a little flour mixture at a time into shortening-sugar mixture and beat after each addition.

Drop spoonfuls of mixture onto unsprayed cookie sheets and bake for about 8 minutes or until done.

Continued next page...

Continued from previous page...

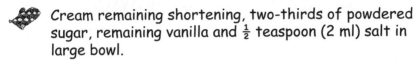 Cream remaining shortening, two-thirds of powdered sugar, remaining vanilla and $\frac{1}{2}$ teaspoon (2 ml) salt in large bowl.

Beat egg whites until stiff. Pour remaining one-third of powdered sugar into egg whites and beat. Add shortening mixture to whites and beat for about 2 minutes.

Make "sandwiches" of the cakes and filling. Wrap each individually and eat right away. Makes 8 to 12 "pies".

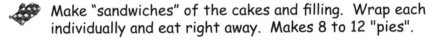

Chocolate-Coconut Cookies

1 cup sweetened condensed milk	*310 g*
4 cups flaked coconut	*340 g*
2/3 cup miniature semi-sweet	
chocolate bits	*115 g*
1 teaspoon vanilla	*5 ml*
1/2 teaspoon almond extract	*2 ml*

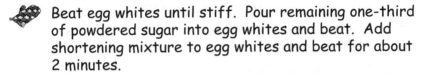 Preheat oven to 325° (165° C). Combine sweetened condensed milk and coconut in bowl. (Mixture will be gooey.)

Add chocolate bits, vanilla and almond extract and stir until blended well. Drop spoonfuls of dough onto sprayed cookie sheet. Bake for 12 minutes.

Store in airtight container. Makes 2 to 3 dozen cookies.

 # Chocolate Crunch Cookies

These cookies are incredibly easy.

1 (18 ounce) box German chocolate
   cake mix with pudding   510 g
1 egg, slightly beaten
½ cup (1 stick) butter, melted   115 g
1 cup rice crispy cereal   25 g

 Preheat oven to 350° (175° C). Combine cake mix, egg and butter in bowl. Add cereal and stir until blended. Shape dough into 1-inch (2.5 cm) balls. Place on sprayed cookie sheet.

 Dip fork in flour and flatten cookies in crisscross pattern. Bake for 10 to 12 minutes and cool. Makes 3 dozen cookies.

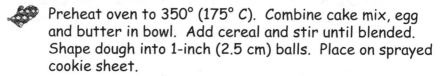

A 16th century British cookie recipe:

To make Fine Cakes.- Take fine flowre and good Damaske water you must have no other liqeur but that, then take sweet butter, two or three yolkes of eggs and a good quantity of Suger, and a few cloves, and mace, as your Cookes mouth shall serve him, and a lyttle saffron, and a little Gods good about a spoonful if you put in too much they shall arise, cutte them in squares lyke unto trenchers, and pricke them well, and let your oven be well swept and lay them uppon papers and so set them into the oven. Do not burne them if they be three or foure days olde they bee the better." From Goode Huswife's Jewell *by Thomas Dawson*

 # Devil's Food Cookies

1 (18 ounce) box devil's food cake mix	510 g
½ cup canola oil	125 ml
2 eggs	
¾ cup chopped pecans	85 g

 Preheat oven to 350° (175° C). Combine cake mix, oil, eggs and pecans in bowl and mix well.

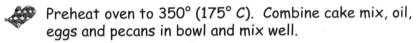 Drop spoonfuls of dough onto non-stick cookie sheet. Bake for 10 to 12 minutes. Cool and remove to wire rack. Makes 3 dozen cookies.

 # Nutty Fudgies

1 (18 ounce) box fudge cake mix	510 g
1 (8 ounce) carton sour cream	225 g
⅔ cup peanut butter chips	115 g
½ cup chopped peanuts	85 g

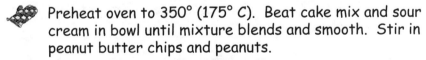 Preheat oven to 350° (175° C). Beat cake mix and sour cream in bowl until mixture blends and smooth. Stir in peanut butter chips and peanuts.

Drop spoonfuls of dough onto sprayed cookie sheet. Bake for 10 to 12 minutes. Remove from oven and cool. Makes 3 dozen cookies.

All-Kids Peanut Butter Cookies

This will make about 22 cookies so if you have a bunch of kids you'd better double the recipe. This was my son's favorite cookie when he was growing up.

½ cup (1 stick) butter, softened	115 g
¼ cup shortening	50 g
⅔ cup sugar	135 g
1 cup packed brown sugar	220 g
1 egg	
1 cup crunchy peanut butter	290 g
1¾ cups flour	210 g
½ teaspoon baking powder	2 ml
¾ teaspoon baking soda	4 ml

 Preheat oven to 350° (175° C).

 Cream butter, shortening, sugar, brown sugar and egg in bowl and beat well. Add peanut butter and mix well. Add flour, baking powder, baking soda and ¼ teaspoon (1 ml) salt and mix well.

 Using small cookie scoop, place cookies onto cookie sheet. Use fork to flatten cookies and criss-cross fork twice. Bake for 12 minutes. Store in airtight container. Makes about 2 dozen cookies.

Easy Peanut Butter Chip Cookies

1 (18 ounce) package sugar cookie dough	510 g
½ cup peanut butter	145 g
½ cup miniature chocolate chips	85 g
½ cup peanut butter chips	85 g
½ cup chopped peanuts	85 g

Preheat oven to 350° (175° C).

Beat cookie dough and peanut butter in large bowl until blended and smooth.

Stir in remaining ingredients. Drop heaping tablespoonfuls of dough onto cookie sheet.

Bake for 15 minutes. Cool on wire rack. Makes 3 dozen cookies.

How do you identify an authentic peanut butter cookie? By the criss-cross design on top, of course! This practice dates back to 1931 in Pillsbury's Balanced Recipes with "Peanut Butter Balls" flattened with a fork before baking.

Peanut Butter-Date Cookies

1 egg, beaten	
⅔ cup sugar	*135 g*
⅓ cup packed brown sugar	*75 g*
1 cup crunchy peanut butter	*290 g*
½ cup chopped dates	*75 g*

 Preheat oven to 350° (175° C).

 Blend egg, sugar, brown sugar and peanut butter in bowl and mix thoroughly. Stir in dates and roll into 1-inch (2.5 cm) balls.

 Place on cookie sheet. Use fork to press ball down to about ½ inch (1.2 cm).

 Bake for about 12 minutes. Cool before storing. Makes 2 dozen cookies.

I cldnuot blviee that I cluod aulaclty uesdnatnrd waht I was rdanieg. The phonemneal pweor of the hmuan mnid. Aoccdrnig to rscheearch at Cmabrigde Uinervtisy, it deosn't mttaer in waht odrer the ltteers in a wrod are, the olny iprmoatnt tnhig is taht the frist and lsat ltteres be in the rghit pclae.

Crunchy Cashew Cookies

1 cup (2 sticks) butter, softened	225 g
1 cup sugar	200 g
¾ cup packed brown sugar	165 g
1 egg	
2¼ cups flour	270 g
½ teaspoon baking soda	2 ml
½ teaspoon cream of tartar	2 ml
2 teaspoons vanilla	10 ml
1 teaspoon almond extract	5 ml
1½ cups chopped cashews	200 g

 Preheat oven to 350° (175° C).

 Combine butter, sugar, brown sugar and egg in bowl and beat well. Blend in flour, baking soda and cream of tartar. Add vanilla, almond extract and cashews and mix thoroughly.

 Drop spoonfuls of dough onto sprayed cookie sheet and bake for 10 to 12 minutes or until golden brown. Makes 3 dozen cookies.

Some people complain because God put thorns on roses, while others praise Him for putting roses among thorns. —Anonymous

 # Orange-Pecan Cookies

The cake mix makes these cookies a breeze because you have a head start.

2 cups pecan halves, divided	*225 g*
1 (18 ounce) box orange cake mix	*510 g*
1 (8 ounce) carton vanilla yogurt	*225 g*
1 egg	
2 tablespoons butter, softened	*30 g*

Preheat oven to 350° (175° C). Chop 1 cup (110 g) pecans and set aside. In large bowl, combine dry cake mix with yogurt, egg and butter. Beat on low speed just until blended.

Stir in chopped pecans. Drop by rounded spoonfuls onto sprayed cookie sheet and press pecan half on top of each cookie.

Bake for 11 to 13 minutes or until light brown. Remove from oven, let cookies cool for 1 minute and transfer to cooling rack. Makes 3 to 4 dozen cookies.

Pecan Dreams

1 cup (2 sticks) butter	225 g
½ cup sugar	100 g
2 teaspoons vanilla	10 ml
2 cups flour	240 g
2 cups chopped pecans	220 g

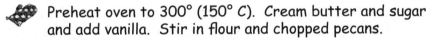 Preheat oven to 300° (150° C). Cream butter and sugar and add vanilla. Stir in flour and chopped pecans.

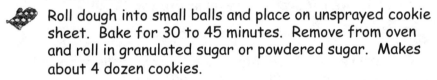 Roll dough into small balls and place on unsprayed cookie sheet. Bake for 30 to 45 minutes. Remove from oven and roll in granulated sugar or powdered sugar. Makes about 4 dozen cookies.

Pecan Puffs

2 egg whites	
¾ cup packed light brown sugar	165 g
1 teaspoon vanilla	5 ml
1 cup chopped pecans	110 g

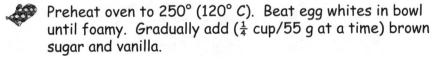 Preheat oven to 250° (120° C). Beat egg whites in bowl until foamy. Gradually add (¼ cup/55 g at a time) brown sugar and vanilla.

Continue beating until stiff peaks form (about 3 or 4 minutes). Fold in pecans. Line cookie sheet with freezer paper.

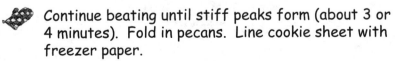 Drop spoonfuls of mixture onto paper. Bake for 45 minutes. Makes 2 dozen cookies.

Coconut Moments

1 cup (2 sticks) butter, softened	225 g
½ cup powdered sugar	60 g
½ cup cornstarch	65 g
1⅓ cups flour	160 g
1 (7 ounce) package flaked coconut	200 g

Beat butter and powdered sugar in bowl until light and fluffy. Add cornstarch and flour and beat until they blend well. Cover and refrigerate for 1 hour.

When ready to bake, preheat oven to 325° (165° C).

Remove and shape into 1-inch (2.5 cm) balls and roll in flaked coconut. Place onto cookie sheet.

Bake for 12 to 15 minutes. Watch closely and don't let coconut burn. Cool for 2 or 3 minutes before removing from pan. Makes 2 dozen cookies.

Coconut Nibbles

2 cups flaky wheat cereal	80 g
1 ¼ cups shredded coconut	105 g
2 large egg whites	
1 ¼ cups sugar	250 g
½ teaspoon vanilla	2 ml

Preheat oven to 350° (175° C). Prepare baking sheet with non-stick spray. Combine cereal and coconut in large bowl and mix well.

In separate bowl, beat egg whites on high speed until soft peaks form. Gradually add sugar and vanilla while mixing.

Fold egg whites into cereal-coconut mixture and mix well. Drop tablespoonfuls of dough about 2 inches (5 cm) apart and bake for about 8 to 10 minutes.

Watch closely and remove from oven when they become golden brown. Do not let them get too brown on bottom. Store in airtight container. Makes 3 dozen cookies.

Coconut Macaroons

2 (7 ounce) packages flaked coconut	2 (200 g)
1 (14 ounce) can sweetened condensed milk	395 g
2 teaspoons vanilla	10 ml
½ teaspoon almond extract	2 ml

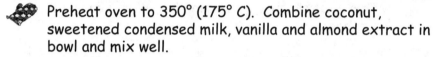 Preheat oven to 350° (175° C). Combine coconut, sweetened condensed milk, vanilla and almond extract in bowl and mix well.

Drop rounded spoonfuls of dough onto foil-lined cookie sheet. Bake for 8 to 10 minutes or until light brown around edges.

Immediately remove from foil. (Macaroons will stick if allowed to cool.) Store at room temperature. Makes 3 dozen cookies.

Family meals teach basic manners and social skills that children need to learn to be successful in life. What they learn will help them in new situations and give them more confidence because they will know how to act and what to say and do.

Macaroons

2 large egg whites	
3 tablespoons sugar	40 g
½ teaspoon vanilla	2 ml
½ teaspoon almond extract	2 ml
½ cup sweetened flaked coconut	45 g

Preheat oven to 300° (150° C). Line large cookie sheet with sprayed and lightly floured foil. (Shake off excess flour.)

In bowl, whisk egg whites, sugar, vanilla, almond extract and a pinch of salt. Stir in coconut.

Drop heaping tablespoons of mixture on cookie sheet about 2 inches (5 cm) apart. Bake about 18 minutes or until tops are light brown in spots.

Carefully transfer foil with cookies from cookie sheet to wire rack and cool completely. Peel macaroons from foil. Makes about 2 dozen cookies.

Family meals offer quality time for all members of the family. A meal should be interactive with each family member sharing something about their day, their friends, their job, soccer practice, etc. Family meals provide stability and a sense of community that children need. By listening to adults, they increase their vocabulary, their social skills and their confidence.

Angel Macaroons

1 (16 ounce) package 1-step angel food cake mix	455 g
1½ teaspoons almond extract	7 ml
2 cups flaked coconut	170 g

Preheat oven to 350° (175° C). Beat cake mix, ½ cup (125 ml) water and almond extract in bowl on low speed for 30 seconds. Scrape bowl and beat on medium for 1 minute.

Fold in coconut. Drop rounded spoonfuls of dough onto parchment paper-lined cookie sheet.

Bake for 10 to 12 minutes or until set. Remove paper with cookies to wire rack to cool. Makes 3 dozen cookies.

Macaroons are light and chewy cookies made with egg whites, almonds or coconut, and sugar. Though macaroons are available in many different flavors and textures, they are most often characterized by their crisp outside and chewy center.

Charlie McRoons

We used to call these Chocolate Macaroons, but a sweet little 3-year-old renamed them for us.

1 (4 ounce) package sweet baking chocolate	115 g
2 egg whites, room temperature	
½ cup sugar	100 g
¼ teaspoon vanilla	1 ml
1 (7 ounce) can flaked coconut	200 g

Preheat oven to 350° (175° C).

Place chocolate in top of double boiler. Stir occasionally until chocolate melts and remove from heat to cool.

Beat egg whites at high speed for 1 minute. Gradually add sugar, 1 tablespoon (15 ml) at a time, beating until stiff peaks form, about 3 minutes.

Add chocolate and vanilla, beat well, and stir in coconut. Drop by spoonfuls onto cookie sheet lined with parchment paper.

Bake for 12 to 15 minutes. Transfer parchment paper to wire rack and allow cookies to cool. Makes about 2 dozen cookies.

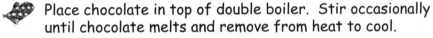

Soft cookies should be stored in an airtight container. Crisp, thin cookies should be covered loosely.

Fast Chocolate Macaroons

These are really fast and delicious cookies.

4 (1 ounce) squares unsweetened baking chocolate, melted	4 (30 g)
1 (14 ounce) can sweetened condensed milk	395 g
2 teaspoons vanilla	10 ml
1 (14 ounce) package flaked coconut	395 g

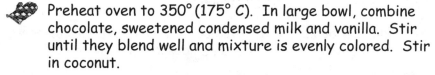

Preheat oven to 350° (175° C). In large bowl, combine chocolate, sweetened condensed milk and vanilla. Stir until they blend well and mixture is evenly colored. Stir in coconut.

Drop dough by heaping spoonfuls about 2 inches (5 cm) apart onto sprayed cookie sheet. Bake for 10 minutes.

Remove from oven and immediately transfer to cooling rack. Makes 3½ dozen cookies.

When beating egg whites, be sure the bowl is spotless and grease-free; metal bowls seem to work better than plastic. Even a tiny speck of fat or egg yolk can cause whipped egg whites to have less volume.

Lemon-Coconut Macaroons

⅔ cup sweetened condensed milk	210 g
1 large egg white	
2 teaspoons lemon juice	10 ml
1 teaspoon grated lemon peel	5 ml
3½ cups shredded sweetened coconut	300 g

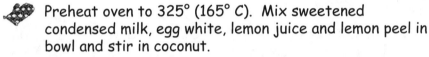 Preheat oven to 325° (165° C). Mix sweetened condensed milk, egg white, lemon juice and lemon peel in bowl and stir in coconut.

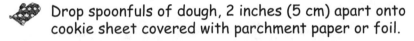 Drop spoonfuls of dough, 2 inches (5 cm) apart onto cookie sheet covered with parchment paper or foil.

Bake for 20 minutes or until light brown. Cool completely and remove carefully from foil or parchment paper. Makes 3 dozen cookies.

One baking step that cannot be done ahead of time is beating egg whites. After 5 minutes they will begin to lose volume. Egg whites will whip better when at room temperature because the protein in the eggs is more elastic and will whip up into more of the tiny air bubbles. If the eggs are colder, they will take longer to beat.

Unfortunately, in high humidity, you sometimes will not be able to get the correct volume no matter what.

Classic Date Log Cookies

1 cup dates	*150 g*
¼ cup sugar	*50 g*
1 (3 ounce) package cream	
* cheese, softened*	*85 g*
½ cup (1 stick) butter	*115 g*
1 cup flour	*120 g*
Powdered sugar	

 Preheat oven to 275° (135° C). Cook dates and sugar in ¼ cup water in saucepan over medium heat until a smooth paste forms.

 Beat cream cheese and butter in bowl until smooth. Add flour and a little salt and mix well. On lightly floured wax paper, roll out dough and cut in 3-inch (7.6 cm) squares.

 Place 1 teaspoon date mixture on each square and roll into logs. Seal ends with fork. Bake for 20 minutes. Roll in powdered sugar and serve. Makes 2 dozen cookies.

 What was Snow White's brother's name?

Egg White! Get the yolk?

Mincemeat Cookies

1 cup (2 sticks) butter, softened	225 g
1⅔ cups sugar	335 g
3 eggs, beaten	
1 teaspoon baking soda	5 ml
3¼ cups flour	390 g
1¼ cups chopped pecans	140 g
1 cup mincemeat	305 g

Preheat oven to 350° (175° C). Cream butter in bowl and add sugar gradually. Add eggs and baking soda after it dissolves in 2 teaspoons (10 ml) hot water. Mix well.

Add ½ teaspoon (2 ml) salt and flour to creamed mixture and mix well. Add pecans and mincemeat.

Drop spoonfuls of mixture onto sprayed cookie sheet and bake for 14 to 15 minutes or until cookies brown. Makes about 4 dozen cookies.

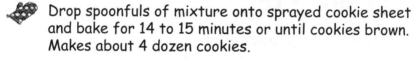

What we call a cookie in the U.S. is called a biscuit in Great Britain and Australia.

Lemon Cookies

½ cup (1 stick) butter, softened	115 g
1 cup sugar	200 g
2 tablespoons lemon juice	30 ml
2 cups flour	240 g

 Preheat oven to 350° (175° C). Cream butter, sugar and lemon juice in bowl and slowly stir in flour.

Drop spoonfuls of dough onto cookie sheet. Bake for 14 to 15 minutes. Makes 2 dozen cookies.

Lemon Drops

½ (8 ounce) carton frozen whipped topping, thawed	½ (225 g)
1 (18 ounce) box lemon cake mix	510 g
1 egg	
Powdered sugar	

Preheat oven to 350° (175° C). Stir whipped topping into lemon cake mix in bowl with spoon. Add egg and mix thoroughly.

Shape into balls and roll in sifted powdered sugar. Bake for 8 to 10 minutes. Do not overcook. Makes 3 dozen cookies.

Old-Fashioned Peach Cookies

1 (20 ounce) can peach pie filling	565 g
1 (18 ounce) box yellow cake mix	510 g
2 eggs	
1 cup finely chopped pecans	110 g
Sugar	

 Preheat oven to 350° (175° C).

 In blender, process pie filling until smooth. In large bowl, combine pie filling, dry cake mix and eggs and blend well. Stir in pecans.

 Drop by tablespoonfuls onto sprayed cookie sheet. Sprinkle with sugar.

 Bake for 15 minutes or until cookies are light brown around edges. Makes 4 dozen cookies.

You can get more juice out of a lemon or lime by rolling it firmly on a countertop or work surface. Or microwave it for 20 to 40 seconds before cutting it.

Mexican Wedding Cookies

1 cup (2 sticks) butter	225 g
1 cup powdered sugar, divided	120 g
½ teaspoon vanilla	2 ml
1¾ cups flour	210 g
½ cup chopped pecans or walnuts	60 g

Cream butter and ¾ cup (90 g) powdered sugar. Beat in vanilla, flour and walnuts. Cover and refrigerate dough for about 1 hour.

When ready to bake, preheat oven to 350° (175° C).

Shape dough into 1-inch (2.5 cm) balls and place 2 inches (5 cm) apart on unsprayed cookie sheet. Bake for 20 minutes.

Remove from oven and transfer to cooling rack. When cool, roll in remaining ¼ cup (30 g) powdered sugar. Makes about 4 dozen cookies.

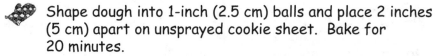

Mexican Wedding Cookies is a universal cookie rich in butter and sugar with different names wherever it appears. Sand Tarts, Pecan Crescents and Russian Tea Cakes are all the same cookie, but called different names.

The name in Mexico is pastelitos de boda *(wedding cookies) and they are traditionally served as a dessert at weddings.*

Sand Tarts

1 cup (2 sticks) butter, softened	225 g
¾ cup powdered sugar	90 g
2 cups sifted flour	240 g
1 cup chopped pecans	110 g
1 teaspoon vanilla	5 ml

Preheat oven to 325° (165° C). Cream butter and powdered sugar in bowl and add flour, pecans and vanilla.

Roll into crescents and place on cookie sheet. Bake for 20 minutes. Roll in extra powdered sugar after tarts cool. Makes 3 dozen cookies.

Scotch Shortbread

1 cup (2 sticks) butter	225 g
2 cups flour	240 g
¾ cup cornstarch	95 g
⅔ cup sugar	135 g

Granulated sugar or colored-sugar sprinkles

Preheat oven to 325° (165° C). Melt butter in saucepan and stir in flour, cornstarch and sugar. Press into sprayed 9-inch (23 cm) square pan.

Bake for 45 minutes. Cut into squares immediately after removing from oven. Sprinkle with granulated sugar or colored-sugar sprinkles. Makes 2 dozen cookies.

Classic Shortbread Cookies

2 cups (4 sticks) butter, softened	455 g
1 cup powdered sugar	120 g
4 cups flour	480 g
Additional powdered sugar	

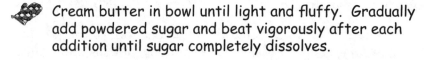

Cream butter in bowl until light and fluffy. Gradually add powdered sugar and beat vigorously after each addition until sugar completely dissolves.

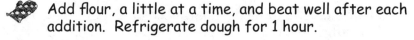

Add flour, a little at a time, and beat well after each addition. Refrigerate dough for 1 hour.

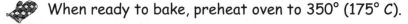

When ready to bake, preheat oven to 350° (175° C).

Sprinkle surface with equal parts of flour and powdered sugar and turn one-third of dough at a time onto surface.

Pat into ½-inch (1.2 cm) thickness and cut cookies with 1½-inch (3.8 cm) biscuit cutter. Place on unsprayed cookie sheet and prick tops of cookies with fork to make a design.

Bake for 15 to 20 minutes or until light golden color. Remove from oven and cool slightly before lightly dusting with powdered sugar. Makes 4 dozen cookies.

Almond-Fudge Shortbread

1 cup (2 sticks) butter, softened	225 g
1 cup powdered sugar	120 g
1 ¼ cups flour	150 g
1 (12 ounce) package chocolate chips	340 g
1 (14 ounce) can sweetened condensed milk	395 g
½ teaspoon almond extract	2 ml
1 (2.5 ounce) package chopped almonds, toasted	70 g

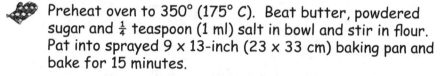 Preheat oven to 350° (175° C). Beat butter, powdered sugar and ¼ teaspoon (1 ml) salt in bowl and stir in flour. Pat into sprayed 9 x 13-inch (23 x 33 cm) baking pan and bake for 15 minutes.

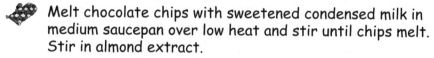 Melt chocolate chips with sweetened condensed milk in medium saucepan over low heat and stir until chips melt. Stir in almond extract.

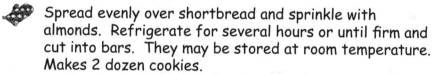 Spread evenly over shortbread and sprinkle with almonds. Refrigerate for several hours or until firm and cut into bars. They may be stored at room temperature. Makes 2 dozen cookies.

Ladyfingers

3 eggs, separated	
1 teaspoon almond extract	5 ml
1/3 cup sugar	65 g
1/2 cup cake flour	45 g
1 teaspoon baking powder	5 ml

Beat egg yolks until thick and lemon colored. Beat in almond extract.

In separate bowl, beat egg whites until stiff peaks form. Continue beating and gradually add sugar until mixture is glossy and stiff.

Fold egg yolk mixture into egg white mixture. Sift flour and baking powder and gently fold into egg mixture.

Fill pastry bag and pipe mixture onto unsprayed cookie sheet in 3-inch (8 cm) lengths about 1-inch (2.5 cm) wide. Bake 10 minutes. Remove from cookie sheet and cool. Makes about 2 dozen ladyfingers.

I totally take back all those times I didn't want to take a nap when I was younger.

Individual Meringues

1 (16 ounce) box powdered sugar	455 g
6 egg whites, room temperature	
1 teaspoon cream of tartar	5 ml
½ teaspoon vanilla	2 ml
1 teaspoon vinegar	5 ml

Preheat oven to 250° (120° C). Beat powdered sugar and egg whites in bowl at high speed for 10 minutes.

Add cream of tartar, vanilla and vinegar and beat for additional 10 minutes.

Spoon individual meringues on sprayed cookie sheet. Bake for 15 minutes.

Increase temperature to 300° (150° C) and bake for additional 12 minutes.

Remove immediately from cookie sheet and store between sheets of wax paper in airtight containers. Serves 12 to 14.

If you are uncertain about the freshness of eggs, cover them with a few inches of water. If eggs sink to the bottom of the container and lay horizontally, they are okay. If they sink, but stand on their ends or they float, discard them.

Amaretti

2 egg whites
1 cup sugar   *200 g*
1 teaspoon almond extract   *5 ml*
1 cup finely ground almonds   *85 g*

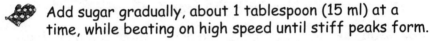 Preheat oven to 300° (150° C). In medium bowl, beat egg whites and a pinch of salt with mixer until frothy.

Add sugar gradually, about 1 tablespoon (15 ml) at a time, while beating on high speed until stiff peaks form.

Fold in almond extract and almonds and drop dough by rounded spoonfuls onto parchment paper-lined cookie sheets.

Bake for 25 to 30 minutes or until cookies are light brown.

Remove from oven and cool cookies. Peel cookies from paper and store in airtight container. Makes 2 to 2½ dozen cookies.

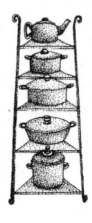

Party Kisses

3 egg whites	
1 cup sugar	200 g
2 teaspoons vanilla	10 ml
½ teaspoon almond extract	2 ml
3⅓ cups Frosted Flakes®	95 g
1 cup chopped pecans	110 g

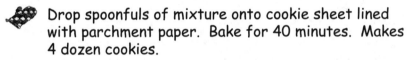

Preheat oven to 350° (175° C). Beat egg whites in bowl until stiff. Gradually add sugar, vanilla and almond extract. Fold in Frosted Flakes® and pecans.

Drop spoonfuls of mixture onto cookie sheet lined with parchment paper. Bake for 40 minutes. Makes 4 dozen cookies.

Potato Chip Crispies

1 cup (2 sticks) butter, softened	225 g
⅔ cup sugar	135 g
1 teaspoon vanilla	5 ml
1½ cups flour	150 g
½ cup crushed potato chips	30 g

 Preheat oven to 350° (175° C). Cream butter, sugar and vanilla in bowl. Add flour and chips and mix well.

 Drop spoonfuls of dough onto cookie sheet. Bake for about 12 minutes or until light brown. Makes 3 dozen cookies.

In 1853 George Crum, a chef at Moon Lake Lodge in Sarasota Springs, New York, tried to please a diner after he sent back the french fries because they were too thick. Crum cut the potatoes paper thin and fried them crisp. To his surprise, the customer was extremely pleased.

These paper-thin potato chips became very popular in the Northeast until in the 1920's Herman Lay began selling the chips from the trunk of his car to restaurants all over the south. Lay's® Potato Chips was the first product to be marketed nationally.

In 1961, the H.W. Lay company merged with the Frito Company (Fritos® Corn Chips) to become Frito-Lay, Inc. Today Americans eat more potato chips, Fritos® and french fries than any other group in the world.

Cakes and Frostings

 # French Vanilla Cake

1 (18 ounce) box French vanilla
    cake mix   510 g
1 pint vanilla ice cream, softened   475 ml
3 eggs, beaten
1 teaspoon vanilla   5 ml

Preheat oven to 350° (175° C). In mixing bowl, beat all
ingredients for 3 minutes on medium speed.

Spoon into sprayed, floured 10-inch (25 cm) bundt pan.
Bake for 35 to 40 minutes or until toothpick inserted in
center comes out clean.

Cool in pan for about 20 minutes and invert onto cake
plate. Cool completely before icing.

Icing:

1 (8 ounce) package cream
    cheese, softened   225 g
¼ cup (½ stick) butter, softened   55 g
2 tablespoons Kahlua® liqueur   30 ml
½ cup powdered sugar   60 g

In mixing bowl, beat cream cheese, butter and Kahlua®
on low speed until light and creamy. Gradually add
powdered sugar and beat for about 2 minutes.

Refrigerate icing until cake cools completely and spread
icing on top and sides of cake. Serves 12 to 16.

 # Creamy Butter Cake

4 eggs, divided
1 (18 ounce) box butter cake mix   510 g
½ cup (1 stick) butter, melted   115 g
1 (16 ounce) box powdered sugar,
    divided   455 g
1 (8 ounce) package cream
    cheese, softened   225 g

Preheat oven to 350° (175° C). Beat 2 eggs with cake mix and butter in bowl. Spread mixture into sprayed, floured 9 x 13-inch (23 x 33 cm) baking pan.

Set aside ¾ cup (90 g) powdered sugar for topping. Mix remaining powdered sugar, 2 remaining eggs and cream cheese in bowl and beat until smooth.

Spread mixture on top of dough. Sprinkle remaining powdered sugar on top. Bake for 40 minutes. Cake will puff up and then go down when it cools. Serves 12 to 16.

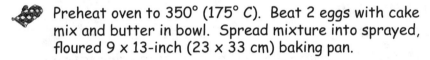

The word cake is derived from the Old Norse word kaka. At one time, bread and cake were interchangeable words with cake implying a small bread. Primitive man made simple "cakes" with flour from pounded grains and water. The ancient Greeks made plakous (the word means flat), a cake made of nuts and honey.

Amaretto Cake

1 ½ cups sliced almonds, divided	285 g
1 (18 ounce) box yellow cake mix	510 g
1 (3 ounce) box vanilla pudding mix	85 g
3 eggs	
⅓ cup corn oil	75 ml
¼ cup amaretto liqueur	60 ml
¾ cup orange juice	175 ml
1 ½ teaspoons almond flavoring	7 ml

Preheat oven to 325° (165° C). Spread almonds on baking sheet and place in oven for 8 to 10 minutes or until golden brown. Remove and set aside.

Sprinkle ½ cup (95 g) almonds in sprayed, floured bundt pan.

Combine cake mix, pudding mix, eggs, oil, amaretto, orange juice and almond flavoring in bowl, mix and beat until fluffy.

Fold in remaining almonds, pour into bundt pan and bake for 1 hour. Cake is done when toothpick inserted in center comes out clean. Invert on cake plate.

Continued next page...

In the 1800's the first bakery was started on the yeast coast.

Continued from previous page...

Glaze:

¼ cup (½ stick) butter	60 g
¾ cup sugar	150 g
⅓ cup amaretto liqueur	75 ml

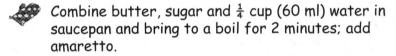 Combine butter, sugar and ¼ cup (60 ml) water in saucepan and bring to a boil for 2 minutes; add amaretto.

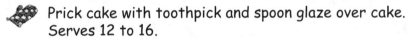 Prick cake with toothpick and spoon glaze over cake. Serves 12 to 16.

Centuries ago cakes were only baked for very special occasions or for the wealthy because the ingredients were so expensive. To this day, we think of cakes when celebrating an anniversary, wedding or birthday.

At one time, yeast was used to make cakes rise, but by the mid-1700s, beaten eggs became popular as a way to raise cakes by beating in air.

The Industrial Revolution with its introduction of mass production along with the transportation provided by railroads made ingredients for baking more available and affordable.

Old-Fashioned Buttermilk Cake

Don't worry about buying buttermilk. Check out the tip below and you won't have to make a special trip to the grocery store.

1 cup buttermilk*	250 ml
3 tablespoons vanilla	45 ml
½ teaspoon baking soda	2 ml
1 cup shortening	190 g
2 cups sugar	400 g
4 eggs	
3 cups flour	360 g
¾ cup chopped walnuts	100 g

Preheat oven to 325° (165° C). Pour buttermilk, vanilla and baking soda in glass and set aside. Place shortening in large bowl and cream until smooth. Add sugar slowly and continue to cream until mixture is fluffy.

Add eggs one at a time and beat after each addition. When mixture is fluffy, stir in buttermilk mixture and gradually add flour and 1 teaspoon (5 ml) salt; stir well after each addition. Fold in nuts.

Pour into sprayed, floured 10-inch (25 cm) tube pan. Bake for about 1 hour or until toothpick inserted in center comes out clean. Serves 12 to 16.

*TIP: To make buttermilk, mix 1 cup (250 ml) milk with 1 tablespoon (15 ml) lemon juice or vinegar and let milk stand for about 10 minutes.

 # Chess Cake

1 (18 ounce) box yellow cake mix   510 g
2 eggs
½ cup (1 stick) butter, softened   115 g

Preheat oven to 350° (175° C). Beat cake mix,
2 eggs and butter in mixing bowl. Press into sprayed
9 x 13-inch (23 x 33 cm) baking pan.

Topping:

2 eggs
1 (8 ounce) package cream
   cheese, softened   225 g
1 (16 ounce) box powdered sugar   455 g

Beat 2 eggs, cream cheese and powdered sugar in
bowl and pour over cake batter. Bake for 35 minutes.
Serves 12 to 16.

Buttermilk does not contain butter, but once
was the liquid left after butter was churned.
Today buttermilk is made by adding a lactic acid to
pasteurized whole, skim or non-fat milk. It ferments
for 12 hours or more. This buttermilk is called
cultured buttermilk.

It is easy to make a buttermilk substitute by
adding 1 tablespoon (15 ml) lemon juice or vinegar to
1 cup (250 ml) milk and letting the milk stand for
about 10 minutes.

Mississippi Mud Cake

2 cups sugar	400 g
2 cups flour	240 g
½ cup (1 stick) butter	115 g
½ cup shortening or canola oil	95 g/125 ml
4 heaping tablespoons cocoa	20 g
½ cup buttermilk*	125 ml
2 eggs, beaten	
1 teaspoon baking soda	5 ml
1 teaspoon ground cinnamon	5 ml
1 teaspoon vanilla	5 ml

 Preheat oven to 350° (175° C).

Combine sugar and flour in bowl. Combine butter, shortening, cocoa and 1 cup (250 ml) water in saucepan and bring to a boil.

Pour over flour and sugar mixture and beat well. Add buttermilk, eggs, baking soda, cinnamon, vanilla and ½ teaspoon (2 ml) salt, mix well and pour into sprayed, floured 9 x 13-inch (23 x 33 cm) pan. Bake for 40 to 45 minutes.

Continued next page...

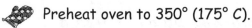

Always stir flour before measuring, then spoon it into a measuring cup and level the top with a knife. Do not shake down the flour or pack it. If you scoop the flour with the cup, it may settle and cause you to have more flour than the recipe calls for.

Continued from previous page...

Frosting:

½ cup (1 stick) butter	115 g
¼ cup cocoa	20 g
6 tablespoons milk	90 ml
1 (16 ounce) box powdered sugar	455 g
1 teaspoon vanilla	5 ml
1 (16 ounce) package miniature marshmallows	455 g
1 cup chopped pecans	110 g
1 (3 ounce) can flaked coconut	85 g

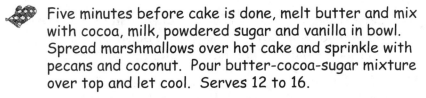

Five minutes before cake is done, melt butter and mix with cocoa, milk, powdered sugar and vanilla in bowl. Spread marshmallows over hot cake and sprinkle with pecans and coconut. Pour butter-cocoa-sugar mixture over top and let cool. Serves 12 to 16.

*TIP: To make buttermilk, mix 1 cup (250 ml) milk with 1 tablespoon (15 ml) lemon juice or vinegar and let milk stand for about 10 minutes.

Dark-colored pans absorb heat and allow foods to brown quicker and develop a good crust. Light-colored pans reflect heat and create foods that are tender and have a light crust. Dark pans are good for breads and light pans are good for cakes and cookies.

Down Home Molasses Cake

½ cup shortening	95 g
½ cup sugar	100 g
3 eggs, separated	
¾ teaspoon baking soda	4 ml
⅔ cup molasses	150 ml
2¼ cups flour	270 g
1 teaspoon ground cinnamon	5 ml
¼ teaspoon ground cloves	1 ml
¼ teaspoon ground mace	1 ml
½ cup milk	125 ml

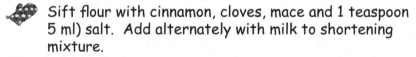 Preheat oven to 350° (175° C). Cream shortening, sugar and egg yolks in bowl. In separate bowl, combine baking soda with molasses and add to shortening mixture.

Sift flour with cinnamon, cloves, mace and 1 teaspoon 5 ml) salt. Add alternately with milk to shortening mixture.

Beat egg whites and stir into batter. Pour batter into sprayed, floured loaf pan and bake for 50 to 60 minutes. Serves 6 to 8.

 # Favorite Cake

1 (18 ounce) box butter pecan cake mix	510 g
1 cup almond-toffee bits	240 g
1 cup chopped pecans	110 g
Powdered sugar	

Preheat oven to 350° (175° C). Prepare cake mix according to package directions. Fold in almond-toffee bits and pecans.

Pour into sprayed, floured bundt pan. Bake for 45 minutes or until toothpick inserted in center comes out clean.

Allow cake to cool several minutes and remove from pan. Dust with sifted powdered sugar. Serves 12 to 16.

Golden Rum Cake

1 (18 ounce) box yellow cake mix with pudding	510 g
3 eggs	
⅓ cup canola oil	75 ml
½ cup rum	125 ml
1 cup chopped pecans	110 g

Preheat oven to 325° (165° C).

Blend cake mix, eggs, 1 cup (250 ml) water, oil and rum in bowl.

Stir in pecans. Pour into sprayed, floured 10-inch (25 cm) tube or bundt pan.

Bake for 1 hour. (If you like, sprinkle sifted powdered sugar over cooled cake.) Serves 12 to 16.

 # Pecan Cake

1 (18 ounce) box butter pecan cake mix	510 g
½ cup (1 stick) butter, melted	115 g
1 egg	
1 cup chopped pecans	110 g
1 (8 ounce) package cream cheese, softened	225 g
2 eggs	
1 (16 ounce) box powdered sugar	455 g

Preheat oven to 350° (175° C).

Combine cake mix, ¾ cup (175 ml) water, butter and egg in bowl; beat well. Stir in pecans.

Pour into sprayed, floured 9 x 13-inch (23 x 33 cm) baking dish.

Beat cream cheese, eggs and powdered sugar in bowl. Pour over cake mixture.

Bake for 40 minutes. Cake is done when toothpick inserted in center comes out clean. Serves 12 to 16.

Poppy Seed Cake

3 cups sugar	600 g
1¼ cups shortening	235 g
6 eggs	
3 cups flour	360 g
¼ teaspoon baking soda	1 ml
1 cup buttermilk*	250 ml
3 tablespoons poppy seeds	25 g
2 teaspoons almond extract	10 ml
2 teaspoons vanilla	10 ml
2 teaspoons butter flavoring	10 ml

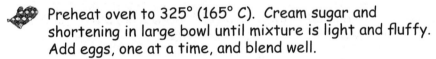 Preheat oven to 325° (165° C). Cream sugar and shortening in large bowl until mixture is light and fluffy. Add eggs, one at a time, and blend well.

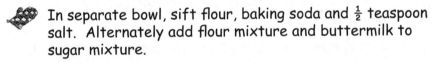 In separate bowl, sift flour, baking soda and ½ teaspoon salt. Alternately add flour mixture and buttermilk to sugar mixture.

Add poppy seeds and flavorings and blend well. Pour into sprayed, floured bundt pan. Bake for 1 hour 15 minutes or when toothpick inserted in center comes out clean.

Continued next page...

What might cause a cake to rise unevenly when baked? The flour may not have been mixed into the batter thoroughly enough; or the oven may heat unevenly; or the cake was baked at too high a temperature.

Continued from previous page...

Glaze:

1½ cups powdered sugar	180 g
⅓ cup lemon juice	75 ml
1 teaspoon vanilla	5 ml
1 teaspoon almond extract	5 ml

 Combine all ingredients in bowl and mix well. Pour over top of cool cake and let some glaze run down sides of cake. Serves 12 to 16.

*TIP: To make buttermilk, mix 1 cup (250 ml) milk with 1 tablespoon (15 ml) lemon juice or vinegar and let milk stand for about 10 minutes.

It takes more than 900,000 poppy seeds to make one pound. They are best toasted under very low heat which brings out their nutty flavor. They are added to many baked goods and are used extensively in Asian and Middle Eastern countries.

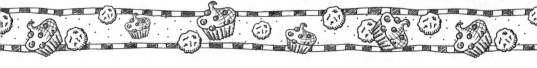

Poppy Seed Bundt Cake

1 (18 ounce) box yellow cake mix	510 g
1 (3.4 ounce) package instant coconut cream pudding mix	100 g
½ cup canola oil	125 ml
3 eggs	
2 tablespoons poppy seeds	20 g
Powdered sugar	

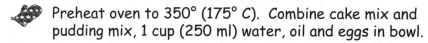 Preheat oven to 350° (175° C). Combine cake mix and pudding mix, 1 cup (250 ml) water, oil and eggs in bowl.

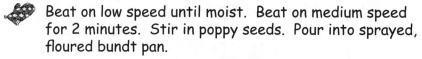 Beat on low speed until moist. Beat on medium speed for 2 minutes. Stir in poppy seeds. Pour into sprayed, floured bundt pan.

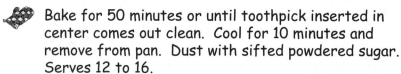 Bake for 50 minutes or until toothpick inserted in center comes out clean. Cool for 10 minutes and remove from pan. Dust with sifted powdered sugar. Serves 12 to 16.

If fruit or nuts sink to the bottom of a cake, the pieces may have been too large; or the fruit or nuts were not dusted with flour before being added; or the batter was too wet; or it was baked at too low a temperature.

 # Chocolate Hurricane Cake

This is easy and very, very yummy.

1 cup chopped pecans	110 g
1 (3 ounce) can sweetened flaked coconut	85 g
1 (18 ounce) box German chocolate cake mix	510 g
⅓ cup canola oil	75 ml
3 eggs	
½ cup (1 stick) butter, melted	115 g
1 (8 ounce) package cream cheese, softened	225 g
1 (16 ounce) box powdered sugar	455 g

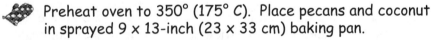 Preheat oven to 350° (175° C). Place pecans and coconut in sprayed 9 x 13-inch (23 x 33 cm) baking pan.

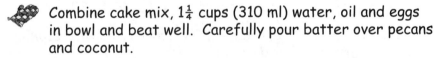 Combine cake mix, 1¼ cups (310 ml) water, oil and eggs in bowl and beat well. Carefully pour batter over pecans and coconut.

Combine butter, cream cheese and powdered sugar in bowl and whip to blend. Spoon mixture over batter and bake for 40 to 42 minutes. (You cannot test for doneness with toothpick because cake will appear sticky even when it is done.) The icing sinks into bottom as it bakes and forms white ribbon inside. Serves 12 to 16.

Cake Pops

1 (18 ounce) box cake mix (your
    choice of flavor)   510 g
1 (16 ounce) can ready-to-serve
    frosting (your choice of flavor)   455 g
2 (16 ounce) packages chocolate
    candy coating   2 (455 g)
Foam block or lollipop stand
40 - 48 lollipop sticks

Prepare cake mix and bake according to package
directions. Allow cake to cool completely.

Crumble into fine pieces by hand and eliminate all
lumps. Mix cake crumbs with two-thirds of ready-made
frosting by hand or spoon.

Form cake mixture into 1 inch to 1½ inch (2.5 to 3.8 cm)
balls. Place on baking sheet covered with wax paper.
Refrigerate for 2 hours or freeze for 15 to 20 minutes.

Optional: After chilling, create different shapes with cookie
            cutters or candy molds.

Use a lollipop stick to make holes in the foam block to
insert cake pops.

Melt candy coating according to package directions. To
prevent waste, melt a portion of candy coating at a time
in small but deep bowl. (This is also helpful to prevent
candy coating from hardening because you can melt
small amounts as you go.) There should be about
3 inches of melted coating in bowl.

Continued next page...

Continued from previous page...

 Dip ½ inch (1.3 cm) of lollipop stick into candy coating, drain excess into bowl and push stick halfway into cake ball. Immerse ball into candy coating to cover thoroughly. Remove gently and allow excess to drain for a few seconds while twirling the stick to allow for even coverage. Place in foam block to dry.

Optional: While candy coating is still wet, attach your choice of decorations.

 Store in airtight container at room temperature or in refrigerator. Cake pops are like cupcakes and are best the first day. Makes 40 to 48 cake pops.

TIP: If coating is too thick, add a little vegetable oil to thin. A little goes a long way so add 1 tablespoon (15 ml) at a time until you reach desired consistency.

TIP: Don't compress crumbs too tightly when forming shapes because they may expand and crack candy coating.

TIP: The easiest method to combine the cake crumbs and frosting is to mix by hand. It's messy but worth it!

TIP: If cake pops are bigger than 1½" (3.8 cm) they can get too heavy and fall off lollipop stick when removing from candy coating dip.

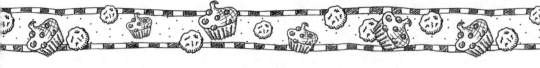

 # Chocolate Pudding Cake

1 (18 ounce) box milk chocolate cake mix	510 g
1¼ cups milk	310 ml
⅓ cup canola oil	75 ml
3 eggs	

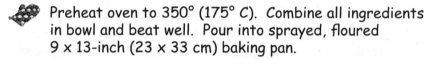 Preheat oven to 350° (175° C). Combine all ingredients in bowl and beat well. Pour into sprayed, floured 9 x 13-inch (23 x 33 cm) baking pan.

 Bake for 35 minutes or when toothpick inserted in center comes out clean.

Icing:

1 (14 ounce) can sweetened condensed milk	395 g
¾ (16 ounce) can chocolate syrup	¾ (455 g)
1 (8 ounce) carton frozen whipped topping, thawed	225 g
⅓ cup chopped pecans, optional	40 g

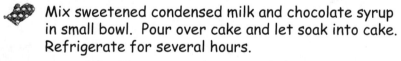 Mix sweetened condensed milk and chocolate syrup in small bowl. Pour over cake and let soak into cake. Refrigerate for several hours.

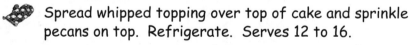 Spread whipped topping over top of cake and sprinkle pecans on top. Refrigerate. Serves 12 to 16.

Chocolate Chip Cake

1 cup self-rising flour	125 g
1 cup sugar	200 g
4 eggs	
½ cup (1 stick) butter	115 g
1 teaspoon vanilla	5 ml
1 (16 ounce) can chocolate syrup	455 g
½ cup semi-sweet chocolate chips	85 g

 Preheat oven to 350° (175° C). Spray and flour bundt pan. Mix all ingredients in large mixing bowl and pour into pan. Bake 50 minutes. Let cool and remove from pan.

Frosting:

1 cup sugar	200 g
½ cup (1 stick) butter	115 g
⅓ cup evaporated milk	75 ml
1 tablespoon peanut butter or	
½ cup nuts, optional	15 ml/85 g
½ cup semi-sweet chocolate chips	85 g

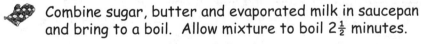 Combine sugar, butter and evaporated milk in saucepan and bring to a boil. Allow mixture to boil 2½ minutes.

 Add peanut butter or nuts and chocolate chips. Beat until glossy. Pour over cake. Serves 12 to 16.

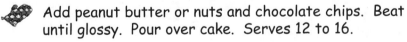

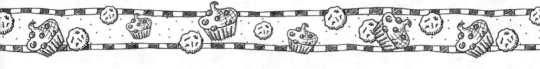

 # Dirt-and-Worms Cake

This fun dessert is easy to make and children love it! This is one mud cake you won't mind them eating! Also, it's fun to put a plastic, toy trowel with it for the "gardener" to use.

1 (18 ounce) chocolate cake mix	510 g
½ cup chocolate syrup	155 g
1 (3 ounce) package instant chocolate fudge pudding mix	85 g
1¾ cups milk	425 ml
1 cup crushed chocolate graham crackers or other chocolate cookies	105 g
7 candy gummy worms	

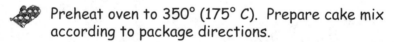 Preheat oven to 350° (175° C). Prepare cake mix according to package directions.

Pour batter into sprayed, floured 9 x 13-inch (23 x 33 cm) baking pan and bake for 30 to 35 minutes.

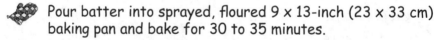 While cake is still hot, poke holes over entire surface with knife. Pour chocolate syrup evenly over cake; cool.

Beat pudding mix and milk in bowl for 2 minutes and set aside for 3 to 5 minutes. Smooth evenly over cake.

Continued next page...

Continued from previous page...

 Sprinkle half graham cracker crumbs over pudding. Score top of cake as you would slice into servings. No need to cut through to bottom until you're ready to serve.

 Push 1 end of each worm gently into crumb mixture and cover lightly with remaining crumbs. (Worms should appear to be poking out of the ground.) Refrigerate until ready to serve. Serves 12 to 16.

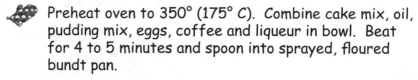Black Russian Cake

1 (18 ounce) box milk-chocolate cake mix	510 g
½ cup canola oil	125 ml
1 (4 ounce) package instant chocolate pudding mix	115 g
4 eggs, room temperature	
⅔ cup strong brewed coffee	150 ml
⅓ cup creme de cacao liqueur	75 ml

  Preheat oven to 350° (175° C). Combine cake mix, oil, pudding mix, eggs, coffee and liqueur in bowl. Beat for 4 to 5 minutes and spoon into sprayed, floured bundt pan.

  Bake for 55 to 60 minutes. Cake is done when toothpick inserted in center comes out clean.

Icing:

1½ cups powdered sugar	180 g
2 tablespoons butter, melted	30 g
Enough Kahlua® liqueur to make icing spreadable	

  Combine powdered sugar and butter in bowl. Add Kahlua®, a little at a time, until icing has consistency for spreading but thin enough to run down sides. Serves 12 to 16.

TIP: It's even better if you add a dip of vanilla ice cream on top.

 # Black Forest Cake

1 (18 ounce) box devil's food
   cake mix   510 g
1 (20 ounce) can cherry pie filling   565 g
1 (3.4 ounce) package vanilla
   instant pudding   100 g
1 cup milk   250 ml
1 (8 ounce) carton frozen
   whipped topping, thawed   225 g

Preheat oven to 350° (175° C). Prepare cake according
to package directions and pour in sprayed, floured
9 x 13-inch (23 x 33 cm) baking pan. Bake as directed.

While cake is still warm, poke top with fork and spread
cherry pie filling over cake. While cake cools, prepare
pudding with milk. Fold in whipped topping.

Spread pudding and whipped topping mixture over cake
and carefully cover cherry pie filling. Refrigerate.
Serves 12 to 16.

*Cakes should be cooled in pans for about 10 to
15 minutes before turning out on a wire rack
to cool. Put a couple of paper towels on the rack to
keep the wires from leaving an imprint on the cake or
breaking the top of the cake.*

 # Rich Turtle Cake

1 (18 ounce) box German chocolate cake mix	510 g
½ cup (1 stick) butter, softened	115 g
½ cup canola oil	125 ml
1 (14 ounce) can sweetened condensed milk, divided	395 g
1 cup chopped pecans	110 g
1 (16 ounce) bag caramels	455 g

Preheat oven to 350° (175° C). Combine cake mix, butter, 1½ cups (375 ml) water, oil and half can sweetened condensed milk in bowl and beat well.

Fold in pecans and pour half batter into sprayed, floured 9 x 13-inch (23 x 33 cm) baking dish. Bake for 25 minutes.

Combine caramels and remaining sweetened condensed milk in saucepan, spread evenly over baked cake and cover with remaining batter. Bake for additional 20 to 25 minutes.

Continued next page...

If no one sees you eat it, do you still have to count the calories?

Continued from previous page...

Frosting:

½ cup (1 stick) butter	115 g
¼ cup cocoa	20 g
4 - 5 tablespoons milk	60 - 75 ml
1 (16 ounce) box powdered sugar	455 g
1 teaspoon vanilla	5 ml

 Melt butter in saucepan, add cocoa and milk and mix well. Add powdered sugar and vanilla and stir well.

 (If frosting seems too stiff, add 1 tablespoon/15 ml milk.) Spread over warm, but not hot, cake. Serves 12 to 16.

History of Cake Mixes

Cakes were time consuming and expensive to bake before World War II, but during the early 1940's, Betty Crocker labs were testing and researching ways to make a simple mix. Their first mixes were tested in homes rather than the lab, and researchers discovered that home bakers preferred to add their own fresh eggs instead of using powdered eggs.

By 1953 Betty Crocker developed one cake mix that produced three different colors and flavors. A cake with whole eggs was yellow. A cake with egg whites was white. And, a cake with spices and whole eggs was spice color.

 # Oreo Cake

1 (18 ounce) box white cake mix	510 g
⅓ cup canola oil	75 ml
4 egg whites	
1¼ cups coarsely chopped Oreo® cookies plus extra for top of cake	155 g

Preheat oven to 350° (175° C). Combine cake mix, oil, 1¼ cups (310 ml) water and egg whites in bowl. Blend on low speed until moist. Beat for 2 minutes at high speed.

Gently fold in coarsely chopped cookies. Pour batter into 2 sprayed, floured 8-inch (20 cm) round cake pans.

Bake for 25 to 30 minutes or until toothpick inserted in center comes out clean. Cool for 15 minutes and remove from pan. Cool completely and frost.

Frosting:

4¼ cups powdered sugar	510 g
1 cup (2 sticks) butter, softened	225 g
1 cup shortening (not butter-flavored)	190 g
1 teaspoon almond flavoring	5 ml

Combine all ingredients in bowl and beat until creamy. Frost first layer of cake and place second layer on top and frost top and sides.

Sprinkle with extra crushed Oreo® cookies on top. Serves 12 to 16.

White Chocolate-Almond Cake

1 (18 ounce) box white cake mix	510 g
4 egg whites	
¼ cup oil	60 ml
1 teaspoon almond extract	5 ml
1 cup chopped almonds	170 g
6 (1 ounce) squares white chocolate, melted	6 (30 g)
1 (16 ounce) can caramel icing	455 g

Preheat oven to 350° (175° C). In mixing bowl, combine cake mix, egg whites, oil, almond extract and 1½ cups (375 ml) water and beat until all ingredients blend well.

Stir in chopped almonds and melted white chocolate and pour into 2 (9 inch/23 cm) round cake pans.

Bake for 30 to 35 minutes or until toothpick inserted in center comes out clean. Spread each layer with half icing. Place second layer on top of first layer Serves 12 to 16.

Always use the right size of pan. Cake batter should fill the pan no more than two-thirds full before baking.

 # Apple Cake

1 (18 ounce) box spice cake mix	*510 g*
1 (20 ounce) can apple pie filling	*565 g*
2 eggs	
⅓ cup chopped walnuts	*45 g*

Preheat oven to 350° (175° C). Combine all ingredients in bowl and mix very thoroughly with spoon. Make sure all lumps from cake mix break up.

Pour into sprayed, floured bundt pan. Bake for 50 minutes or until toothpick inserted in center comes out clean. Serves 12 to 16.

TIP: You may substitute any other pie filling for this cake.

Yummy Dutch Apple Cake

4 apples, peeled, chopped	
2¾ cups sugar, divided	550 g
1½ teaspoons ground cinnamon, divided	7 ml
1½ teaspoons baking powder	7 ml
1 cup shortening	190 g
3 eggs	
½ teaspoon vanilla	2 ml
1 yeast cake	
1 cup milk	250 ml
4 cups flour	480 g

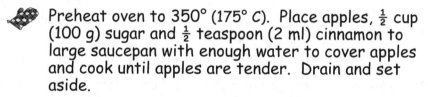 Preheat oven to 350° (175° C). Place apples, ½ cup (100 g) sugar and ½ teaspoon (2 ml) cinnamon to large saucepan with enough water to cover apples and cook until apples are tender. Drain and set aside.

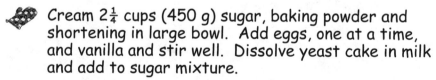 Cream 2¼ cups (450 g) sugar, baking powder and shortening in large bowl. Add eggs, one at a time, and vanilla and stir well. Dissolve yeast cake in milk and add to sugar mixture.

Add flour and remaining cinnamon a little at a time and mix well. Pour mixture into sprayed, floured 9 x 13-inch (23 x 33 cm) baking pan. Spread apples over top of cake.

Bake for about 30 minutes or until toothpick inserted in center comes out clean. Let stand for 15 minutes before serving. Serves 12 to 16.

Old-Fashioned Applesauce Spice Cake

1 (18 ounce) box spice cake mix	*510 g*
3 eggs	
1¼ cups applesauce	*320 g*
⅓ cup canola oil	*75 ml*
1 cup chopped pecans	*110 g*
1 (16 ounce) can vanilla frosting	*455 g*
½ teaspoon ground cinnamon	*2 ml*

Preheat oven to 350° (175° C). Combine cake mix, eggs, applesauce and oil in bowl. Beat at medium speed for 2 minutes. Stir in pecans.

Pour into sprayed, floured 9 x 13-inch (23 x 33 cm) baking pan. Bake for 40 minutes. Cake is done when toothpick inserted in center comes out clean. Cool.

Mix vanilla frosting and cinnamon. and frost cake Serves 12 to 16.

Harry Baker was the first to develop a cake using vegetable oil and it became very popular. In 1959 Betty Crocker developed the first cake mix using vegetable oil in its Betty Crocker® chiffon cake mix.

 # Banana Butter Cake

1 (18 ounce) box yellow cake mix	510 g
2 ripe bananas	
3 (2 ounce) Butterfinger® candy bars, chopped, divided	3 (55 g)
½ cup chopped pecans	55 g
1 (16 ounce) can white frosting	455 g

Preheat over to 350° (175° C). Prepare cake batter according to package directions.

Mash bananas and stir into batter. Fold in about ¾ cup (175 ml) chopped Butterfinger® and chopped pecans.

Pour into sprayed, floured 9 x 13-inch (23 x 33 cm) baking pan. Bake for 40 to 50 minutes or until toothpick inserted in center comes out clean.

Cool thoroughly, remove from pan and spread with frosting. Sprinkle remaining chopped Butterfinger® over top. Serves 12 to 16.

While there are many variations on cake throughout the world, the cake we know in the U.S. is primarily of British origin. Romans baked the first fruitcakes.

 # Blackberry Cake

1 (18 ounce) box white cake mix with pudding	510 g
1 (3 ounce) package black raspberry gelatin	85 g
1 cup canola oil	250 ml
½ cup milk	125 ml
4 eggs	
1 cup fresh or frozen blackberries	150 g
1 cup flaked coconut	85 g
1 cup chopped pecans	110 g

 Preheat oven to 350° (175° C). Combine cake mix, gelatin, oil and milk in bowl and mix well. Add eggs. Fold in blackberries, coconut and pecans.

 Pour into 3 (9 inch/23 cm) cake pans. Bake for about 45 minutes or until done. Cool before removing from pans.

Frosting:

½ cup (1 stick) butter, softened	115 g
1 (16 ounce) box powdered sugar	455 g
1 cup blackberries	150 g
½ cup flaked coconut	45 g
½ cup chopped pecans	55 g

 Cream butter in bowl and add powdered sugar. Crush blackberries and add to butter-powdered sugar mixture. Add coconut and pecans.

 Frost each layer and stack on top of each other. Use remaining frosting to cover sides. Serves 12 to 16.

 # Brandy-Spiced Peach Cake

1 (20 ounce) can peach pie filling	565 g
1 (18 ounce) box yellow cake mix	510 g
3 eggs	
½ cup brandy	125 ml
¼ cup vegetable oil	60 ml

Preheat oven to 350° (175° C).

In blender, process pie filling until smooth. In large bowl, combine pie filling, dry cake mix, eggs, brandy and oil and blend well.

Pour into sprayed, floured 10-inch (25 cm) tube pan. Bake for 1 hour or until cake springs back when lightly touched. Serves 12 to 16.

TIP: Sprinkle with powdered sugar before serving.

The fastest and easiest way to flour and grease a cake pan is to use the baker's spray that has non-stick spray and flour in the can.

 # Carrot Cake

1 (18 ounce) box spice cake mix	510 g
2 cups shredded carrots	220 g
1 cup chopped walnuts or pecans	130 g / 110 g

Prepare cake mix according to package directions. Stir in carrots and nuts.

Bake according to package directions in sprayed, floured 9 x 13-inch (23 x 33 cm) pan. Cool before frosting.

Frosting:

½ cup (1 stick) butter, softened	115 g
1 (8 ounce) package cream cheese, softened	225 g
1 (16 ounce) box powdered sugar	455 g

Combine butter and cream cheese and beat until creamy. Stir in powdered sugar and beat. Spread on carrot cake. Serves 12 to 16.

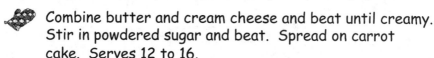

The good news about carrots is they are very low in saturated fat and cholesterol. They are also very good for fiber, vitamins A, C and K, as well as potassium. The bad news is that most of their calories come from sugar. The sugar content is one reason carrots are so good for cake.

 # Cherry-Nut Cake

1 (18 ounce) box French vanilla cake mix	510 g
½ cup (1 stick) butter, melted	115 g
2 eggs	
1 (20 ounce) can cherry pie filling	565 g
1 cup chopped pecans	110 g
Powdered sugar, optional	

 Preheat oven to 350° (175° C). In large bowl, mill all ingredients by hand. Pour into sprayed, floured bundt or tube pan.

 Bake for 1 hour. (Sprinkle some powdered sugar on top of cake if you would like a sweeter cake.) Serves 12 to 16.

Wedding cakes have evolved dating as far back as the Roman Empire, but the cakes then were more like breads and not the sweet elaborate cakes we have today. At some time, probably in the Middle Ages, guests brought small cakes to the wedding, stacked them all together and the bride and groom would kiss over the cakes. This was probably the origin of the custom of having the bride and groom figures on top of wedding cakes.

From the stacked small cakes, multi-tiered cakes with icing evolved and the ceremony of the bride and groom cutting the cake to mark their first act as a married couple continues today.

Cherry-Pineapple Cake

1 (20 ounce) can crushed pineapple, drained	565 g
1 (20 ounce) can cherry pie filling	565 g
1 (18 ounce) box yellow cake mix	510 g
1 cup (2 sticks) butter, softened	225 g
1¼ cups chopped pecans	140 g

Preheat oven to 350° (175° C). Place all ingredients in bowl and mix with spoon.

Pour into sprayed, floured 9 x 13-inch (23 x 33 cm) baking dish. Bake for 1 hour 10 minutes. Serves 12 to 16.

Two antennas met on a roof, fell in love and got married. The ceremony wasn't much, but the reception was excellent.

 # Chocolate-Cherry Cake

1 (18 ounce) box milk-chocolate
   cake mix   510 g
1 (20 ounce) can cherry pie filling 565 g
3 eggs

 Preheat oven to 350° (175° C). Combine cake mix, pie filling and eggs in bowl and mix with spoon.

 Pour into sprayed, floured 9 x 13-inch (23 x 33 cm) baking pan and bake for 35 to 40 minutes. Cake is done when toothpick inserted in center comes out clean.

Icing:

⅓ cup (⅔ stick) butter   75 g
1 ¼ cups sugar   250 g
½ cup milk   125 ml
1 (6 ounce) package chocolate
   chips   170 g

 When cake is done, combine butter, sugar and milk in saucepan. Bring to a boil for 1 minute and stir constantly.

 Add chocolate chips, stir until chips melt and pour over hot cake. Serves 12 to 16.

Christmas Lemon-Pecan Cake

1 (1.5 ounce) bottle lemon extract	*45 g*
4 cups pecan halves	*450 g*
2 cups (4 sticks) butter, softened	*455 g*
3 cups sugar	*600 g*
3½ cups flour, divided	*420 g*
1½ teaspoons baking powder	*7 ml*
6 eggs	
½ pound candied green pineapple, chopped	*225 g*
½ pound candied red cherries, halved	*225 g*

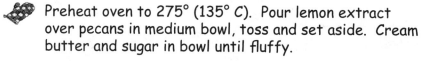 Preheat oven to 275° (135° C). Pour lemon extract over pecans in medium bowl, toss and set aside. Cream butter and sugar in bowl until fluffy.

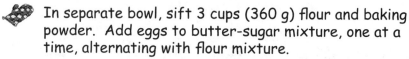 In separate bowl, sift 3 cups (360 g) flour and baking powder. Add eggs to butter-sugar mixture, one at a time, alternating with flour mixture.

Add ½ cup (60 g) flour to pineapple and cherries and mix to coat well with flour. Fold fruit and pecans into batter and pour into sprayed tube pan.

Bake for 2 hours 30 minutes or until done. Cool and remove carefully from pan. Serves 12 to 16.

 # Sweet Coconut Cake Deluxe

This cake is really moist and delicious and freezes nicely.

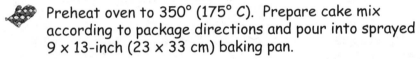

1 (18 ounce) box yellow cake mix	510 g
1 (14 ounce) can sweetened condensed milk	395 g
1 (15 ounce) can cream of coconut	445 ml
1 (3 ounce) can flaked coconut	85 g
1 (8 ounce) carton frozen whipped topping, thawed	225 g

 Preheat oven to 350° (175° C). Prepare cake mix according to package directions and pour into sprayed 9 x 13-inch (23 x 33 cm) baking pan.

Bake for 30 to 35 minutes or until toothpick inserted in center comes out clean.

While cake is warm, punch holes in cake about 2 inches (5 cm) apart. Pour sweetened condensed milk over cake and spread around until all milk soaks into cake.

Pour cream of coconut over cake and sprinkle coconut over top. Cool and frost with whipped topping. Serves 12 to 16.

An excellent health tip: Read More Books Than You Did Last Year.

Coconut-Pecan Cake

2 cups flour	240 g
1½ cups sugar	300 g
2 teaspoons baking soda	10 ml
1 (20 ounce) can crushed pineapple with juice	565 g

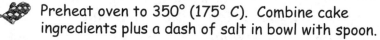 Preheat oven to 350° (175° C). Combine cake ingredients plus a dash of salt in bowl with spoon.

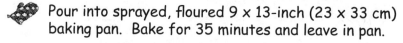 Pour into sprayed, floured 9 x 13-inch (23 x 33 cm) baking pan. Bake for 35 minutes and leave in pan.

Icing:

1½ cups sugar	300 g
1 (5 ounce) can evaporated milk	150 ml
½ cup (1 stick) butter	115 g
1 cup flaked coconut	85 g
1 cup chopped pecans	110 g
1 teaspoon vanilla	5 ml

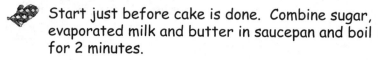 Start just before cake is done. Combine sugar, evaporated milk and butter in saucepan and boil for 2 minutes.

Add coconut, pecans, vanilla and dash of salt and pour mixture over cake as soon as it comes out of oven.

When cake cools, cover with foil. Cut into squares to serve. Serves 12 to 16.

 # Delightful Pear Cake

1 (15 ounce) can pears in light
    syrup   425 g
1 (18 ounce) box white cake mix   510 g
2 egg whites
1 egg
Powdered sugar

Preheat oven to 350° (175° C). Drain pears, set aside juice and chop pears.

Place pears and juice in bowl and add cake mix, egg whites and egg. Beat on low speed for 30 seconds. Beat on high for 4 minutes.

Pour batter into sprayed, floured 10-inch (25 cm) bundt pan.

Bake for 50 to 55 minutes. Cook until toothpick inserted in center comes out clean. Cool in pan for 10 minutes. Remove cake and dust with powdered sugar. Serves 12 to 16.

"Plump up" dried fruits or raisins before adding to a mixture by pouring boiling water over them and soak them for about 30 minutes. Drain and dry completely with paper towels. Then dust the fruit or raisins with flour so they will not sink to the bottom of the cake.

Easy Pineapple Cake

2 cups sugar	400 g
2 cups flour	240 g
1 (20 ounce) can crushed	
pineapple with juice	565 g
1 teaspoon baking soda	5 ml
1 teaspoon vanilla	5 ml

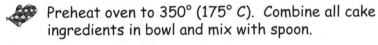 Preheat oven to 350° (175° C). Combine all cake
ingredients in bowl and mix with spoon.

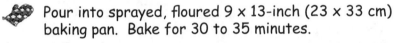 Pour into sprayed, floured 9 x 13-inch (23 x 33 cm)
baking pan. Bake for 30 to 35 minutes.

Easy Pineapple Cake Icing:

1 (8 ounce) package cream	
cheese, softened	225 g
½ cup (1 stick) butter, melted	115 g
1 cup powdered sugar	120 g
1 cup chopped pecans	110 g

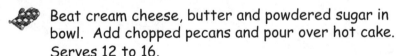 Beat cream cheese, butter and powdered sugar in
bowl. Add chopped pecans and pour over hot cake.
Serves 12 to 16.

*If you want butter to be room temperature, but
you forgot to take it out of the refrigerator,
just cut into small pieces and place on a plate. It will
warm up quickly and you won't have to melt it.*

Fruit Cocktail Cake

2 cups sugar	400 g
2 cups flour	240 g
1 teaspoon baking soda	5 ml
2 (15 ounce) cans fruit cocktail, divided	2 (425 g)

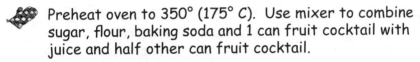 Preheat oven to 350° (175° C). Use mixer to combine sugar, flour, baking soda and 1 can fruit cocktail with juice and half other can fruit cocktail.

Drain remaining can fruit cocktail and add half fruit to sugar mixture. (Set aside half can fruit cocktail.) Beat several minutes with mixer (fruit will be chopped up).

Pour into sprayed, floured 9 x 13-inch (23 x 33 cm) baking pan and bake for 30 to 35 minutes. Cake is done when toothpick inserted in center comes out clean.

Frosting:

1 (8 ounce) package cream cheese	225 g
½ cup (1 stick) butter	115 g
1 cup flaked coconut	85 g
1 cup powdered sugar	120 g
Remaining fruit cocktail	

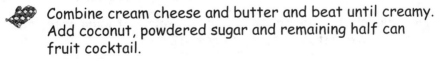 Combine cream cheese and butter and beat until creamy. Add coconut, powdered sugar and remaining half can fruit cocktail.

Beat several minutes until fruit chops well and pour mixture over hot cake. When cool, store in refrigerator. Serves 12 to 16.

TIP: Pecans can be substituted for coconut.

 # Hawaiian Dream Cake

1 (20 ounce) can crushed pineapple
     with juice, divided   565 g
1 (18 ounce) box yellow cake mix   510 g
4 eggs
¾ cup canola oil   175 ml

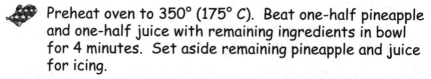 Preheat oven to 350° (175° C). Beat one-half pineapple and one-half juice with remaining ingredients in bowl for 4 minutes. Set aside remaining pineapple and juice for icing.

 Pour into sprayed, floured 9 x 13-inch (23 x 33 cm) baking pan.

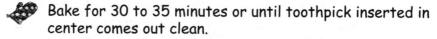 Bake for 30 to 35 minutes or until toothpick inserted in center comes out clean.

Icing:

Remaining pineapple with juice
½ cup (1 stick) butter   115 g
1 (16 ounce) box powdered sugar   455 g
1 (7 ounce) can flaked coconut   200 g

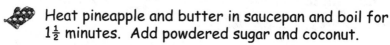 Heat pineapple and butter in saucepan and boil for 1½ minutes. Add powdered sugar and coconut.

 Punch holes in cake with knife. Pour hot icing over cake. Refrigerate to store. Serves 12 to 16.

 # Hawaiian Pineapple Cake

1 (20 ounce) can crushed pineapple, drained	565 g
1 (20 ounce) can cherry pie filling	565 g
1 (18 ounce) box yellow cake mix	510 g
1 cup (2 sticks) butter, softened	225 g
1¼ cups chopped pecans	140 g

 Preheat oven to 350° (175° C).

 Place all ingredients in large bowl and mix by hand.

 Pour into sprayed, floured 9 x 13-inch (23 x 33 cm) baking dish.

 Bake for 1 hour 10 minutes. Serves 12 to 16.

Pineapple is native to South America and was given its name because of its resemblance to a pinecone. Christopher Columbus discovered pineapple in 1493 on the island of Guadeloupe. James Cook introduced pineapple to Hawaii in 1770, but commercial harvesting of pineapple did not begin until the development of the steam engine. It wasn't until the 1880's that shipping pineapples to the mainland was feasible with the steamship.

By 1903 James Dole began canning pineapples in Hawaii and business boomed by the 1920's. he last pineapple crop in Hawaii was harvested in 2008 to make room for Hawaii's ever expanding tourist industry.

 # Lemon-Pineapple Cake

1 (18 ounce) box lemon cake mix   510 g
1 (20 ounce) can crushed
      pineapple with juice   565 g
3 eggs
⅓ cup canola oil   75 ml

 Preheat oven to 350° (175° C). Combine all ingredients in bowl. Blend on low speed to moisten and beat on medium for 2 minutes.

Pour batter into sprayed, floured 9 x 13-inch (23 x 33 cm) baking pan.

Bake for 30 minutes. Cake is done when toothpick inserted in center comes out clean. When cake is baking, start topping for cake. Cool for about 15 minutes.

Topping:

1 (14 ounce) can sweetened
      condensed milk   395 g
1 cup sour cream   240 g
¼ cup lemon juice   60 ml

Combine all ingredients in medium bowl. Stir and blend well. Pour over warm cake. Refrigerate. Serves 12 to 16.

Lemony Sponge Cake

4 eggs
1 (18 ounce) box yellow cake mix   510 g
½ cup plus 2 tablespoons
    vegetable oil   155 mℓ
1 tablespoon lemon extract   15 mℓ
⅔ cup apricot nectar   150 mℓ

Preheat oven to 350° (175° C). In small bowl, crack eggs
and beat slightly to mix. In large bowl, combine dry
cake mix and eggs until eggs absorb into mixture.

Pour in oil, lemon extract and apricot nectar and mix
well. Pour batter in sprayed, floured cake pan.

Bake for 40 to 45 minutes. Serves 12 to 16.

TIP: A lemon glaze is wonderful poured over top of this cake.
Mix juice of 2 lemons and 1½ cups (180 g) powdered sugar
until smooth and pour over cake after it cools slightly.

Sponge cakes are light, airy cakes used for
trifles, madeleines and some shortcakes. The
typical sponge cake is a mixture of eggs beaten
with sugar with flour gently folded into mixture.
Sometimes baking powder is included, sometimes it is
not. Before the cake cools, it is very flexible and can
be rolled.

Miracle Cake

1 (18 ounce) box lemon cake mix	510 g
3 eggs	
⅓ cup canola oil	75 ml
1 (20 ounce) can crushed	
pineapple with juice	565 g

Preheat oven to 350° (175°C). Combine all ingredients in bowl. Blend on low speed and beat on medium for 2 minutes.

Pour batter into sprayed, floured 9 x 13-inch (23 x 33 cm) baking dish. Bake for 30 to 35 minutes or until toothpick inserted in center comes out clean.

Miracle Cake Topping:

1 (14 ounce) can sweetened	
condensed milk	395 g
¼ cup lemon juice	60 ml
1 (8 ounce) carton frozen	
whipped topping, thawed	225 g

 Blend all ingredients in bowl and mix well. Spread over cake. Refrigerate. Serves 12 to 16.

Sweetened condensed milk has 50% of the water removed. The remaining mixture is 40% sugar and is very sticky and sweet.

Nutty Cherry Cake

2 cups sugar	400 g
1/2 cup (1 stick) butter, softened	115 g
2 eggs	
2 1/2 cups flour	300 g
2 teaspoons baking soda	10 ml
1 (16 ounce) can bing cherries, drained	455 g
1 cup chopped pecans	110 g

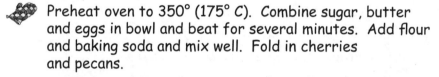

 Preheat oven to 350° (175° C). Combine sugar, butter and eggs in bowl and beat for several minutes. Add flour and baking soda and mix well. Fold in cherries and pecans.

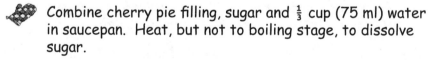 Pour into sprayed, floured 9 x 13-inch (23 x 33 cm) baking pan and bake for 35 minutes. Cake is done when toothpick inserted in center comes out clean.

Cherry Sauce:

1 (16 ounce) can cherry pie filling	455 g
1/3 cup sugar	65 g

Combine cherry pie filling, sugar and 1/3 cup (75 ml) water in saucepan. Heat, but not to boiling stage, to dissolve sugar.

When ready to serve, pour 1/3 cup (75 ml) hot sauce over each piece of cake. Serves 12 to 16.

Orange-Date Cake

Don't worry about buying buttermilk. Check the tip below.
The cake is great.

4 cups flour	480 g
1 teaspoon baking soda	5 ml
1 cup (2 sticks) butter, softened	225 g
2½ cups sugar	500 g
4 eggs	
1½ cups buttermilk*	375 ml
1 teaspoon orange extract	5 ml
1 tablespoon grated orange peel	15 ml
1 (11 ounce) can mandarin oranges	310 g
1 (8 ounce) package chopped dates	225 g
1 cup chopped pecans	110 g

 Preheat oven to 350° (175° C).

 Sift flour and baking soda in bowl and set aside. In separate bowl, cream butter and sugar, add eggs one at a time and beat well.

 Add buttermilk and dry ingredients alternately and end with dry ingredients. Add orange extract and peel and beat well. Stir in oranges, dates and pecans.

 Pour into sprayed bundt pan and bake for 1 hour 15 minutes or until toothpick inserted in center comes out clean. Remove from oven and pour glaze over cake while still in pan.

Continued next page...

Continued from previous page...

Glaze:

½ cup orange juice	125 ml
1¼ cups sugar	250 g
1 teaspoon grated orange peel	5 ml
½ teaspoon orange extract	2 ml

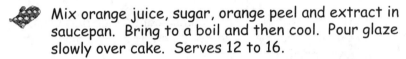 Mix orange juice, sugar, orange peel and extract in saucepan. Bring to a boil and then cool. Pour glaze slowly over cake. Serves 12 to 16.

*TIP: To make buttermilk, mix 1 cup (250 ml) milk with 1 tablespoon (15 ml) lemon juice or vinegar and let milk stand for about 10 minutes.

Pure flavor extracts are always best to use in baking recipes. Imitation or synthetic flavorings may have a bitter aftertaste. Pure flavor extracts are available for fruits, nuts, flowers, liquors and more. Some of the most common include vanilla, almond, lemon, orange, lime, peppermint, banana, allspice, butter, apricot, rose, lavender, brandy, cognac, butter rum and hazelnut, to mention just a few.

Orange-Butter Cake

2 cups sugar	400 g
1 cup (2 sticks) butter, softened	225 g
3 eggs	
2 cups flour	240 g
2 tablespoons orange juice	30 ml

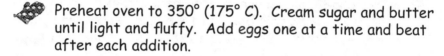 Preheat oven to 350° (175° C). Cream sugar and butter until light and fluffy. Add eggs one at a time and beat after each addition.

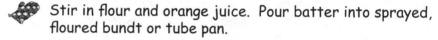 Stir in flour and orange juice. Pour batter into sprayed, floured bundt or tube pan.

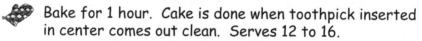 Bake for 1 hour. Cake is done when toothpick inserted in center comes out clean. Serves 12 to 16.

The modern butter cake is a lighter, fluffier version of the traditional pound cake which used equal weights of butter, sugar, flour and eggs. The pound cake is a heavy, dense cake that originated in England.

Butter cakes came along after baking powder and baking soda hit the market. These leavening agents made it possible to use the same traditional ingredients but resulted in a lighter, fluffier cake.

Common flavors of butter cakes include apple cinnamon, banana, berry, butterscotch, pecan, caramel, cherry, chocolate, coconut and many more.

Peaches 'n Cream

1 (18 ounce) box yellow cake mix	510 g
½ cup (1 stick) butter, melted	115 g
3 eggs, divided	
1 (20 ounce) can peach pie filling	565 g
1 (1 pint) carton sour cream	500 ml

Preheat oven to 350° (175° C). In large bowl, combine dry cake mix, butter and 2 eggs and blend well. Pour into sprayed 9 x 13-inch (23 x 33 cm) baking pan.

Bake for 25 minutes. Remove from oven.

Spoon pie filling over cake. In small bowl, combine sour cream and remaining egg.

Pour mixture over pie filling. Bake additional 15 minutes or until sour cream topping sets. Cut into 3-inch (8 cm) squares. Serves 12 to 16.

Butter cakes, as well as all cakes, are better if all ingredients are room temperature. If eggs are cold, the batter may curdle and not mix well. If butter is cold, it doesn't reach a creamy, smooth texture and you cannot beat air into the mixture properly.

While sifting flour reduces the chances of lumps in batter, many flours today come presifted and just need to be stirred lightly before measuring.

Overbeating the batter results in a tough texture instead of a soft, moist texture.

 # Pina Colada Cake

1 (18 ounce) box pineapple
  cake mix   *510 g*
3 eggs
⅓ cup canola oil   *75 ml*

 Preheat oven to 350° (175° C). Combine cake mix, eggs, 1¼ cups (325 ml) water and oil in bowl.

 Beat for 3 to 4 minutes and pour into sprayed, floured 10 x 15-inch (25 x 38 cm) baking pan. Bake for 35 minutes.

 When cake is done, punch holes in top with fork so frosting will soak into cake.

Frosting:

1 (14 ounce) can sweetened
  condensed milk   *395 g*
1 (15 ounce) can cream of coconut   *445 ml*
1 cup flaked coconut   *85 g*
1 (8 ounce) can crushed
  pineapple, drained   *225 g*
1 (8 ounce) carton frozen
  whipped topping, thawed   *225 g*

 Mix sweetened condensed milk, cream of coconut, coconut and pineapple in bowl.

While cake is still warm, pour mixture over top of cake. Refrigerate for about 1 hour, spread whipped topping over cake and return to refrigerator. Serves 12 to 16.

Pineapple Upside-Down Cake

½ cup (1 stick) butter	115 g
2 cups packed light brown sugar	440 g
1 (20 ounce) can crushed pineapple, drained	565 g
10 maraschino cherries, quartered	
1 (18 ounce) box pineapple cake mix	510 g

 Preheat oven to 350° (175° C). In small saucepan, melt butter and brown sugar until creamy. Divide mixture evenly between 2 sprayed, floured 9-inch (23 cm) cake pans.

 Spread pineapple and cherries evenly over brown sugar mixture in each pan. Prepare cake batter according to package directions and pour over pineapple.

 Bake for 35 to 40 minutes or until toothpick inserted in center of cake comes out clean. Remove cake from oven and cool for 10 minutes.

 Put plate on top of cake pan, turn cake pan upside down and tap bottom of cake pan several times with knife. Gently lift cake pan off cake. Serves 12 to 16.

Upside-down cakes were common when cakes were cooked in cast-iron skillets. Fruits, nuts and sugar were mixed together and poured on the bottom of large skillets. Cake batter was then poured on top and cooked over the fire. The natural way to remove the cake was by flipping it upside down onto a plate.

Pink Lady Cake

1 (18 ounce) box strawberry cake mix	510 g
3 eggs	
1 teaspoon lemon extract	5 ml
1 (20 ounce) can strawberry pie filling	565 g

Preheat oven to 350° (175° C). Beat cake mix, eggs and lemon extract in bowl. Fold in pie filling.

Pour in sprayed, floured 9 x 13-inch (23 x 33 cm) baking pan. Bake for 30 to 35 minutes. Cake is done when toothpick inserted in center comes out clean. Serves 12 to 16.

TIP: *Add a prepared vanilla frosting or frozen whipped topping, thawed.*

Pie fillings are some of the more popular convenience foods on grocery store shelves today. Pie fillings include apple, cherry, lemon, blueberry and many other flavors that are parts of a lot of desserts today With its strawberry pie filling, Pink Lady Cake is just one recipe that shows pie fillings are not just for pies.

Pumpkin Chess Cake

1 (18 ounce) box yellow cake mix	510 g
¾ cup (1½ sticks) butter, softened, divided	170 g
4 eggs, divided	
1 (15 ounce) can pumpkin	425 g
2 teaspoons ground cinnamon	10 ml
½ cup packed brown sugar	110 g
⅔ cup milk	150 ml
½ cup sugar	100 g
⅔ cup chopped pecans	85 g

 Preheat oven to 350° (175° C). Set aside 1 cup (250 ml) cake mix. Mix rest of cake mix, ½ cup (115 g) butter and 1 egg and press into sprayed, floured 9 x 13-inch (23 x 33 cm) baking pan.

 Mix pumpkin, 3 eggs, cinnamon, brown sugar and milk in bowl and pour over batter in pan.

Use remaining cake mix, sugar, remaining butter and pecans to make topping and crumble over cake. Bake for 1 hour. Serves 12 to 16.

Pumpkin-Rum Cake

1 (18 ounce) box white cake mix	510 g
1 (15 ounce) can pumpkin	425 g
3 eggs	
½ cup rum	125 ml
¾ cup chopped pecans, toasted	85 g

Preheat oven to 325° (165° C). In large bowl, combine dry cake mix, pumpkin, eggs and rum. Beat on low speed to blend. Beat on medium speed for 2 minutes.

Fold in pecans and pour batter into sprayed, floured 12-cup (3 L) bundt pan.

Bake for 45 to 50 minutes or when toothpick inserted in center comes out clean. Cool 10 minutes. Turn out onto serving platter and frost with Orange Glaze.

Orange Glaze:

1 cup powdered sugar	120 g
2 tablespoons plus ½ teaspoon orange juice	32 ml
1 tablespoon orange zest	15 ml

Mix all ingredients until smooth. Spoon over top of cake and allow glaze to run down sides of cake. Serves 12 to 16.

 # Quick Fruitcake

1 (15.6 ounce) package cranberry or blueberry quick-bread mix	440 g
½ cup chopped pecans	55 g
½ cup chopped dates	75 g
¼ cup chopped maraschino cherries	60 g
¼ cup crushed pineapple, drained	60 g

Preheat oven to 350° (175° C). Prepare quick-bread batter according to package directions. Stir in remaining ingredients. Pour into sprayed 9 x 5-inch (23 x 13 cm) loaf pan.

Bake for 60 minutes or until toothpick inserted in center comes out clean. Cool 10 minutes before removing from pan. Serves 12 to 16.

Fruitcakes date back to Roman times when seeds, nuts and raisins were mixed with grain mash. As dried fruits became more plentiful and were shipped from the Mediterranean to Europe, more and more fruits and nuts were added to the cake until they were quite heavy and dense. In the early 1700's fruitcakes were considered decadent because they were tantalizingly good; they were declared sinful and against the law in most of Europe.

Shortcakes

2½ cups plus 2 tablespoons flour	315 g
2½ teaspoons baking powder	12 ml
⅓ cup sugar	65 g
½ cup (1 stick) butter, softened, sliced	115 g
1 cup milk	250 ml

Preheat oven to 400° (205° C). In bowl, combine flour, baking powder, sugar and butter. Stir and mix with fork until mixture resembles coarse meal.

Add milk and mix until dough forms. Place dough on lightly floured surface and with lightly floured hands, pat dough into 4 x 6-inch (10 x 15 cm) rectangle.

Cut dough into 8 squares and place on sprayed baking sheet. Bake 30 minutes or until light brown.

To serve, cut shortcakes in half and serve with sugared strawberries or raspberries and top with whipped topping. Serves 16.

Pecans contain no cholesterol and add essential fiber, vitamin E, magnesium, thiamin and copper to the diet. They are also high in monounsaturated fats that help lower LDL cholesterol blood levels.

 # Strawberry Cake

1 (18 ounce) box white cake mix	510 g
1 tablespoon flour	15 ml
1 (3 ounce) box strawberry gelatin	85 g
1 (10 ounce) package frozen strawberries, thawed, divided	285 g
1 cup corn oil	250 ml
4 eggs	

 Preheat oven to 350° (175° C). Spray and flour 2 (8 or 9 inch/20 or 23 cm) round pans.

 Combine cake mix, flour and gelatin in bowl and mix well. In separate bowl, mix ¾ cup (165 g) strawberries, ½ cup (125 ml) water and corn oil. Add to cake mixture and blend well.

Add eggs one at a time and beat for 1 minute after each egg. Pour into pans and bake for 35 minutes.

Frosting:

½ cup (1 stick) butter	115 g
2½ - 3 cups powdered sugar	300 - 360 g
2 tablespoons milk	30 ml

 Cream butter and sugar with milk in bowl. Add small amount of remaining strawberries for color.

 (If frosting is too thin, add more powdered sugar.) Frost cake and refrigerate for several hours before serving. Serves 12 to 16.

Strawberry Shortcake

Shortcakes:

2½ cups biscuit mix	300 g
¼ cup sugar	50 g
3 tablespoons butter, softened	40 g
½ cup milk	125 ml

Preheat oven to 350° (175° C).

In mixing bowl, combine biscuit mix and sugar; cut in butter until mixture is crumbly. Add milk and stir just until soft dough forms.

Drop heaping tablespoonfuls of batter onto sprayed baking sheet. Bake about 15 minutes or until light brown.

Strawberry Glaze:

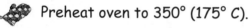

1 tablespoon cornstarch	15 ml
1 teaspoon almond extract	5 ml
¾ cup sugar	150 g
1 (16 ounce) container frozen strawberries, thawed	455 g
1 (8 ounce) carton frozen whipped topping, thawed	225 g

Place cornstarch, almond extract, sugar and 2 tablespoons (30 ml) water in saucepan.

Continued next page...

Continued from previous page...

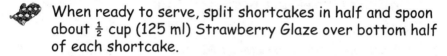 Add strawberries, bring mixture to a boil and stir constantly. Reduce heat, cook and stir until mixture thickens. Remove from heat and refrigerate.

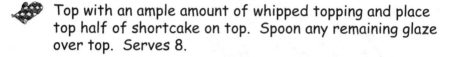 When ready to serve, split shortcakes in half and spoon about ½ cup (125 ml) Strawberry Glaze over bottom half of each shortcake.

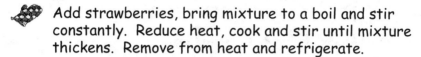 Top with an ample amount of whipped topping and place top half of shortcake on top. Spoon any remaining glaze over top. Serves 8.

Shortcakes originally meant cakes made with shortening or butter and were heavy, dense cakes similar to scones. Strawberry shortcake has probably been around as long as cakes have been around. It wouldn't take a stroke of genius to put berries over a cake for a nice dessert.

In the 1860's in the U.S. when railroads went coast to coast, the popularity of strawberries spread along their routes and strawberry shortcakes depicted a celebration of the beginning of summer. Strawberry shortcake in its present form, whether an original shortcake or today's sponge cake, is typically considered to be an American invention.

 # Watermelon Cake with Lime Frosting

1 (3 ounce) package watermelon gelatin	85 g
1 (18 ounce) box white cake mix	510 g
4 eggs	
½ cup vegetable oil	125 ml
Several drops of red food coloring (optional)	

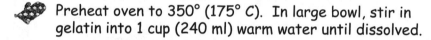

Preheat oven to 350° (175° C). In large bowl, stir in gelatin into 1 cup (240 ml) warm water until dissolved.

Add cake mix, eggs and oil. (At this point, you can add several drops of red food coloring, if desired, to color the batter a deeper pink or red.). Beat on low speed to moisten, then beat on medium for 2 minutes.

Divide batter between 2 sprayed, floured round cake pans. Bake for 30 minutes or until toothpick inserted in center comes out clean. Cool and frost with Lime Frosting.

Continued next page...

Watermelons probably originated in Africa and seeds were found dating from as early as 2000 BC in the tombs of Egyptian pharaohs, including Tutankhamen. European explorers and African slaves probably introduced watermelons to the Native Indians and colonists in the New World as well as in countries across the globe.

Continued from previous page...

Lime Frosting:

½ cup (1 stick) butter, softened	115 g
3 - 3½ cups powdered sugar, divided	360 - 420 g
¼ cup fresh lime juice	60 ml
1 teaspoon lime zest (grated lime rind)	5 ml
1 teaspoon clear vanilla*	5 ml
Several drops of green food coloring, optional	

In medium bowl, cream butter with 1 cup (120 g) powdered sugar. Add lime juice, zest and vanilla. Blend well.

Gradually add remaining powdered sugar, beating well after each addition until frosting reaches spreading consistency. (If desired, add a few drops of green food coloring.) Serves 12 to 16.

*TIP: Clear vanilla can be found in cake decorating supply stores or online. Regular vanilla can be used but will change the color of the icing.

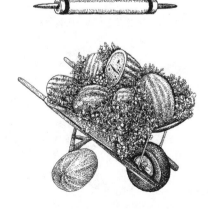

A Really Great Pound Cake

½ cup shortening	95 g
1 cup (2 sticks) butter	225 g
3 cups sugar	600 g
5 eggs	
3½ cups flour	420 g
½ teaspoon baking powder	2 ml
1 cup milk	250 ml
1 teaspoon rum flavoring	5 ml
1 teaspoon coconut flavoring	5 ml

 Preheat oven to 325° (165° C).

 Cream shortening, butter and sugar in bowl. Add eggs and beat well.

 In separate bowl, mix flour and baking powder. Add dry ingredients and milk alternately to butter mixture, beginning and ending with flour.

 Add rum and coconut flavorings. Pour into large sprayed, floured tube pan.

 Bake for 1 hour 30 minutes to 1 hour 45 minutes. (Do not open door during baking.)

 Cake is done when toothpick inserted in center comes out clean.

Continued next page...

Continued from previous page...

Glaze:

⅓ cup sugar   70 g
½ teaspoon almond extract   2 ml

Right before cake is done, combine 1 cup (250 ml) water and sugar in saucepan and bring to a rolling boil. Remove from heat and add almond extract.

While cake is still in pan and right out of the oven, pour glaze over cake and let stand for about 30 minutes before removing from pan. Serves 12 to 16.

Pound cakes have been in the South long before the first recorded recipes in the 18th century. They were named Pound Cakes because of the equal weight of each of the ingredients: 1 pound flour, 1 pound butter, 1 pound sugar and 1 pound eggs (approximately 8 large).

In The Virginia Housewife published in 1824, Mary Randolph uses these ingredients and measurements and suggests adding grated lemon peel, nutmeg and brandy. She also suggests baking the mixture as a cake, baking it as a pudding in a large mold, or boiling it served with butter and sugar.

Rum-Brown Sugar Pound Cake

1½ cups (3 sticks) butter, softened	345 g
1 (16 ounce) package brown sugar	455 g
1 cup sugar	200 g
5 large eggs	
¾ cup milk	175 ml
¼ cup rum	60 ml
2 teaspoons vanilla	10 ml
3 cups flour	360 g
1 teaspoon baking powder	5 ml
1½ cups chopped pecans	165 g

Preheat oven to 325° (165° C).

Beat butter, brown sugar and sugar in bowl on medium speed for 5 minutes. Add eggs, one at a time and beat just until yellow disappears.

Combine milk, rum and vanilla in bowl.

In separate bowl, combine flour, baking powder and ¼ teaspoon (1 ml) salt. Add half flour mixture and mix. Add milk mixture and mix. Add remaining flour mixture, beat at low speed and fold in pecans.

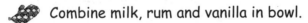

Pour into sprayed, floured tube pan and bake for 1 hour 25 minutes. Cake is done when toothpick inserted in center comes out clean. Cool in pan for 20 minutes, remove from pan and cool completely. Serves 12 to 16.

TIP: If you don't want to use rum, add another ¼ cup (60 ml) milk and 2 teaspoons (10 ml) rum flavoring.

Chocolate Pound Cake

3 cups sugar	600 g
1 cup (2 sticks) butter, softened	225 g
½ cup shortening	95 g
5 eggs	
3 cups flour	360 g
½ cup cocoa	40 g
½ teaspoon baking powder	2 ml
1 cup milk	250 ml
1 teaspoon vanilla	5 ml
Powdered sugar	

 Preheat oven to 350° (175° C).

 Cream sugar, butter and shortening in bowl on medium speed. Add eggs, one at a time, and beat well after each addition.

 In separate bowl, sift flour, cocoa, baking powder and ¼ teaspoon (1 ml) salt. Reduce speed to low and add one-half dry ingredients, milk and vanilla and beat well after each addition. Add remaining dry ingredients and beat well.

 Pour into sprayed, floured 10-inch (25 cm) bundt pan and bake for 1 hour 20 minutes. Cool for 10 minutes in pan, turn on rack or plate to cool and sprinkle powdered sugar over top. Serves 12 to 16.

Double Chocolate Pound Cake

1 cup (2 sticks) butter, softened	225 g
½ cup shortening	95 g
1 (3 ounce) package cream cheese, softened	85 g
3 cups sugar	600 g
2 teaspoons vanilla	10 ml
5 large eggs	
½ cup cocoa	40 g
3 cups flour	360 g
1 teaspoon baking powder	5 ml
1 cup buttermilk*	250 ml
1 (6 ounce) package chocolate chips	170 g
Powdered sugar	

 Preheat oven to 325° (165° C).

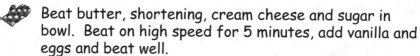 Beat butter, shortening, cream cheese and sugar in bowl. Beat on high speed for 5 minutes, add vanilla and eggs and beat well.

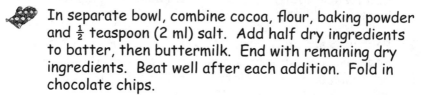 In separate bowl, combine cocoa, flour, baking powder and ½ teaspoon (2 ml) salt. Add half dry ingredients to batter, then buttermilk. End with remaining dry ingredients. Beat well after each addition. Fold in chocolate chips.

Continued next page...

Continued from previous page...

 Pour into sprayed, floured 10-inch (25 cm) tube pan, bake for 1 hour 30 minutes and cake is done when toothpick inserted in center comes out clean.

 Cool cake in pan for 15 minutes, then turn onto cake plate and cool completely. Dust with powdered sugar Serves 12 to 16.

TIP: To make buttermilk, mix 1 cup (250 ml) milk with 1 tablespoon (15 ml) lemon juice or vinegar and let milk stand for about 10 minutes.

Life Lessons:

Don't spend money until you get it.

It's not what you say but how you say it.

Life is not a dress rehearsal.

Be it ever so humble, there's no place like home.

Red Velvet Pound Cake

3 cups sugar	600 g
¾ cup shortening	140 g
6 eggs	
1 teaspoon vanilla	5 ml
3 cups flour	360 g
1 cup milk	250 ml
2 (1 ounce) bottles red food coloring	2 (30 g)

 Preheat oven to 325° (165° C).

Cream sugar and shortening in bowl and add eggs, one at a time, and beat after each addition. Add vanilla and mix.

Add ¼ teaspoon (1 ml) salt, flour and milk and alternate each, beginning and ending with flour. Add food coloring and beat until smooth.

Bake in sprayed, floured tube pan for 1 hour 30 minutes or until toothpick inserted in center comes out clean.

Set aside in pan for 10 minutes. Remove cake from pan, cool completely and frost.

Continued next page...

Continued from previous page...

Frosting:

1 (16 ounce) box powdered sugar   455 g
1 (3 ounce) package cream cheese,
   softened   85 g
¼ cup (½ stick) butter, softened   55 g
3 tablespoons milk   45 ml
Red sprinkles

 Beat powdered sugar, cream cheese, butter and milk in bowl and mix well. Frost cake and top with a few red sprinkles. Serves 12 to 16.

Cooking Terms Make Baking a Little Easier.

Beat: Beat usually means an electric mixer set on medium speed unless specified differently or beat by hand with large spoon or fork. Baking doesn't require electric mixers, but you can figure about 100 strokes by hand to one minute with an electric mixer.

Cream: Cream, used as a verb, means to blend two or more ingredients until they are smooth and no longer identifiable. Butter and sugar are usually creamed to a smooth, silky texture. You can cream ingredients by hand or with an electric mixer.

Fold: Fold means to place a light mixture on top of a heavier mixture and gently mix the two by folding one over the other. The purpose is to put air into the mixture while combining all ingredients.

Peanut Butter Pound Cake

1 cup (2 sticks) butter	225 g
2 cups sugar	400 g
1 cup packed light brown sugar	220 g
½ cup peanut butter	145 g
5 eggs	
1 tablespoon vanilla	15 ml
3 cups flour	360 g
½ teaspoon baking powder	2 ml
½ teaspoon baking soda	2 ml
1 cup whipping cream	250 ml

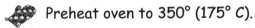

Preheat oven to 350° (175° C).

Cream butter, sugar, brown sugar and peanut butter in bowl and beat until fluffy. Add eggs one at a time and beat well after each addition. Add vanilla and blend.

In separate bowl, sift dry flour, baking powder, baking soda and ½ teaspoon (2 ml) salt and add alternately with whipping cream.

Pour mixture into large, sprayed tube pan and bake for 1 hour 10 minutes. Cake is done when toothpick inserted in center comes out clean.

Continued next page...

Continued from previous page...

Frosting:

¼ cup (½ stick) butter, softened	60 g
3 - 4 tablespoons milk	45 - 60 ml
⅓ cup creamy or crunchy peanut butter	95 g
1 (16 ounce) box powdered sugar	455 g

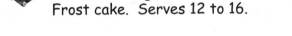

Combine all ingredients in bowl and beat until smooth. Frost cake. Serves 12 to 16.

Cooking Terms Make Baking a Little Easier.

Cut in: "Cut in" refers to adding butter or a creamy ingredient to dry ingredients. By putting some of the butter on top of the dry mixture, you can cut through both by hand or with a pastry blender or fork. The point is to mix all ingredients to achieve a course texture.

Whisking: A wire whisk is a kitchen tool with a series of wire loops connected to a handle. It is used to whip air into ingredients such as whipping cream or egg whites. Wire whisks come in several different sizes and are great tools for many uses.

Greasing and Flouring: The easy way to grease and flour a baking pan is to use the all-purpose bakers' spray that has non-stick cooking spray and flour in it. The messy way is to put shortening or butter on your fingers or on wax paper and rub it all over the baking pan.

Nutty Pound Cake

1 cup (2 sticks) butter, softened	225 g
2 cups sugar	400 g
5 large eggs	
1 teaspoon vanilla	5 ml
1 teaspoon butter flavoring	5 ml
1 teaspoon almond extract	5 ml
2 cups flour, divided	240 g
2 cups chopped pecans	220 g
Powdered sugar	

 Preheat oven to 325° (165° C).

 Cream butter and sugar in bowl and beat in eggs, one at a time.

 Stir in vanilla, butter and almond flavorings. Add 1¾ cups (425 g) flour and beat well.

 Combine remaining flour with pecans and fold into batter.

 Bake in sprayed, floured bundt pan for 70 to 75 minutes. Cool, remove cake from pan and dust with powdered sugar. Serves 12 to 16.

If you drink a diet soda and eat a candy bar, will they cancel each other out?

If you eat standing up, do all the calories go to your feet and get walked off?

 # Blueberry Pound Cake

1 (18 ounce) box yellow cake mix   510 g
1 (8 ounce) package cream cheese,
    softened   225 g
½ cup canola oil   125 ml
4 eggs
1 (15 ounce) can whole blueberries,
    drained   425 g
Powdered sugar

 Preheat oven to 350° (175° C).

 Combine all ingredients in bowl except blueberries and
beat for 3 minutes. Gently fold in blueberries. Pour
into sprayed, floured bundt or tube pan.

 Bake for 50 minutes. Cake is done when toothpick
inserted in center comes out clean.

Sprinkle sifted powdered sugar over top of cake.
Serves 12 to 16.

*If you eat food off someone else's plate,
does it count?*

*If you scrape the batter out of the bowl, does it
have any calories?*

Lemon Pound Cake

2 cups sugar	400 g
1 cup (2 sticks) butter	225 g
6 eggs	
2 cups flour	240 g
1 teaspoon lemon extract	5 ml

 Preheat oven to 350° (175° C).

 Cream sugar and butter until light and fluffy.

 Add eggs one at a time and beat well after each addition. Gradually add flour and lemon extract.

 Pour batter into sprayed tube or bundt pan and bake for 50 to 60 minutes. Cake is done when toothpick inserted in center and comes out clean. Serves 12 to 16.

Familiar Mom-isms

Who said life was going to be easy?

Are you kids trying to drive me crazy?

Answer me when I ask you a question.

A little soap and water never killed anyone.

 # Strawberry Pound Cake

1 (18 ounce) box strawberry
　　cake mix   510 g
1 (3.4 ounce) package instant
　　vanilla pudding mix   95 g
⅓ cup canola oil   75 ml
4 eggs
1 (3 ounce) package strawberry
　　gelatin   85 g

Preheat oven to 350° (175° C).

Mix all ingredients plus 1 cup (250 ml) water in bowl and
beat for 2 minutes at medium speed.

Pour into sprayed, floured bundt pan.

Bake for 55 to 60 minutes. Cake is done when toothpick
inserted in center comes out clean.

Cool for 20 minutes before removing cake from pan.
If you would like an icing, use prepared vanilla icing.
Serves 12 to 16.

TIP: If you like coconut better than pineapple, use coconut
cream pudding mix.

Pumpkin-Pie Pound Cake

1 cup shortening	190 g
1¼ cups sugar	250 g
¾ cup packed brown sugar	165 g
5 eggs, room temperature	
1 cup canned pumpkin	245 g
2½ cups flour	300 g
2 teaspoons ground cinnamon	10 ml
1 teaspoon ground nutmeg	5 ml
1 teaspoon baking soda	5 ml
½ cup orange juice, room temperature	125 ml
2 teaspoons vanilla	10 ml
1½ cups chopped pecans	165 g

Preheat oven to 325° (165° C).

Cream shortening, sugar and brown sugar in bowl for about 4 minutes. Add eggs, one at a time and mix well after each addition. Blend in pumpkin.

In separate bowl, mix flour, spices, ¼ teaspoon (1 ml) salt and baking soda and mix well.

Gradually beat dry ingredients into batter until ingredients mix well.

Fold in orange juice, vanilla and pecans. Pour into sprayed, floured bundt pan.

Continued next page...

Continued from previous page...

 Bake for 70 to 75 minutes or until toothpick inserted in center comes out clean.

 Allow cake to stand in pan for about 15 minutes. Turn cake out onto rack to cool completely before frosting.

Frosting:

1 (16 ounce) box powdered sugar	455 g
6 tablespoons (¾ stick) butter, melted	85 g
¼ teaspoon orange extract	1 ml
2 - 3 tablespoons orange juice	30 - 45 ml

 Thoroughly mix all ingredients in bowl using only 2 tablespoons (30 ml) orange juice. Add more orange juice if frosting seems too stiff. Serves 12 to 16.

The World's Largest Pumpkin Pie recorded in the Guinness Book of World Records was baked in 2010 in New Bremen, Ohio. It was 20 feet in diameter and weighed 3,699 pounds. Here's the filling recipe.

1,212 pounds canned pumpkin
233 dozen (2796) eggs
109 gallons evaporated milk
525 pounds sugar
14.5 pounds cinnamon
7 pounds salt

Old Southern Praline Sauce

Great poured over pound cake!

2 eggs	
1 (16 ounce) box light brown sugar	455 g
2 tablespoons flour	15 g
½ cup (1 stick) butter	115 g
1 teaspoon vanilla	5 ml
1½ cups chopped pecans	165 g

Beat eggs and combine with brown sugar. Add flour and mix.

In skillet, melt butter and stir in brown sugar mixture, stirring constantly. Remove from heat and stir in vanilla and pecans. Pour over pound cake (or ice cream).

Amaretto Sauce for Pound Cake

1 (3.4 ounce) package French vanilla pudding mix (not instant)	95 g
1 cup milk	250 ml
1 (8 ounce) carton whipping cream, whipped	250 ml
¼ cup amaretto liqueur	60 ml

Cook pudding with milk according to package directions. Cover and cool to room temperature.

With wire whisk, stir in whipped cream and amaretto. Pour over pound cake (or ice cream).

Cupcakes
and
Decorations

Easy Basic Cupcakes

½ cup shortening	95 g
1 cup sugar	200 g
3 eggs	
1¾ cups flour	310 g
2 teaspoons baking powder	10 ml
½ cup milk	125 ml
1 teaspoon vanilla	5 ml

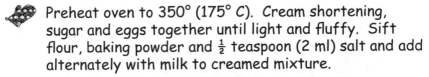 Preheat oven to 350° (175° C). Cream shortening, sugar and eggs together until light and fluffy. Sift flour, baking powder and ½ teaspoon (2 ml) salt and add alternately with milk to creamed mixture.

Add vanilla. Beat thoroughly. Pour into paper liners in cupcake pans. Bake for 15 to 20 minutes. Makes 18 cupcakes.

Decorations:

1 (12 ounce) can ready-to-serve vanilla frosting	340 g
1 (10 ounce) package prepared cake icing	285 g

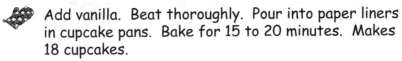 Spread cupcakes with vanilla frosting using icing spatula or back of spoon. Draw your favorite designs on each cupcake using cake icing in a squeezable tube with small nozzle tip.

TIP: Make your own pastry bag with a medium-size plastic bag. Cut small hole in one of the bottom corners. Repeat steps for pastry bag. You don't have to have special tips unless you want pretty swirls and designs.

 # Butter Pecan Cupcakes

1 (18 ounce) box butter-pecan cake mix	510 g
1/3 cup canola oil	75 ml
3 eggs, slightly beaten	
1/2 cup finely chopped pecans	55 g

 Preheat oven to 350° (175° C).

 Beat cake mix, oil, 1 cup (250 ml) water and beaten eggs in bowl for 2 minutes on low speed. Stir in pecans.

Pour two-thirds batter into 24 muffin cups with paper linings and bake for 20 to 22 minutes or until toothpick inserted in center comes out clean.

Glaze:

1 tablespoon butter, softened	15 ml
2 tablespoons maple syrup	30 ml
1/3 cup powdered sugar	40 g
1/4 cup very finely chopped pecans	30 g

 Combine butter, maple syrup and powdered sugar in bowl and beat thoroughly. Stir in pecans and drizzle over hot cupcakes. Makes 24 cupcakes.

Using an ice cream scoop that holds about 1/4 to 1/3 cup (60 to 75 ml) of cupcake batter makes filling cupcake pans much faster. Pans should be filled about three-fourths full.

Spiced Cupcakes

½ cup shortening	95 g
1 cup sugar	200 g
2 eggs, separated	
⅓ cup chopped, seeded raisins	40 g
⅓ cup chopped currants	50 g
⅓ cup chopped nuts	45 g
1 teaspoon baking soda	5 ml
2½ cups flour	300 g
½ teaspoon ground cloves	2 ml
½ teaspoon ground mace	2 ml
1½ teaspoons ground cinnamon	7 ml
¾ cup sour cream	180 g

Preheat oven to 350° (175° C). Cream shortening, sugar and egg yolks in bowl. Add raisins, currants and nuts. Dissolve baking soda in 1 tablespoon (15 ml) hot water and stir in.

Sift flour, ½ teaspoon (2 ml) salt, cloves, mace and cinnamon together and add alternately with sour cream to first mixture.

Fold in 1 stiffly beaten egg white. (Use the other egg white in scrambled eggs or other dish.) Pour in sprayed, floured muffin cups and bake for 15 to 20 minutes. Makes 18 cupcakes.

Cupcakes do not have to be round. There are cupcake molds in the shape of stars, hearts, flowers, etc.

Sour Cream Cupcakes

1 tablespoon shortening	*15 ml*
1 cup sugar	*200 g*
2 eggs	
½ teaspoon baking soda	*2 ml*
½ cup sour cream	*120 g*
1½ cups flour	*180 ml*
½ teaspoon cream of tartar	*2 ml*
⅛ teaspoon mace	*.5 ml*

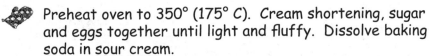

Preheat oven to 350° (175° C). Cream shortening, sugar and eggs together until light and fluffy. Dissolve baking soda in sour cream.

Sift flour, 1½ teaspoons (7 ml) salt, cream of tartar and mace together and add alternately with cream to first mixture. Beat thoroughly.

Bake in sprayed cupcake pans for 18 to 22 minutes. Makes 18 cupcakes.

Decorations:

1 (12 ounce) can ready-to-serve	
vanilla frosting	*340 g*
1 fresh orange	
¼ cup sugar	*50 g*

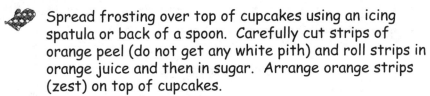

Spread frosting over top of cupcakes using an icing spatula or back of a spoon. Carefully cut strips of orange peel (do not get any white pith) and roll strips in orange juice and then in sugar. Arrange orange strips (zest) on top of cupcakes.

Maple-Cream Cupcakes

1½ cups flour	180 g
⅓ cup sugar	65 g
1 tablespoon baking powder	15 ml
1 teaspoon ground cinnamon	5 ml
1 teaspoon ground nutmeg	5 ml
¼ cup shortening	95 g
¾ cup quick-cooking oats	60 g
1 egg, beaten	
½ cup milk	125 ml
½ cup maple syrup	125 ml

Preheat oven to 350° (175° C). Place paper baking cups in 16 muffin cups. Sift flour, sugar, baking powder, ¼ teaspoon (1 ml) salt, cinnamon and nutmeg in bowl.

Cut in shortening until mixture resembles coarse crumbs. Stir in oats; add egg, milk and maple syrup, stir only until dry ingredients are moist. Fill muffin cups one-half full.

Bake for 18 to 21 minutes. Let stand in pan for about 5 minutes. Cool completely before frosting. Makes 16 cupcakes.

Continued next page...

Jay: Did you hear the joke about the broken egg?

Alfred: Yes, it cracked me up!

Continued from previous page...

Frosting:

*1 (12 ounce) can ready-to-serve
    buttercream frosting*   340 g
2 tablespoons maple syrup   30 ml
1 tablespoon butter, melted   15 ml
Ground cinnamon

 Place buttercream frosting in small bowl, stir in maple
syrup and melted butter; blend well. Frost cupcakes and
sprinkle with cinnamon.

 # Pumpkin Cupcakes

1 (18 ounce) box spice cake mix   510 g
1 (15 ounce) can pumpkin   425 g
3 eggs
⅓ cup canola oil   75 ml

 Preheat oven to 350° (175° C). Blend cake mix,
pumpkin, eggs, oil and ⅓ cup (75 ml) water in bowl.
Beat for 2 minutes.

 Pour batter into 24 paper-lined muffin cups and fill
three-fourths full.

 Bake for 18 to 20 minutes or until toothpick inserted in
center comes out clean. (You might want to spread with
commercial icing.) Makes 24 cupcakes.

Harvest Pumpkin Cupcakes

1 (15 ounce) can pumpkin	425 g
3 eggs, slightly beaten	
½ cup oil	125 ml
1½ teaspoons ground cinnamon	7 ml
1 teaspoon baking soda	5 ml
1 (18 ounce) box yellow cake mix	510 g
½ cup chopped walnuts	65 g
1 (16 ounce) can ready-to-serve buttercream frosting	455 g

Preheat oven to 350° (175° C). Place paper baking cups in 24 muffin cups. Combine pumpkin, eggs, oil, cinnamon and baking soda in bowl and mix well.

Add cake mix, ¼ cup (60 ml) water and beat for 1 minute on low speed. Increase speed to high and beat for 2 minutes. Fold in walnuts.

Fill muffin cups two-thirds full and bake for 19 to 22 minutes or until toothpick inserted in center comes out clean.

Cool for 10 minutes in pan; remove from pan and cool completely before frosting. Makes 24 cupcakes.

Cooking times and the number each recipe makes will vary based on the muffin pan used, how much batter is in each cup, additions of nuts, raisins, etc., and of course, altitude.

 # Carrot Cake Cupcakes

1 (18 ounce) box carrot cake mix	510 g
3 eggs	
½ cup canola oil	125 ml
1 (8 ounce) can crushed pineapple with juice	225 g
¾ cup chopped pecans	85 g

 Preheat oven to 350° (175° C).

 Place paper baking cups in 24 muffin cups. Mix cake mix, eggs, oil, pineapple and ½ cup (125 ml) water in bowl and beat on low speed for 1 minute.

 Increase speed to medium and beat for 2 minutes. Fold in pecans and spoon into muffin cups.

 Bake for 19 to 23 minutes or until toothpick inserted in center comes out clean. Cool in pan for 5 minutes. Remove cupcakes from pan and cool completely before frosting. Makes 24 cupcakes.

Decorations:

1 (16 ounce) container ready-to-serve cream cheese frosting	455 g
Powdered sugar, optional	
Pecan pieces, optional	

 Frost cupcakes with frosting and sprinkle powdered sugar and pecan pieces over tops.

Zucchini Cupcakes

These are not too sweet — just right for a quick, healthy lunch box or snack treat.

1½ cups self-rising flour	190 g
1 teaspoon baking soda	5 ml
1½ teaspoons pumpkin pie spice	7 ml
3 egg whites or ¾ cup egg substitute	185 g
¾ cup packed brown sugar	165 g
½ cup canola oil	125 ml
2 cups peeled, grated zucchini	250 g
Cream cheese frosting, optional	

Preheat oven to 350° (175° C). Combine flour, baking soda and pumpkin pie spice in small bowl.

In separate bowl beat eggs, brown sugar and oil for about 3 minutes. Add zucchini and stir until they blend well. Add flour mixture and stir until ingredients combine thoroughly.

Fill sprayed non-stick muffin cups three-fourths full and bake for 20 to 25 minutes. Cool completely before frosting. Makes 12 cupcakes.

TIP: *You can make a carrot topper by adding orange food coloring to a little frosting, squeeze frosting out of plastic freezer bag and make the shape of carrot. Use green food coloring to make the stem.*

 # Banana-Nut Cupcakes

1 (16 ounce) box banana nut cake mix with walnuts, separated	455 g
⅔ cup milk	150 g
2 tablespoons canola oil	30 ml
1 egg	
1 (12 ounce) can ready-to-serve buttercream frosting	340 g

Preheat oven to 350° (175° C). Place paper baking cups in 12 muffin cups. Combine cake mix, milk, oil and egg in medium bowl. Stir mixture just until they blend well. (Batter will be slightly lumpy.)

Divide batter among muffin cups and sprinkle walnuts from cake mix evenly over batter.

Bake for about 20 minutes or until golden brown and tops spring back when touched. Cool in pan for 10 minutes; cool completely before frosting. Makes 12 cupcakes.

Small muffin-shaped cakes were first made because it took so long to bake a cake in a hearth oven.

Cupcakes probably got their name because small cups were used for faster baking and the ingredients were measured in cups rather than by pounds.

Caramel-Apple Cupcakes

1 (18 ounce) box carrot cake mix	510 g
3 cups chopped, peeled tart apples	375 g
1 (12 ounce) package butterscotch chips	340 g
1 cup finely chopped pecans	110 g

Preheat oven to 350° (175° C). Prepare cake mix according to package directions. Fold in apples. Fill 12 sprayed or paper-lined jumbo muffin cups three-fourths full.

Bake for 20 minutes or until toothpick inserted in center comes out clean.

Melt butterscotch chips in saucepan on very low heat. Spread over cupcakes and sprinkle with chopped pecans. Makes 12 cupcakes.

The origin and creator of cupcakes cannot be pinpointed in culinary history, but it can be assumed that the name "cupcake" derived from its measurements. The basic cupcake recipe started out with 1 cup butter, 1 cup sugar and 1 cup flour. This was similar to the traditional pound cake named for its measurements of 1 pound butter, 1 pound sugar, 1 pound flour and 1 pound eggs.

 # Fresh Lemon Cupcakes

1 (18 ounce) box lemon cake mix	510 g
1/3 cup canola oil	75 ml
3 eggs	
1 (8 ounce) can crushed pineapple, drained	225 g
1 (16 ounce) can ready-to-serve lemon frosting	455 g

Preheat oven to 350° (175° C).

Place paper baking cups in 24 muffin cups. Combine cake mix, 1¼ cups water, oil and eggs in bowl and beat on low speed for 30 seconds.

Increase mixer speed to medium and beat for 2 minutes. Stir in pineapple and mix well. Spoon into muffin cups and bake for 18 to 22 minutes or until toothpick inserted in cupcakes comes out clean.

Cool in pan for about 5 minutes. Cool to room temperature before frosting. Makes 24 cupcakes.

Another theory for the origin of cupcakes is that cupcakes got their names for how they were baked. Instead of a large cake pan, cups and small earthenware vessels were used to make individual cakes.

Sweet Orange Cupcakes

½ cup (1 stick) unsalted butter, softened	115 g
1 ¼ cups sugar	250 g
2 large eggs	
1 (8 ounce) carton plain yogurt	225 g
2 cups flour	240 g
1 teaspoon baking soda	5 ml
½ cup chopped pecans	55 g
½ cup orange marmalade	160 g
1 teaspoon orange extract	5 ml

 Preheat oven to 350° (175° C).

 Cream butter and sugar in bowl. Beat in eggs and yogurt for 1 minute. Add flour and baking soda and stir into creamed mixture; stir just until mixture is moist. Fold in pecans, orange marmalade and orange extract.

 Place paper baking cups in 18 muffin cups and fill muffin cups three-fourths full. Bake for 18 to 21 minutes or until toothpick inserted in center comes out clean.

 Cool in pan for about 5 minutes. Remove from pan and cool before frosting. Makes 18 cupcakes.

Continued next page...

I always knew looking back on the tears would make me laugh. But I never knew looking back on the laughs would make me cry.
—Unknown

Continued from previous page...

Decorations:

1 (16 ounce) can ready-to-serve
    cream cheese frosting   455 g
Orange sanding sugar
Fresh orange slices

 Frost cupcakes using a pastry bag fitted with a round
tip between number 10 or 12, depending on the size
you want. Sprinkle with sugar and garnish with
orange slices.

*Lives of great men all remind us
We can make our lives sublime,
And, departing, leave behind us
Footprints on the sands of time.*
Henry Wadsworth Longfellow: "A Psalm of Life"

*Don't walk in front of me, I may not follow. Don't
walk behind me, I may not lead. Just walk beside me
and be my friend.*
                                        —Unknown

 # Strawberry Delight

1 (18 ounce) box strawberry cake mix	510 g
3 eggs	
⅓ cup canola oil	75 ml
1 (6 ounce) package white chocolate chips	170 g

 Preheat oven to 350° (175° C).

 Place paper baking cups in 24 muffin cups. Combine cake mix, eggs, oil and 1¼ cups water in bowl and beat on low speed for about 30 seconds.

 Increase speed to medium and beat for 2 minutes. Stir in white chocolate chips and spoon about ¼ cup batter into each muffin cup.

 Bake for 19 to 23 minutes or until toothpick inserted in center comes out clean. Cool in pan for 5 to 10 minutes. Cool completely before frosting. Makes 24 cupcakes.

Continued next page...

Hostess® CupCakes were first made in 1919, but they were a small snack cake. It wasn't until 1950 when they were filled with a crème center that they became the Hostess® CupCake of today.

Hostess® CupCakes are the best-selling cupcakes in the U.S. Americans eat more than 500 million Hostess® CupCakes every year.

Continued from previous page...

Decorations:

*1 (16 ounce) can ready-to-serve
    strawberry frosting*   455 g
*1 (2 ounce) bottle multi-colored
    sprinkles*   55 g

 Use a pastry bag fitted with an open star tip number 21. Squeeze bag evenly around cupcake from outside to inside. Top with multi-colored sprinkles.

 If you can't find the right color for your cupcakes, don't hesitate to use food coloring. Just remember, a drop or two can be a lot of color.

The 10 Most Popular Flavors of Cupcakes:

1. *Chocolate and Vanilla*
2. *Red Velvet*
3. *Carrot Cake*
4. *Peanut Butter*
5. *Lemon*
6. *Chocolate*
7. *Coffee*
8. *Banana*
9. *Pumpkin*
10. *Vanilla*

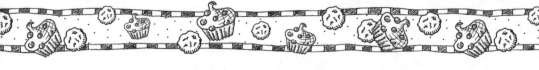

 # Chocolate-Strawberry Cupcakes

1 (18 ounce) box milk chocolate cake mix	510 g
⅓ cup canola oil	75 g
3 eggs	
1 teaspoon almond extract	5 g
1 cup white chocolate chips	170 g

 Preheat oven to 350° (175° C).

 Place paper baking cups in 24 muffin cups. Combine cake mix, 1¼ cups (310 ml) water, oil, eggs and almond extract in bowl.

 Beat on low speed for 30 seconds; increase speed to medium and beat for 2 minutes. Stir in white chocolate chips and spoon into 24 muffin cups.

 Bake for 18 to 22 minutes or until toothpick inserted in center comes out clean. Cool for 10 minutes; then let cool completely for 30 minutes before frosting. Makes 24 cupcakes.

Continued next page...

When asked about chocolate, about 90% of people questioned will say they like milk chocolate more than dark chocolate.

Continued from previous page...

Decorations:

1 (16 ounce) can ready-to-serve
    strawberry frosting   455 g
1 (3 ounce) container chocolate
    sprinkles   85 g

Use a pastry bag fitted with an open star tip number 21 or 199. Squeeze bag evenly around cupcake from outside to inside. Top with sprinkles.

For a special touch, dip one whole strawberry with stem in melted chocolate about half-way to stem and place on top of cupcakes.

The Toothpick Test

The toothpick test is a great way to test cupcakes to know when they are done. Insert a toothpick into the center of the cupcake. If it comes out clean, it is done. If it has cake stuck to it, it needs to bake a little longer.

If you are out of toothpicks to test cupcakes to see if they are done, use the touch method. Lightly touch the top of the cupcake. If it springs back, it is done. If it does not spring back, it needs to bake a little longer.

 # Cherry-Chocolate Cupcakes

1 (18 ounce) box devil's food cake mix	510 g
3 large eggs	
⅓ cup oil	75 ml
1 teaspoon almond extract	5 ml
2 (6 ounce) bottle maraschino cherries, drained, divided	2 (170 g)
1 cup white chocolate chips	170 g

Preheat oven to 350° (175° C).

 Place paper baking cups in 24 muffin cups. Combine cake mix, eggs, oil, almond extract and 1¼ cups (310 ml) water in bowl and beat on low speed for about 30 seconds. Increase speed to medium and beat mixture for 2 minutes.

 Drain 1 bottle of maraschino cherries and chop. Stir in chopped cherries and white chocolate chips and mix well, but gently.

 Pour into muffin cups and bake for 19 to 23 minutes or until toothpick inserted in center comes out clean. Cool on wire rack for 5 to 10 minutes; cool completely before frosting. Makes 24 cupcakes.

Decorations:

1 (16 ounce) can ready-to-serve cherry frosting	455 g
Remaining maraschino cherries with stems	

 Spread cherry frosting over cupcakes using knife in swirling motion and top each with 1 cherry with stem.

 # White and Dark Chocolate Cupcakes

1 (18 ounce) box French vanilla cake mix	510 g
⅓ cup canola oil	75 ml
3 eggs	
1 teaspoon vanilla	5 ml
1 cup white chocolate chips or 1 cup dark chocolate chips or ½ cup white chocolate and ½ cup dark chocolate	170 g
1 (16 ounce) can ready-to-serve chocolate frosting	455 g

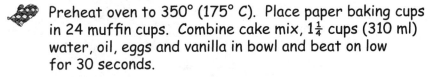

Preheat oven to 350° (175° C). Place paper baking cups in 24 muffin cups. Combine cake mix, 1¼ cups (310 ml) water, oil, eggs and vanilla in bowl and beat on low for 30 seconds.

Increase speed to medium and beat for 2 minutes. Stir in chocolate chips. Spoon into muffin cups.

Bake for 18 to 23 minutes or until toothpick inserted in center comes out clean.

Cool for 5 minutes before removing from pan. Cool for 30 minutes before frosting. Makes 24 cupcakes.

TIP: Instead of the decorations on top of your cupcakes, you can always use a Hershey's® bar and a potato peeler to make some chocolate curls.

 # Chocolate Cupcakes Topped with White Chocolate and Brickle Bits

1 (18 ounce) box devil's food cake mix	510 g
3 eggs	
⅓ cup canola oil	75 ml
1 cup chocolate chips	170 g

 Preheat oven to 350° (175° C).

 Place paper baking cups in 24 muffin cups. Combine cake mix, 1¼ cups (310 ml) water, eggs and oil in bowl and beat on low speed for 30 seconds.

 Increase speed to medium and beat for 2 minutes. Stir in chocolate chips and pour batter into muffin cups.

 Bake for 21 to 25 minutes or until toothpick inserted in center comes out clean. Cool for 10 minutes before removing from pan. Cool for additional 30 minutes before frosting. Makes 24 cupcakes.

Continued next page...

If icing gets too thick while you're spreading it on cupcakes, just add several drops of lemon juice, stir well and continue icing.

Continued from previous page...

Decorations:

1 cup white chocolate chips	*170 g*
(16 ounce) can ready-to-serve	
creamy chocolate frosting	*455 g*
1 cup white chocolate shavings	*100 g*
1 cup brickle bits	*250 ml*

Microwave white chocolate chips in microwave-safe bowl on medium speed for about 2½ minutes and stir after 1 or 2 minutes. Stir until smooth and cool for 5 minutes. Stir in frosting until mixture blends well.

Immediately frost cupcakes. Use a pastry bag fitted with an open star tip between number 17 or 21. Squeeze bag evenly around cupcake from outside to inside.

These cupcakes are extra pretty sprinkled with white chocolate shavings and brickle bits on top.

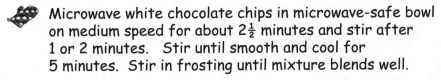
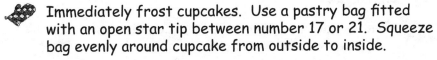

Chocolate comes from cacao. The first people to use cacao were the Olmecs who ruleed from 1500 BC to 400 BC. They are the oldest known people in North America.

Cacao was so valuable that the Aztec and Mayan Indians traded it for goods and services. It became a form of money.

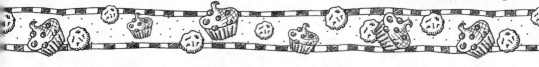

 # Chocolate-Filled Cupcakes

1 (18 ounce) box devil's food cake mix	510 g
1⅓ cups buttermilk*	325 ml
4 eggs, divided	
⅓ cup canola oil	75 ml
1 cup mini semi-sweet chocolate chips, divided	170 g
1 (8 ounce) package cream cheese, softened	225 g
½ cup sugar	100 g

 Preheat oven to 350° (175° C). Combine cake mix, buttermilk, 3 eggs and oil in large bowl.

 Beat on low speed to blend, then beat on medium for 2 minutes. Stir ½ cup (85 g) chocolate chips into batter and set aside.

 In separate bowl, beat cream cheese, sugar and remaining egg until mixture is smooth. Melt remaining chocolate chips in saucepan and add to cream cheese mixture. Beat mixture until it blends well.

Continued next page...

When asked what the meaning of life is, the old woman quickly answered, "Chocolate".

Continued from previous page...

Prepare 24 muffin cups by either spraying and flouring or using paper baking liners. Fill each cup half full with batter.

Drop 1 tablespoon (15 ml) chocolate-cream cheese mixture in center of each and spoon remaining batter evenly over each. Bake for 25 minutes. Makes 24 cupcakes.

*TIP: To make buttermilk, mix 1 cup (250 ml) with 1 tablespoon (15 ml) lemon juice or vinegar and let milk stand for about 10 minutes.

You can use a plastic bag as a decorating or piping bag. Cut a small piece off a bottom corner, fill with icing and squeeze from the top to decorate or to ice with swirls.

Just about every cake recipe can work for cupcakes. Just check the baking time carefully. Cupcakes will not have to bake as long as cakes bake because they are smaller.

Batter for an 8-inch (20 cm) cake pan makes about 20 cupcakes. Fill cupcake molds about ⅔ to ¾ full and bake at 350° (175° C) for about 20 minutes or until toothpick inserted in center comes out clean.

 # Chocolate Peanut Butter Yummies

1 (21 ounce) package double fudge brownie mix	595 g
2 eggs	
3 (9 ounce) packages miniature peanut butter cups	3 (255 g)
1 (16 ounce) can ready-to-serve buttercream frosting	455 g
½ cup peanut butter	145 g

Preheat oven to 350° (175° C). Prepare brownie mix according to package directions using 2 eggs. Spoon into miniature cupcake liners in mini-muffin pans; fill three-fourths full.

Place peanut butter cup in center of each and push into batter. Bake for 15 to 20 minutes or until toothpick inserted in center comes out clean.

Place buttercream frosting in small bowl, stir in peanut butter and mix well. Spread frosting generously over cupcakes. Makes about 60 to 70 mini cupcakes.

Cupcakes are best the day you bake them.

 # Cream-Filled Chocolate Cupcakes

1 (18 ounce) box double chocolate
   cake mix   510 g
½ cup canola oil   125 ml
1 egg
1 (16 ounce) can ready-to-serve
   vanilla frosting   455 g

Preheat oven to 350° (175° C). Place paper baking cups
in 24 muffin cups. Stir cake mix, 1 cup water, oil and egg
in medium bowl just until they blend and divide batter
among muffin cups.

Bake for 18 to 22 minutes. Cool in pan for 10 minutes,
remove from pan and cool for additional 30 minutes.

Cut off tops of cupcakes. Create a small well in the
center of each cupcake and fill with frosting. Place top
of cupcake on top of frosting. Makes 24 cupcakes.

TIP: For a special touch, sprinkle with powdered sugar and
garnish with your favorite fruit.

 *Easy frosting: Just dip the top of the cupcake
in a bowl of frosting and swirl until covered.*

 # Chocolate-Peanut Cupcakes

1 (18 ounce) box butter-fudge
    cake mix   510

3 eggs

⅓ cup canola oil   75 ml

1 (6 ounce) package butter-brickle
    chips   170 g

 Preheat oven to 350° (175° C).

 Place paper baking cups in 24 muffin cups. Combine cake
mix, eggs, oil and 1¼ cups water in bowl and beat on low
speed for about 30 seconds.

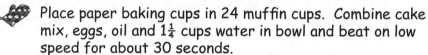 Increase speed to medium and beat for 2 minutes. Stir
in butter brickle chips. Fill muffin cups two-thirds full.
Bake for 19 to 23 minutes.

Cool on wire rack before removing from pan. Cool
completely before frosting. Makes 24 cupcakes.

Decorations:

1 (16 ounce) can ready-to-serve
    buttercream frosting   455 g

½ cup peanut butter   145 g

24 chocolate-covered peanuts,
    optional

 Place buttercream frosting in small bowl, stir in peanut
butter and mix well.

 Use a pastry bag fitted with a round tip number 8 or
10. Squeeze bag evenly around cupcake from outside to
inside. Top with chocolate-covered peanuts.

 # Chocolate Chip Cupcakes

1 (18 ounce) box yellow cake mix	510 g
3 eggs	
⅓ cup canola oil	75 ml
1 teaspoon vanilla	5 ml
1 (12 ounce) package chocolate chips	340 g

Preheat oven to 350° (175° C). Place paper baking cups in 24 muffin cups. Combine cake mix, 1¼ (310 g) cups water, eggs, oil and vanilla in bowl.

Beat on low speed for 30 seconds, increase speed to medium and beat for 2 minutes. Fold in chocolate chips and pecans and spoon into all muffin cups.

Bake for 19 to 22 minutes or until toothpick inserted in center comes out clean. Cool for 5 to 10 minutes in pan.

Remove from pan and place cupcakes on wire rack to cool completely before storing. Makes 24 cupcakes.

To avoid crumbs in frosting, dust the top of cupcakes with your finger to remove loose crumbs. Spread a thin layer of frosting before putting the final layer of frosting down to avoid crumbs resurfacing. Wash knife with hot water when too much frosting sticks to it.

Double Rich Chocolate Cupcakes

½ cup cocoa	40 g
1⅔ cups flour	200 g
1½ cups sugar	300 g
½ teaspoon baking soda	2 ml
½ cup shortening	95 g
2 eggs	
1 (6 ounce) package chocolate chips	170 g

 Preheat oven to 350° (175° C).

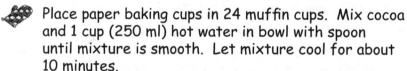 Place paper baking cups in 24 muffin cups. Mix cocoa and 1 cup (250 ml) hot water in bowl with spoon until mixture is smooth. Let mixture cool for about 10 minutes.

Add flour, sugar, baking soda, shortening and eggs and beat on low speed for 2 minutes. Increase speed and beat for 2 minutes. Stir in chocolate chips and mix well. Fill muffin cups half full.

Bake for 18 to 20 minutes or until toothpick inserted in center comes out clean. Cool completely for at least 30 minutes. Makes 24 cupcakes.

Continued next page...

 It is a good idea to add 1 teaspoon (5 ml) butter to chocolate when melting it because it will create a better consistency.

Continued from previous page...

Decorations:

1 (16 ounce) can ready-to-serve
    dark chocolate frosting   455 g
Chocolate bar, optional

 Use a pastry bag fitted with a closed star tip between number 28 or 30. Squeeze bag evenly around cupcake from outside to inside. Slice chocolate curls from a chocolate bar with a potato peeler to put on top of the dark chocolate frosting.

Fillings in cupcakes are an added surprise to any bite. Use a plastic freezer bag to inject icings, custards and crèmes into the center of cupcakes or dig out a small hole, fill with crème, etc. and replace a piece of cake in the hole.

 # Triple Chocolate Cupcakes

1 (18 ounce) box triple chocolate fudge cake mix	510 g
1/3 cup canola oil	75 ml
3 eggs	
1 (12 ounce) package swirled chocolate and white chocolate chips	340 g

 Preheat oven to 350° (175° C).

 Place paper baking cups in 24 muffin cups. Combine cake mix, 1¼ cups (310 ml) water, oil and eggs in bowl. Beat on low speed for 30 seconds. Increase speed to medium and beat for 2 minutes. Stir in chocolate chips and spoon into muffin cups.

Bake for 19 to 23 minutes or until toothpick inserted in center comes out clean. Cool in pan for about 10 minutes. Cool completely before frosting. Makes 24 cupcakes.

Continued next page...

To keep icing from melting and sliding off the top of the cupcake, let cupcakes cool completely before icing.

Continued from previous page...

Decorations:

1 (16 ounce) can chocolate fudge
*   frosting*   *455 g*

 Spread frosting in swirling motions on each cupcake.

For chocolate lovers, reserve about ¾ cup (125 g) swirled chocolate and white chocolate chips (don't add to batter) and sprinkle 5 to 8 chips on top of frosting — looks great!

No Extra Trip to the Grocery Store!

Red velvet cupcakes are really popular and fast to make with a red velvet cake mix, but what if you don't have a red velvet mix? You can use a butter cake mix or a white cake mix. Add cocoa and red food coloring and you've got red velvet cake mix!

Taste a little bit of the batter. If you can still taste the butter or white cake flavor, add a little more cocoa. Simple and just think of the time you have saved!

 # White Truffle-Chocolate Cupcakes

1 (18 ounce) box chocolate cake mix	510 g
3 large eggs	
⅓ cup canola oil	75 ml
1 teaspoon almond extract	5 ml
⅓ cup flaked coconut	30 g
1 (12 ounce) package white chocolate chips	340 g
1 (16 ounce) can ready-to-serve whipped white frosting	455 g

Preheat oven to 350° (175° C). Place paper baking cups in 24 muffin cups. Combine cake mix, eggs, oil, almond extract and 1¼ cups (310 ml) water and beat on low speed for 30 seconds.

Increase speed to medium and beat for 2 minutes. Stir in coconut and white chocolate chips.

Pour into muffin cups and bake for 19 to 23 minutes. Cool in pan for about 5 minutes. Cool completely before frosting. Makes 24 cupcakes.

First Lesson in Spreading Frosting:

Place a big blob of frosting on the center of a cupcake. Don't be skimpy with the frosting! Use a knife or back of spoon to make a swirling motion from the inside to the outside. If it feels easier to swirl from the outside in, try that too and use the one you like the best.

 # Nutty Red Velvet Cupcakes

1 (18 ounce) box red velvet cake mix	510 g
3 eggs	
1/3 cup canola oil	75 ml
1 (6 ounce) package white chocolate chips	170 g
1/2 cup chopped walnuts	65 g

 Preheat oven to 350° (175° C).

 Place paper baking cups in 24 muffin cups. Blend cake mix, 1¼ cups (310 ml) water, eggs and oil in bowl on low speed for 30 seconds.

 Beat on medium speed for 2 minutes. Stir in white chocolate chips and walnuts and pour into muffin cups.

 Bake for 19 to 23 minutes or until toothpick inserted in center in center comes out clean. Let stand on wire rack for 30 minutes. Remove each cupcake from pan and cool completely before frosting. Makes 24 cupcakes.

Decorations:

1 (16 ounce) can ready-to-serve whipped frosting	455 g

Use a pastry bag fitted with a closed star tip number 28 or 30 or just a knife in a swirling motion.

Cupcake Sundaes

1 (18 ounce) box milk chocolate
    cake mix   510 g
⅓ cup canola oil   75 ml
3 eggs

Preheat oven to 350° (175° C). Place paper baking cups in 24 muffin cups. Combine cake mix, 1¼ cup (310 ml) water, oil and eggs in bowl.

Beat on low speed for 30 seconds; increase speed to medium and beat for 2 minutes. Spoon into muffin cups.

Bake for 19 to 22 minutes or until toothpick inserted in center comes out clean. Cool for 5 minutes before removing from pan.

Cool for 30 minutes before spreading frosting. Makes 24 cupcakes.

Continued next page...

You can freeze cupcakes for up to three months. Decorated cupcakes don't freeze as well, but you can always freeze the cupcakes and spread icing and apply decorations later.

Continued from previous page...

Decorations:

½ cup vegetable oil	125 ml
1 tablespoon egg white	15 ml
2 tablespoons milk	30 ml
3 cups powdered sugar, sifted	360 ml
Chocolate syrup	
1 (6 ounce) jar maraschino cherries	170 g

 Lightly beat vegetable oil, egg white and milk in large bowl. Add half powdered sugar and beat. Add remaining powdered sugar and beat on high for several minutes.

 Use ice cream scoop to put frosting on cupcake. Drizzle chocolate over cupcake and top with cherry.

November 10th is National Vanilla Cupcake Day!

December 15th is National Cupcake Day!

December 16th is National Chocolate-Covered Anything Day!

Heavenly Chocolate Cupcakes

1 (18 ounce) box devil's food cake mix	510 g
⅓ cup canola oil	75 ml
3 large eggs	
1 cup cold milk	250 ml
1 (3.4 ounce) box instant vanilla pudding mix	95 g
½ cup peanut butter	145 g
1 (16 ounce) can milk chocolate frosting	455 g

 Preheat oven to 350° (175° C). Place paper baking cups in 24 muffin cups. Place cake mix in bowl; add oil, eggs and 1 cup (250 ml) water and beat for 2½ minutes.

In separate bowl, pour cold milk and add pudding mix. Whisk for 2 minutes or until creamy and mixture blends well.

Stir in peanut butter and mix well. Stir mixture into cake mix-eggs mixture.

Spoon into muffin cups and bake for 19 to 22 minutes or until toothpick inserted in center comes out clean.

Cool for 10 minutes in pan; cool completely before frosting. Makes 24 cupcakes.

 # Children's Cake Cones

1 (9 ounce) package chocolate
   cake mix   255 g
2 (12 count) boxes flat bottom ice
   cream cones
1 (12 ounce) can frosting (your
   choice of flavor)   340 g

Preheat oven to 350° (175° C). Prepare cake batter according to package directions.

Fill ice cream cones two-thirds full.

Set cones in muffin cups and bake for 25 to 30 minutes. (Place crumpled foil in bottom of muffin cups to stabilize cones.) Cool and frost. Makes 24 cones.

What kind of cake do bats like?

Upside down cake.

What type of cake do jockeys like?

Carrot cake.

Why type of cake "grows" in orchards?

Fruit cake.

Fun Cupcakes

1 (18 ounce) box white cake mix	510 g
2 (24 count) boxes flat-bottom ice cream cones	
1 - 2 (16 ounce) cans confetti frosting	1 - 2 (455 g)
½ cup fruit Skittles® candies	85 g

Preheat oven to 325° (165° C). Prepare cake mix according to package directions.

Place ice cream cones in muffin cups on baking sheet and fill each cone two-thirds full with batter. (Place crumpled foil in bottom of muffin cups to stabilize cones.)

Bake for 25 to 30 minutes and cool completely.

Frost each fun cake with confetti frosting and sprinkle 3 to 5 Skittles® on top of each cupcake. Makes 24 cupcake cones.

You know you're getting old when you get that one candle on the cake. It's like, "See if you can blow this out."

—Jerry Seinfeld

Pies, Tarts, Cobblers and Cheesecakes

Old-Fashioned Apple Pie

*The best way to save time with this apple pie is to buy
1 (15 ounce/425 g) package refrigerated double piecrusts.
Modern conveniences are great to have around.*

Piecrust:

2 cups flour	*240 g*
⅔ cup shortening	*140 g*

 Combine flour and 1 teaspoon salt in large bowl. Add shortening a little at a time and stir until lumps are small.

 Slowly pour in 3 tablespoons (45 ml) cold water and stir until it mixes well. Divide dough into 2 pieces and place on floured, countertop.

 Roll out each half of dough to about ⅛-inch (3 mm) thick. Place 1 in 9-inch (23 cm) pie pan. Save remaining half for top crust.

Continued next page...

During the 1700's when times were tough, thrifty families, probably in the Northeast, created a Mock Apple Pie using soda crackers. The recipe was popular and its use continues even to today.

In 1935 the Nabisco Company introduced Ritz crackers and printed a recipe for Mock Apple Pie on the box using Ritz crackers. The popularity of the pie recipe helped Ritz crackers gain national prominence. Nabisco continues to print the recipe for Mock Apple Pie on the Ritz box today.

Continued from previous page...

Pie Filling:

2 tablespoons lemon juice	30 ml
6 cups peeled, cored, sliced Gala apples	720 g
1 cup plus 1 tablespoon sugar	415 g
2 tablespoons flour	15 g
1½ teaspoons ground cinnamon	7 ml

Preheat oven to 425° (220° C). Sprinkle lemon juice over apples and stir to mix with all slices in bowl.

In separate bowl, mix sugar, flour and cinnamon. Pour over apples and stir in. Pour pie filling into piecrust.

Place second piecrust over top and seal edges of piecrusts. Cut slits in top piecrust. Bake for 60 minutes and cool before serving. Serves 8.

"As American as Apple Pie" is a very familiar phrase and references apples as a symbol of America. The fact is that apples are not native to America, nor is the apple pie an American invention.

The apple came to the New World by way of European settlers who colonized the new land. Apples became so plentiful that they were served in some fashion at almost every meal during the colonial period.

When America became the world's largest producer of apples, the apple became universally accepted as a symbol of America and what can be accomplished.

Apricot Pie

2 (15 ounce) cans apricot halves,
    drained   2 (425 g)
1 (9 inch) piecrust   23 cm
1¼ cups sugar   250 g
¼ cup flour   30 g
1 (8 ounce) carton whipping
    cream, whipped   250 ml

 Preheat oven to 325° (165° C).

 Cut each apricot half into 2 pieces and arrange evenly in
   piecrust.

 Combine sugar and flour in bowl and sprinkle over
   apricots. Pour whipped cream over pie.

 Place 1-inch (2.5 cm) strips of foil over edge of
   piecrust to prevent excessive browning. Bake for
   1 hour 20 minutes. Serves 6.

TIP: *You might want to place pie on cookie sheet to catch any
     possible spillovers.*

Creamy Blackberry Pie

4 cups fresh blackberries	575 g
1 (9 inch) refrigerated piecrust	23 cm
1 cup sugar	200 g
⅓ cup flour	40 g
2 eggs, beaten	
½ cup sour cream	120 g

 Preheat oven to 350° (175° C). Place blackberries in piecrust. Combine sugar and flour in bowl.

 In separate bowl, blend eggs and sour cream and add sugar mixture to eggs. Spoon over blackberries.

Topping:

½ cup sugar	100 g
½ cup flour	60 g
¼ cup (½ stick) butter	55 g

 Combine sugar, flour and butter in bowl. Mix well. Crumble evenly over sour cream mixture. Bake for 1 hour or until light brown. Serves 8.

Old-Fashioned Blueberry Pie

4 cups fresh blueberries	575 g
¾ cup sugar	150 g
¼ cup flour	30 g
2 tablespoons lemon juice	30 ml
2 (9 inch) piecrusts	2 (23 cm)
2 tablespoons butter	30 g

Preheat oven to 425° (220° C). In large bowl, gently mix blueberries and sugar. (If blueberries are tart, add a little more sugar.)

Stir in flour and lemon juice. Spoon mixture into pie pan over bottom crust. Dot with butter and place top crust over pie filling.

Fold edges of top crust under edges of bottom crust to seal. Flute edges with fingers and cut several slits in top crust.

Bake for 15 minutes and remove pie from oven. Cover edges of piecrust with strips of foil to prevent excessive browning.

Return to oven and bake for 30 to 40 minutes or until pie is bubbly and crust is golden brown. Serves 8.

Old-Fashioned Cherry Pie

4 cups pitted cherries	615 g
1¼ cups sugar	250 g
¼ cup flour	30 g
¼ teaspoon cinnamon	1 ml
2 (9 inch) piecrusts	2 (23 cm)
2 tablespoons butter	30 g

Preheat oven to 425° (220° C). In large bowl, gently mix cherries and sugar. Stir in flour and cinnamon. Spoon mixture into pie pan over bottom crust.

Dot with butter and place top crust over pie filling.

Fold edges of top crust under edges of bottom crust to seal. Flute edges with fingers and cut several slits in top crust.

Bake for 15 minutes and remove pie from oven. Cover edges of piecrust with strips of foil to prevent excessive browning.

Return to oven and bake for 20 to 25 minutes or until pie is bubbly and crust is golden brown. Serves 8.

Nothing feels exactly like the moment during an argument when you realize you are wrong.

Lemon Meringue Pie

1½ cups sugar	300 g
⅓ cup flour	40 g
4 large egg yolks, beaten	
⅓ cup lemon juice	75 ml
1 (9 inch) baked piecrust	23 cm

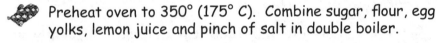 Preheat oven to 350° (175° C). Combine sugar, flour, egg yolks, lemon juice and pinch of salt in double boiler.

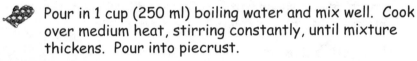 Pour in 1 cup (250 ml) boiling water and mix well. Cook over medium heat, stirring constantly, until mixture thickens. Pour into piecrust.

Meringue:

4 large egg whites	
¼ teaspoon cream of tartar	1 ml
¼ cup sugar	60 ml

Beat egg whites and cream of tartar in bowl until soft peaks form. Gradually add sugar and beat well. Spread on pie filling.

Bake for 12 minutes or until meringue is golden brown. Serves 8.

Don't make meringues on a rainy day.

Use fresh eggs for best meringues.

Lemon Chess Pie

1 ¼ cups sugar	250 g
3 large eggs	
½ cup corn syrup	125 ml
1 tablespoon cornmeal	15 ml
¾ cup sour cream	180 g
½ teaspoon vanilla	2 ml
¼ cup lemon juice	60 ml
1 (9 inch) refrigerated piecrust	23 cm

 Preheat oven to 350° (175° C). Beat sugar and eggs in bowl and mix well. Fold in corn syrup, cornmeal, sour cream, vanilla and lemon juice and mix well. Pour into piecrust.

Cut 1½-inch (4 cm) strips of foil and cover edges of crust to keep crust from excessive browning.

Bake for 45 to 50 minutes or until knife inserted in center comes out clean. Serves 8.

The tiniest speck of egg yolk dooms meringue.

Cold eggs are easier to separate, but should be at room temperature when used in a recipe.

Lemon-Pecan Chess Pie

2¼ cups sugar	450 g
2 tablespoons flour	15 g
1 tablespoon cornmeal	15 ml
4 eggs, lightly beaten	
2 tablespoons grated lemon peel	20 g
¼ cup lemon juice	60 ml
¾ cup chopped pecans	85 g
1 (9 inch) refrigerated piecrust	23 cm

Preheat oven to 400° (205° C). Combine sugar, flour and cornmeal in large bowl and toss lightly. Add eggs, lemon peel and lemon juice and mix until smooth.

Add pecans to mixture and pour into piecrust. Cover crust edges with strips of foil to prevent excessive browning.

Bake for 10 minutes. Reduce temperature to 325° (165° C) and bake for 40 to 45 minutes or until center is not shaky. Serves 8.

Chess pie is a long-time Southern favorite based on eggs, sugar, butter and a little flour. Originally it was regarded as similar to a cheeseless cheesecake because the custard-like filling had the texture of cheese.

Pistachio-Lime Pie

A bridge club favorite!

2 cups vanilla wafer crumbs	320 g
¾ cup chopped pistachios, divided	90 g
¼ cup (½ stick) butter, melted	60 g
1 (8 ounce) package cream cheese, softened	225 g
1 (14 ounce) can sweetened condensed milk	395 g
¼ cup lime juice from concentrate	60 ml
1 (3 ounce) package instant pistachio pudding mix	85 g
1 (8 ounce) can crushed pineapple with juice	225 g
1 (8 ounce) carton frozen whipped topping, thawed	225 g

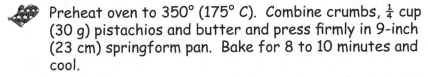

Preheat oven to 350° (175° C). Combine crumbs, ¼ cup (30 g) pistachios and butter and press firmly in 9-inch (23 cm) springform pan. Bake for 8 to 10 minutes and cool.

Beat cream cheese in bowl until fluffy. Gradually beat in sweetened condensed milk, lime juice and pudding mix and mix until smooth.

Stir in remaining pistachios and pineapple and fold in whipped topping. Pour into springform pan and refrigerate overnight. Keep refrigerated. Serves 8.

Margarita Pie

1 (14 ounce) can sweetened condensed milk	395 g
2 eggs, separated	
¾ cup sugar, divided	150 g
⅓ cup fresh lime juice	75 ml
¼ cup tequila	60 ml
¼ cup triple sec liqueur	60 ml
1 (6 ounce) ready graham cracker piecrust	170 g
1 (8 ounce) carton whipping cream	250 ml
Lime slices for garnish	

Preheat oven to 325° (165° C). Combine sweetened condensed milk, egg yolks, ½ cup (100 g) sugar, lime juice, tequila and triple sec in bowl and mix well.

In separate bowl, beat egg whites until slightly stiff and fold into egg-sugar mixture. Spoon mixture into piecrust, bake for 25 minutes or until set and cool.

In separate bowl, beat whipping cream, add remaining ¼ cup (50 g) sugar and spread over cooled pie.

Refrigerate for several hours or overnight. When ready to serve, slice lime very thin and make cut to center of each lime slice, twist and place on each serving for garnish. Serves 6.

Old-Fashioned Peach Pie

5 cups peeled, sliced fresh peaches	770 g
¾ cup sugar	150 g
⅓ cup flour	40 g
1 tablespoon lemon juice	15 ml
2 (9 inch) piecrusts	2 (23 cm)
2 tablespoons butter	30 g

Preheat oven to 425° (220° C). In large bowl, gently mix peaches and sugar. (If peaches are tart, add a little more sugar.)

Stir in flour and lemon juice. Spoon mixture into pie pan over bottom crust. Dot with butter and place top crust over pie filling.

Fold edges of top crust under edges of bottom crust to seal. Flute edges with fingers and cut several slits in top crust.

Bake for 15 minutes and remove pie from oven. Cover edges of piecrust with foil to keep them from burning.

Return to oven and bake for 15 to 20 minutes or until pie is bubbly and crust is light golden brown. Serves 8.

Old-Time Pineapple Chess Pie

1 ½ cups sugar	300 g
1 tablespoon cornmeal	15 ml
2 tablespoons flour	15 g
6 tablespoons (¾ stick) butter, melted	85 g
2 eggs, beaten	
1 (8 ounce) can crushed pineapple with juice	225 g
1 (9 inch) refrigerated piecrust	23 cm

 Preheat oven to 350° (175° C). Combine sugar, cornmeal, flour and pinch of salt in bowl and mix.

Stir in butter, eggs and pineapple and beat. Pour into piecrust and bake for 45 minutes. Serves 8.

Chess pies are Southern specialties dating back to African-American cooks on southern plantations. They are a simple mixture of sugar, butter, eggs and a little flour with variations of flavorings such as lemon, vanilla and chocolate.

Easy Pumpkin Pie

2 eggs
3¼ cups (30 ounce can) pumpkin
   pie mix   795 g
⅔ cup evaporated milk   150 ml
1 (9 inch) refrigerated deep-dish
   piecrust   23 cm

Preheat oven to 400° (205° C). Beat eggs lightly in large
bowl. Stir in pumpkin pie mix and evaporated milk. Pour
into piecrust.

Cut 2-inch (5 cm) wide strips of foil and cover crust
edges to prevent excessive browning. Bake for
15 minutes.

Decrease temperature to 350° (175° C) and bake for
additional 50 minutes or until knife inserted in center
comes out clean. Cool. Serves 6 to 8.

The first Thanksgiving was held at Plymouth
Colony located on Cape Cod in Massachusetts
in 1621. George Washington declared a one-
time national holiday to give thanks in 1789, but
Thanksgiving Day did not become a permanent
national holiday until 1863 under Abraham Lincoln.

Party Pumpkin Pie

1 (15 ounce) can pumpkin	425 g
1 cup sugar	200 g
3 eggs, slightly beaten	
½ teaspoon ground cinnamon	2 ml
¼ teaspoon ground ginger	1 ml
¼ teaspoon ground nutmeg	1 ml
¼ teaspoon ground allspice	1 ml
1½ cups half-and-half cream	375 ml
2 tablespoons bourbon	30 ml
½ cup flaked coconut	45 g
1 (9 inch) refrigerated piecrust	23 cm

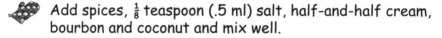 Preheat oven to 350° (175° C). Combine pumpkin, sugar and eggs in bowl and beat well.

Add spices, ⅛ teaspoon (.5 ml) salt, half-and-half cream, bourbon and coconut and mix well.

Pour into piecrust and bake for 35 to 40 minutes or until center is set. Serves 8.

It is not known if turkey was served at the first Thanksgiving, but venison, codfish, oysters, duck, cornbread, onions, succotash and cranberries were in ample supply. It is recorded that on the third Thanksgiving, turkey, dressing and cranberries, and possibly pumpkin, were on the menu.

Sweet Potato Pie

1 (14 ounce) can sweet potatoes, drained, mashed	395 g
¾ cup milk	175 ml
1 cup packed brown sugar	220 g
2 eggs	
½ teaspoon ground cinnamon	2 ml
1 (9 inch) refrigerated piecrust	23 cm

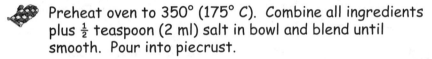 Preheat oven to 350° (175° C). Combine all ingredients plus ½ teaspoon (2 ml) salt in bowl and blend until smooth. Pour into piecrust.

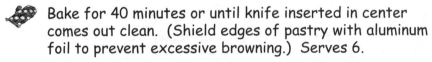 Bake for 40 minutes or until knife inserted in center comes out clean. (Shield edges of pastry with aluminum foil to prevent excessive browning.) Serves 6.

The sweet potato, a Southern favorite, is one of the most nutritious vegetables we have. It is fat-free and cholesterol-free, is full of fiber and has significant amounts of vitamin C and vitamin E. Sweet potatoes can be baked, grilled, sautéed, fried, boiled, steamed and eaten raw in appetizers, salads, side dishes, main dishes, breads and desserts.

Cheesecake Pie

2 (8 ounce) packages cream cheese	2 (225 g)
3 eggs	
1 cup sugar, divided	200 g
1½ teaspoons vanilla, divided	7 ml
1 (6 ounce) graham cracker piecrust	170 g
1 (8 ounce) carton sour cream	225 g

Preheat oven to 350° (175° C). Combine cream cheese, eggs, ¾ cup (150 g) sugar and ½ teaspoon (2 ml) vanilla in bowl. Beat for 5 minutes.

Pour into piecrust and bake for 25 minutes. Cool for 20 minutes.

Combine sour cream, remaining sugar and remaining vanilla. Pour over cooled pie and bake for additional 10 minutes.

Refrigerate for at least 4 hours. Serve with your favorite fruit topping. Serves 8.

There are nine regional cuisines that are distinctively different in the United States. They are Southern, Tex-Mex, Southwest, Cajun-Creole, Pacific Rim, Midwest, New England, Pennsylvania Dutch and Floribbean.

Chess Pie

½ cup (1 stick) butter, softened	115 g
2 cups sugar	400 g
1 tablespoon cornstarch	15 ml
4 eggs	
1 (9 inch) refrigerated piecrust	23 cm

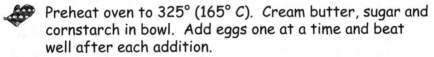 Preheat oven to 325° (165° C). Cream butter, sugar and cornstarch in bowl. Add eggs one at a time and beat well after each addition.

Pour mixture in piecrust. Cover piecrust edges with strips of foil to prevent excessive browning. Bake for 45 minutes or until center sets. Serves 6 to 8.

Cherry-Pecan Pie

1 (14 ounce) can sweetened condensed milk	395 g
¼ cup lemon juice	60 ml
1 (8 ounce) carton frozen whipped topping, thawed	225 g
1 cup chopped pecans	110 g
1 (14 ounce) can cherry pie filling	395 g
2 (6 ounce) graham cracker piecrusts	2 (170 g)

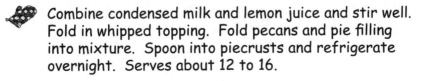 Combine condensed milk and lemon juice and stir well. Fold in whipped topping. Fold pecans and pie filling into mixture. Spoon into piecrusts and refrigerate overnight. Serves about 12 to 16.

Famous Shoo-Fly Pie

1 cup flour	120 g
½ cup packed brown sugar	110 g
1 teaspoon baking soda	5 ml
Shortening	
½ cup molasses	125 ml
1 (9 inch) frozen piecrust, unbaked	23 cm

Preheat oven to 350° (175° C). Mix flour, brown sugar, baking soda and a pinch of salt in bowl. Add just enough shortening to make mixture crumbly.

Mix molasses and ½ cup (125 ml) boiling water in saucepan. While hot pour into piecrust. Spread crust crumbles over top of molasses.

Bake until firm in middle and toothpick inserted in center comes out clean. Serves 8.

Lancaster County, Pennsylvania was settled mostly by Germans who became known as "Pennsylvania Dutch". They included many people seeking freedom from religious persecution. Rural communities of Mennonites, Amish and the Brethren still practice a simple life today, primarily living on family farms. Among the original specialty foods that the Pennsylvania Dutch shared with the nation are scrapple, cheese steaks, shoo fly pie and funnel cakes.

Farmhouse Buttermilk Pie

4 eggs	
1 cup sugar	200 g
3 tablespoons flour	25 g
2 tablespoons butter, melted	30 g
3 tablespoons lemon juice	45 ml
1¼ cups buttermilk*	310 ml
½ teaspoon lemon extract	2 ml
1 (9 inch) baked piecrust, chilled	23 cm

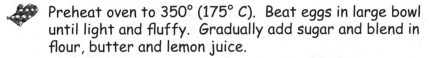 Preheat oven to 350° (175° C). Beat eggs in large bowl until light and fluffy. Gradually add sugar and blend in flour, butter and lemon juice.

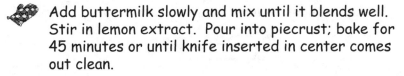 Add buttermilk slowly and mix until it blends well. Stir in lemon extract. Pour into piecrust; bake for 45 minutes or until knife inserted in center comes out clean.

Serve room temperature or chilled, but refrigerate any leftovers. Serves 8.

*TIP: To make buttermilk, mix 1 cup (250 ml) milk with 1 tablespoon (15 ml) lemon juice or vinegar and let milk stand for about 10 minutes.

Chocolate-Amaretto Pie

2 (7 ounce) milk chocolate candy bars with almonds	2 (200 g)
⅓ cup amaretto liqueur	75 ml
2 (8 ounce) cartons whipping cream, whipped	2 (250 ml)
1 (6 ounce) shortbread piecrust	170 g

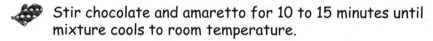

Melt chocolate in double boiler over low heat. Remove from heat and pour in amaretto.

Stir chocolate and amaretto for 10 to 15 minutes until mixture cools to room temperature.

Fold in whipped cream. Pour mixture into piecrust. Refrigerate for several hours before serving. Serves 8.

Pantry Secrets: *Keep these items in the pantry for a quick throw together sweet any time day or night!*

> *Brownie mix*
> *Pudding mix*
> *Cake mix*
> *Ice cream sauces*
> *Sprinkles*

Chocolate-Coconut Pie

1½ cups flaked coconut	130 g
1½ cups chopped pecans	165 g
1 (12 ounce) package chocolate chips	340 g
1 (6 ounce) graham cracker piecrust	170 g
1 (14 ounce) can sweetened condensed milk	395 g

Preheat oven to 350° (175° C). Combine coconut, pecans and chocolate chips. Sprinkle mixture over piecrust.

Spoon sweetened condensed milk evenly over coconut mixture. Bake for 25 to 30 minutes. Cool before serving. Serves 8.

Freezer Secrets: Keep these items in the freezer for a quick throw together sweet any time day or night!

Chopped nuts
Candy bars
Ice cream

German Chocolate Pie

1 (4 ounce) package German sweet chocolate	115 g
½ cup (1 stick) butter	115 g
1 (12 ounce) can evaporated milk	355 ml
1½ cups sugar	300 g
3 tablespoons cornstarch	25 g
2 eggs	
1 teaspoon vanilla	5 ml
1 (9 inch) refrigerated piecrust	23 cm
1 (3.5 ounce) can flaked coconut	100 g
½ cup chopped pecans	55 g

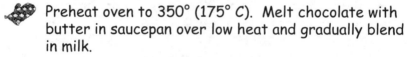 Preheat oven to 350° (175° C). Melt chocolate with butter in saucepan over low heat and gradually blend in milk.

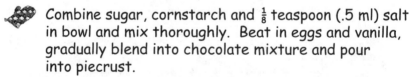 Combine sugar, cornstarch and ⅛ teaspoon (.5 ml) salt in bowl and mix thoroughly. Beat in eggs and vanilla, gradually blend into chocolate mixture and pour into piecrust.

Combine coconut and pecans in bowl and sprinkle over filling. Bake for 45 to 50 minutes. Filling will be soft but will set while cooking. Cool for at least 4 hours before slicing. Serves 8.

Million-Dollar Pie

24 round, buttery crackers, crumbled
1 cup chopped pecans   110 g
4 egg whites (absolutely no yolks
   at all)
1 cup sugar   200 g

Preheat oven to 350° (175° C).

Mix cracker crumbs with pecans in bowl.

In separate bowl, beat egg whites until stiff and slowly add sugar while still mixing.

Gently fold crumbs and pecan mixture into egg whites. Pour into pie pan and bake for 20 minutes. Cool before serving. Serves 6.

If you hide some chopped nuts and candy bars in the freezer, you can always make ice cream special.

Southern Pecan Pie

2 tablespoons flour	15 g
3 tablespoons butter, melted	45 g
3 eggs, beaten	
1 cup packed brown sugar	220 g
1 cup corn syrup	250 ml
1 teaspoon vanilla	5 ml
1 cup chopped pecans	110 g
1 (9 inch) refrigerated piecrust	23 cm

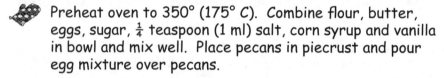 Preheat oven to 350° (175° C). Combine flour, butter, eggs, sugar, ¼ teaspoon (1 ml) salt, corn syrup and vanilla in bowl and mix well. Place pecans in piecrust and pour egg mixture over pecans.

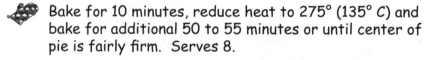 Bake for 10 minutes, reduce heat to 275° (135° C) and bake for additional 50 to 55 minutes or until center of pie is fairly firm. Serves 8.

TIP: *For Amaretto Pecan Pie, add 2 tablespoons (30 ml) amaretto liqueur instead of vanilla. Also you could add 1 teaspoon (5 ml) ground cinnamon and ½ teaspoon (2 ml) ground nutmeg to recipe for a touch of spice.*

Pecan pie has its origin with the French settlement of New Orleans in the early 18th century. Native Americans introduced pecan trees to the French and it didn't take long for French cooking to do the rest. The pecan tree is the only nut tree native to North America.

Mama's Pecan Pie

1 cup pecan halves	110 g
1 (9 inch) refrigerated piecrust	23 cm
2 cups dark corn syrup	500 ml
1 cup sugar	200 g
3 tablespoons butter, melted	45 g
1 teaspoon vanilla	5 ml
4 eggs, slightly beaten	

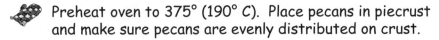 Preheat oven to 375° (190° C). Place pecans in piecrust and make sure pecans are evenly distributed on crust.

Combine corn syrup, sugar and butter in saucepan and bring to a boil; stir constantly for 2 minutes. Remove from heat. In bowl, mix vanilla, eggs and a dash of salt. Add hot mixture a little at a time, stirring constantly so the eggs do not cook; mix well. Pour into piecrust and rearrange pecans, if necessary.

Place 1-inch (2.5 cm) strips of foil around edges of piecrust to prevent excessive browning.

Bake for 10 minutes, reduce heat to 325° (165° C) and bake for 45 minutes or until center sets. Serves 8.

TIP: There are lots of variations to the basic pecan pie. Once you decide which basic pecan pie you like best you can begin your search for the perfect variation. For a Chocolate-Bourbon Pecan Pie, add 2 tablespoons (30 ml) bourbon and $\frac{1}{2}$ cup (85 g) mini chocolate chips.

Creamy Pecan Pie

1½ cups light corn syrup	375 ml
1 (3 ounce) package vanilla instant pudding	85 g
3 eggs	
2½ tablespoons butter, melted	20 g
2 cups pecan halves	225 g
1 (10 inch) deep-dish piecrust	25 cm

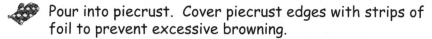 Preheat oven to 325° (165° C). Combine corn syrup, pudding, eggs and butter in bowl, mix well and stir in pecans.

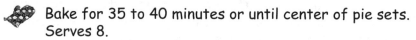 Pour into piecrust. Cover piecrust edges with strips of foil to prevent excessive browning.

 Bake for 35 to 40 minutes or until center of pie sets. Serves 8.

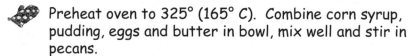

Pecan trees are spread throughout the South where a major pecan market was established. Today more than 400 million pounds of pecans are sold annually, 80% of which are shelled.

While the U.S. produces more than 90% of the world crop, pecans are also grown commercially in southern Europe, Israel, Australia and South Africa.

Pecans contain more than 19 vitamins and minerals, including vitamin A, E and several Bs, as well as folic acid, calcium, magnesium, phosphorus and potassium. Pecans also contain very few carbohydrates.

Fluffy Pecan Pie

3 large egg whites
1 teaspoon cream of tartar   5 ml
1 cup sugar   200 g
12 soda crackers, crushed
1½ teaspoons vanilla   7 ml
1½ cups chopped pecans   165 g

Preheat oven to 350° (175° C). Beat egg whites with cream of tartar in bowl until frothy. Gradually add sugar and continue beating until stiff peaks form.

Fold in crackers, vanilla and pecans mix well. Pour into 9-inch (23 cm) glass pie pan.

Bake for about 30 minutes or until pie is firm. Serves 8.

In the early 1900's the Corn Products Refining Company of New York introduced Karo® syrup made with corn and generically known as corn syrup. Until this syrup was introduced, housewives took syrup containers to the grocery store for the grocer to fill their containers from barrels.

Because of the development of corn syrup, the modern pecan pie came into its own. A corporate executive's wife, made a Karo® Pie, which became the modern-day Pecan Pie. The recipe helped propel Karo® syrup nationwide to make pecan pie's popularity go well beyond the South.

Cinnamon-Almond Pecan Pie

A little change from the traditional pecan pie, but a good one!

⅔ cup sugar	135 g
1 tablespoon flour	15 ml
2½ teaspoons ground cinnamon	12 ml
4 eggs, lightly beaten	
1 cup light corn syrup	250 ml
2 tablespoons butter, melted	30 g
1 tablespoon vanilla	15 ml
1½ teaspoons almond extract	7 ml
1 cup coarsely chopped pecans	110 g
½ cup slivered almonds	85 g
1 (9 inch) refrigerated piecrust	23 cm

Preheat oven to 400° (205° C). Combine sugar and flour in bowl. Add cinnamon, eggs, corn syrup, butter, vanilla and almond extract and mix well.

Stir in pecans and slivered almonds. Pour filling into piecrust. Cover crust edges with strips of foil to prevent excessive browning.

Bake for 10 minutes, reduce temperature to 325° (165° C) and bake for additional 40 to 45 minutes or until pie barely shakes in center. Cool completely before serving. Serves 8.

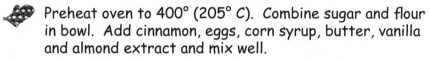

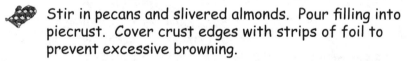

Shelled pecans can be kept in the refrigerator in an air-tight container for nine months. They will keep in the freezer for up to two years. Pecans can be refrozen multiple times.

Apple Tarts

1 (10 ounce) package frozen puff pastry shells	285 g
½ cup Craisins®	60 g
¼ cup apple brandy	60 ml
¼ cup sugar	50 g
1 (20 ounce) can apple pie filling	565 g
½ teaspoon cinnamon	2 ml

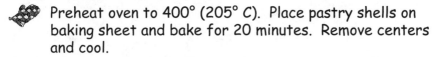

Preheat oven to 400° (205° C). Place pastry shells on baking sheet and bake for 20 minutes. Remove centers and cool.

Combine Craisins®, apple brandy and sugar in saucepan and let soak for 10 minutes.

Add pie filling and cinnamon to saucepan and mix well. Fill each pastry shell with mixture. Serves 8.

TIP: If you like, serve the tarts with a dollop of whipped topping or a scoop of vanilla ice cream.

Washington State produces more apples than any other state.

Fresh Lemon Tarts

1 (8 ounce, 8 count) package frozen tart shells	225 g
⅔ cup fresh lemon juice	150 ml
½ cup sugar	100 g
3 tablespoons sour cream	45 ml
4 eggs	

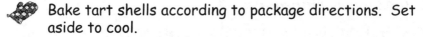 Bake tart shells according to package directions. Set aside to cool.

Preheat oven to 375° (190° C).

Whisk lemon juice and sugar in medium bowl. Whisk in sour cream. Add eggs 2 at a time and whisk until mixture blends well. Pour mixture into tart shells.

Bake tarts until filling sets, about 30 minutes. Cool tarts completely on wire rack and refrigerate at least 1 hour. Serves 8.

TIP: Garnish each tart with dollop of whipped cream and lemon slices.

Lemony Cheese Tarts

1 (8 ounce, 8 count) package frozen tart shells, thawed	225 g
2 large lemons	
3 eggs	
¾ cup sugar, divided	150 g
1 (8 ounce) container mascarpone cheese, softened	225 g

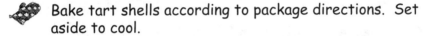

Bake tart shells according to package directions. Set aside to cool.

Squeeze ½ cup (125 ml) juice from lemons and grate 1 tablespoon (15 ml) of zest from peel. Set aside.

Beat eggs lightly and place in top of double boiler. Whisk in ½ cup (100 g) sugar, lemon juice and lemon zest.

Cook in double boiler over simmering water, whisking constantly, until mixture is smooth and slightly thickened, about 10 minutes. (The mixture is ready when it coats the back of a spoon and a trail is left when you run your finger across it.)

Remove top of double boiler from heat and set aside to cool.

In medium bowl, beat cheese until light and fluffy. Gradually beat in remaining ¼ cup (50 g) sugar.

Fold cooled lemon mixture into cheese mixture in several additions. Refrigerate and divide among prepared tart shells. Serves 8.

Lime-Cheesecake Tarts

2 small limes
1 (8 ounce) package cream cheese,
    softened   225 g
⅓ cup sugar   65 g
1 egg
1 (4 ounce, 6 count) package
    miniature graham cracker
    piecrusts   115 g

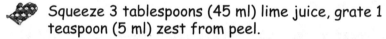 Squeeze 3 tablespoons (45 ml) lime juice, grate 1
teaspoon (5 ml) zest from peel.

Preheat oven to 325° (165° C). In mixing bowl, beat
cream cheese until smooth. Add sugar and beat until
light and fluffy.

Beat in egg, then lime juice and lime zest. Spoon
mixture into piecrusts.

Bake for 30 to 35 minutes or until knife inserted in
center comes out clean. Remove from oven and cool.
Refrigerate until ready to serve. Serves 6.

TIP: Serve with dollop of whipped cream and sprinkle of lime
    zest on top.

Fresh Peach Tarts

1 (8 ounce, 8 count) package frozen tart shells, thawed	225 g
⅔ cup ground pecans	85 g
7 tablespoons brown sugar, divided	95 g
2 tablespoons butter, melted	30 g
2 large, firm, ripe peaches	
8 pecan halves	

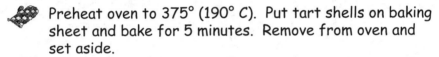

Preheat oven to 375° (190° C). Put tart shells on baking sheet and bake for 5 minutes. Remove from oven and set aside.

Increase temperature to 400° (205° C). Place ground pecans in small bowl and add 6 tablespoons (85 g) brown sugar and butter. Stir well and set aside.

Slice peaches into ¼-inch (6 mm) wedges and cut wedges in half to make pieces small enough to fit easily into tart shells.

Combine with remaining 1 tablespoon (15 ml) brown sugar and stir until peaches are coated. Divide peach mixture among tart shells.

Spoon pecan topping evenly over peaches. Place whole pecan half on top of each tart for garnish.

Bake 15 minutes or until topping and edges of tart are golden brown. Remove from oven and cool to room temperature before serving. Makes 8 tarts.

Pecan Tassies

1 (8 ounce) package cream cheese, softened	225 g
5 tablespoons butter, softened	75 g
1¾ cups flour	210 g
3 eggs, beaten	
2 cups packed brown sugar	440 g
¼ cup (½ stick) butter, melted	55 g
2 teaspoons vanilla	10 ml
1¾ cups coarsely chopped pecans	195 g

Preheat oven to 325° (165° C). Beat cream cheese and butter in bowl until light and fluffy. Add flour a little at a time and mix well.

Form about 36 (1 inch/2.5 cm) balls. Press into miniature muffin cups so sides and bottoms form tart shape.

Beat eggs, brown sugar, melted butter and vanilla in bowl. Divide pecans equally into 36 tarts.

Fill tarts with egg-sugar mixture and bake for 25 minutes. Cool and remove tarts from pans very carefully. Makes 36 miniature tarts.

The American Journal of Clinical Nutrition found that eating pecans may increase metabolic rates and decrease hunger sensations.

Homestead Date-Pecan Tarts

1 (8 ounce) package pitted, chopped dates	225 g
1½ cups milk	375 ml
½ cup flour	60 g
1½ cups sugar	300 g
3 eggs, beaten	
1 teaspoon vanilla	5 ml
1 cup chopped pecans	110 g
8 tart shells, baked, cooled	
1 (8 ounce) carton whipping cream	250 ml
3 tablespoons powdered sugar	25 g

Combine dates, milk, flour and sugar in heavy saucepan and cook for about 3 minutes, stirring constantly.

Stir in eggs and ¼ teaspoon (1 ml) salt and continue cooking, stirring constantly, for additional 5 minutes. Stir in vanilla and pecans. Pour into baked tart shells and cool.

Whip cream in bowl, add powdered sugar, top each tart with whipped cream and refrigerate. Serves 8.

Go easy on yourself. Serving ice cream or sorbet for dessert is a great idea. For a personal touch offer bowls of different toppings and let guests create their own sundae.

Blue Ribbon Apricot Cobbler

This is another one of those recipes that is really quick and easy plus really delicious.

1 (20 ounce) can apricot pie filling	565 g
1 (20 ounce) can crushed pineapple with juice	565 g
1 cup chopped pecans	110 g
1 (18 ounce) box yellow cake mix	510 g
1 cup (2 sticks) butter, melted	225 g
Frozen whipped topping, thawed	

Preheat oven to 375° (190° C). Pour apricot pie filling into sprayed 9 x 13-inch (23 x 33 cm) baking dish and spread out.

Spoon crushed pineapple and juice over pie filling. Sprinkle pecans over pineapple then sprinkle cake mix over pecans. Do not stir.

Pour melted butter over cake mix and bake for 40 minutes or until light brown and crunchy. To serve, top with whipped topping. Serves 10.

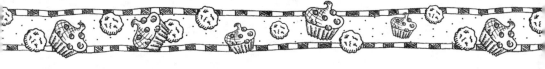

Blueberry Cobbler

½ cup (1 stick) butter, melted	115 g
1 cup self-rising flour	125 g
1¼ cups sugar	250 g
1 cup milk	250 ml
1 (20 ounce) can blueberry pie filling	565 g
Frozen whipped topping, thawed	

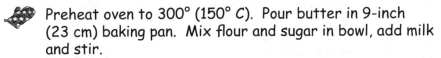 Preheat oven to 300° (150° C). Pour butter in 9-inch (23 cm) baking pan. Mix flour and sugar in bowl, add milk and stir.

Pour mixture over melted butter but do not stir. Spoon pie filling over batter and bake for 1 hour. To serve, top with whipped topping. Serves 8.

Cobblers are an American invention straight out of the settlers' necessity. After Europeans arrived in America, they tried to duplicate their dishes, but didn't have all the ingredients. Cooks used whatever they found in the area and whatever food, fruits and nuts were in season.

Because there were no English ovens in the settlements, foods were cooked over open fires in heavy cast-iron skillets and pots. The natural evolution for the first pies in the New World was the cobbler.

Fruit and berries were put in a deep-dish skillet and biscuit dough was dropped on top. The skillet was covered and when the top was brown the dish was ready.

Blueberry-Streusel Cobbler

1 (14 ounce) package frozen blueberries, thawed	395 g
1 (14 ounce) can sweetened condensed milk	395 g
2 teaspoons grated lemon peel	10 ml
¾ cup (1½ sticks) plus 2 tablespoons butter, softened	200 g
2 cups biscuit mix, divided	240 g
⅔ cup firmly packed brown sugar	150 g
2 tablespoons butter	30 g
¾ cup chopped pecans	85 g

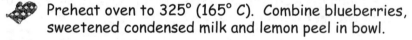 Preheat oven to 325° (165° C). Combine blueberries, sweetened condensed milk and lemon peel in bowl.

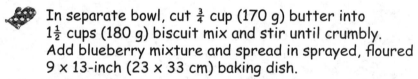 In separate bowl, cut ¾ cup (170 g) butter into 1½ cups (180 g) biscuit mix and stir until crumbly. Add blueberry mixture and spread in sprayed, floured 9 x 13-inch (23 x 33 cm) baking dish.

Combine remaining biscuit mix and brown sugar in bowl. Cut in remaining 2 tablespoons (30 g) butter until crumbly, add pecans and sprinkle over cobbler. Bake for 55 to 60 minutes or when toothpick inserted in center comes out clean.

Continued next page...

Continued from previous page...

Blueberry Sauce:

½ cup sugar	100 g
1 tablespoon cornstarch	15 ml
½ teaspoon ground cinnamon	2 ml
¼ teaspoon ground nutmeg	1 ml
1 (14 ounce) package frozen	
blueberries, thawed	395 g
Vanilla ice cream	

 Combine sugar, cornstarch, cinnamon and nutmeg in small saucepan and gradually add ½ cup (125 ml) water. Cook and stir until thick. Stir in blueberries.

 Serve square of cobbler with ice cream on top and pour blueberry sauce over all. Serves 10.

Cobbler-type dishes have been called a variety of names: crisps, crumbles, Brown Bettys, grunts and slumps. They all were based on a fruit filling with biscuit or pastry cooked on top.

Crisps have crumbs on top and are called crumbles in England. Apple Brown Betty was very popular in the 17th and 18th centuries and had crumbs between layers of apples.

 # Cherry-Strawberry Cobbler

1 (20 ounce) can strawberry pie filling	565 g
1 (20 ounce) can cherry pie filling	565 g
1 (18 ounce) box white cake mix	510 g
1 cup (2 sticks) butter, melted	225 g
¾ cup slivered almonds	125 g
Frozen whipped topping, thawed	

 Preheat oven to 350° (175° C).

 Spread pie fillings in sprayed 9 x 13-inch (23 x 33 cm) baking dish and sprinkle cake mix over pie fillings.

 Drizzle melted butter over top and sprinkle with almonds. Bake for 55 minutes. Top with whipped topping. Serves 15.

Cobblers were also called grunts and slumps. Some stories say that the sound berries and fruits made when cooking sounded like grunts, hence the name. Slumps probably referred to the way the dish looked.

Pandowdy was also a type of cobbler. The fruit filling was usually on the bottom and a crust on top.

 # Cinnamon-Apple Cobbler

2 (20 ounce) cans apple pie filling	2 (565 g)
½ cup packed brown sugar	110 g
1½ teaspoons ground cinnamon	7 ml
1 (18 ounce) box yellow cake mix	510 g
½ cup (1 stick) butter, melted	115 g

Preheat oven to 350° (175° C).

Spread apple pie filling in sprayed 9 x 13-inch baking dish.

Sprinkle with brown sugar and cinnamon and top with dry cake mix. Drizzle melted butter over top of cake mix. Do not stir.

Bake for 50 minutes or until light brown and bubbly. Serves 16.

The early cobblers created by American colonists used whatever ingredients they had on hand. When fruits were in season, one of the easiest desserts they could make was the cobbler. They placed fruit in the bottom of a heavy cast-iron skillet and dropped biscuit dough on top. They covered the dish and cooked the cobbler over an open fire.

Today's cobblers have more of a pastry on top than a heavy biscuit or scone topping.

Double-Berry Cobbler

1 (12 ounce) package frozen raspberries	340 g
1 (12 ounce) package frozen blackberries	340 g
⅓ cup sugar	65 g
⅓ cup flour	40 g
¼ cup (½ stick) butter, melted	115 g
½ (15 ounce) package refrigerated piecrust	½ (425 g)

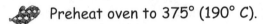
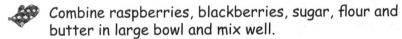

Preheat oven to 375° (190° C).

Combine raspberries, blackberries, sugar, flour and butter in large bowl and mix well.

Spoon berry mixture into sprayed 9 x 13-inch baking dish. Roll 1 piecrust to fit on top of berry mixture and sprinkle with extra sugar. Cut slits in crust.

Bake for 1 hour or until golden brown and bubbly. Serves 16.

Apple Capital of the World
Wenatchee, Washington

Cherry Capital of the World
Traverse City, Michigan

Cranberry Capital of the World
Middleboro, Massachusetts

Date Capital of the World
Indio, California

 # Easy Cherry Cobbler

2 (20 ounce) cans cherry pie filling   2 (565 g)
1 (18 ounce) box white cake mix   510 g
¾ cup (1½ sticks) butter, melted   170 g
1 (4 ounce) package slivered
    almonds   115 g
Frozen whipped topping, thawed

 Preheat oven to 350° (175° C).

Spread pie filling in sprayed 9 x 13-inch (23 x 33 cm) baking pan. Sprinkle cake mix over pie filling.

Drizzle butter over top and sprinkle with almonds. Do not stir.

Bake for 45 minutes. Top with whipped topping to serve. Serves 16.

Raisin Capitals of the World
Fresno and Selma, California

Strawberry Capital of the World
Oxnard, California

Watermelon Capitals of the World
Weatherford, Texas; Hope, Arkansas;
Rush Springs, Oklahoma

Peanut Capitals of the World
Dothan, Alabama; Terrell County, Georgia;
Sylvester, Georgia; Suffolk, Virginia

Peach Capital of the World
Johnston, South Carolina

 # Express Fruit Cobbler

Use any kind of fruit pie filling to create this fast, last-minute cobbler for a great dessert.

2 (20 ounce) cans blueberry pie filling	2 (565 g)
½ cup (1 stick) butter, softened	115 g
1 (18 ounce) box white cake mix	510 g
1 egg	

 Preheat oven to 350° (175° C).

 Spread pie filling in 9 x 13-inch (23 x 33 cm) baking pan.

 In large bowl, cream butter to smooth texture. Add dry cake mix and egg and blend well. (Mixture will be very stiff.)

 Spoon mixture over pie filling. Bake for 40 minutes or until golden brown. Cut into squares. Serves 16.

Early Pennsylvania Dutch pottery shows many examples of pie plates and suggests that the Pennsylvania Dutch were extraordinary pie bakers. Early pies were mostly savory with meat and vegetables, but sweet pies gained popularity rapidly.

After the Revolutionary War, many men who served in southeastern Pennsylvania took recipes and stories of wonderful sweet pies home. The Pennsylvania Dutch contributed much to America's heritage of delicious sweet pies.

Peachy Ginger Cobbler

2 tablespoons cornstarch	15 g
2 tablespoons butter	30 g
1½ cups sugar	300 g
¼ teaspoon ground cinnamon	1 ml
3 cups fresh peaches, peeled, sliced	460 g
¼ cup chopped crystallized ginger (no substitution)	60 ml

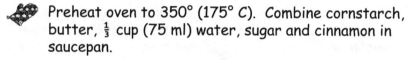 Preheat oven to 350° (175° C). Combine cornstarch, butter, ⅓ cup (75 ml) water, sugar and cinnamon in saucepan.

Heat and stir constantly until mixture is thick. Stir in peaches and crystallized ginger. Pour into sprayed 9 x 13-inch (23 x 33 cm) baking dish.

Topping:

1 cup flour	120 g
½ cup sugar	100 g
½ cup packed brown sugar	110 g
½ teaspoon baking powder	2 ml
1 egg	
¼ cup (½ stick) butter, melted	55 g
1 cup chopped pecans	110 g

Combine all ingredients and ¼ teaspoon (1 ml) salt in bowl and dot teaspoonfuls over peaches. Bake for 40 to 45 minutes or until golden brown. Serves 10.

Texas Peach Cobbler

½ cup (1 stick) butter, melted	115 g
1 cup flour	120 g
2¼ cups sugar, divided	450 g
2 teaspoons baking powder	10 ml
1 cup milk	250 ml
3 - 4 cups fresh, ripe sliced peaches	460 - 615 g
1 teaspoon ground cinnamon	5 ml

Preheat oven to 350° (175° C). Combine butter, flour, 1 cup (200 g) sugar, baking powder and ¼ teaspoon (1 ml) salt in bowl; mix in milk and blend well.

Spoon into sprayed 9 x 13-inch (23 x 33 cm) glass baking dish. Combine sliced peaches, remaining 1¼ cups (250 g) sugar and cinnamon and pour over dough.

Bake for 1 hour. Crust will come to top. Serves 10 to 12.

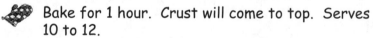

Just about any fruit will work in cobblers. Some of the best choices include peaches, apricots, berries of any kind, pears, plums and of course, apples. It is difficult to mix fruits because the firmer fruits need to cook longer than berries or peaches, as examples.

Washington Apple Crisp

5 cups peeled, cored, sliced apples	900 g
½ cup (1 stick) butter, melted	115 g
1 cup quick-cooking oats	80 g
½ cup packed brown sugar	110 g
⅓ cup flour	40 g

Preheat over to 375° (190° C). Place apple slices in 8-inch or 9-inch (20 or 23 cm) square baking pan.

Combine butter, oats, brown sugar and flour in bowl and sprinkle mixture over apples.

Bake for 40 to 45 minutes or until apples are tender and topping is golden brown. Serves 9.

TIP: For a change, add 1 teaspoon (5 ml) cinnamon and ½ cup (80 g/60 g) raisins or dried cranberries to apples before sprinkling with topping.

The top apple producing states are Washington, New York, Michigan, Pennsylvania, California and Virginia. Washington produces more than all the others combined.

Blueberry Buckle

Excellent for brunch!

2 cups flour	240 g
3 cups sugar	600 g
2 teaspoons baking powder	10 ml
1 egg	
½ cup milk	125 ml
¼ cup (½ stick) butter, softened	115 g
2 cups blueberries	150 g

 Preheat oven to 375° (190° C). Combine flour, sugar, baking powder, egg, ½ teaspoon (2 ml) salt, milk and butter in large bowl. Carefully fold in blueberries.

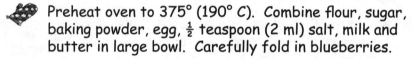 Spread in sprayed 9-inch (23 cm) square pan.

Topping:

¼ cup (½ stick) butter, softened	55 g
⅓ cup flour	40 g
½ cup sugar	100 g
½ teaspoon ground cinnamon	2 ml

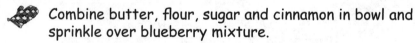 Combine butter, flour, sugar and cinnamon in bowl and sprinkle over blueberry mixture.

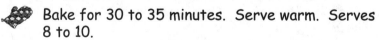 Bake for 30 to 35 minutes. Serve warm. Serves 8 to 10.

 # Blueberry Crumble

1 (13 ounce) box wild blueberry muffin mix with blueberries, separated	370 g
⅓ cup plus ¼ cup sugar	65 g/50 g
½ teaspoon ground cinnamon	2 ml
¼ cup (½ stick) butter, melted	55 g
⅔ cup chopped pecans	75 g
1 (16 ounce) can blueberry pie filling	455 g
1 teaspoon ground cinnamon	5 ml
Vanilla ice cream	

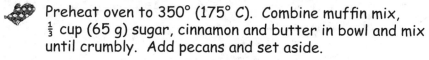

Preheat oven to 350° (175° C). Combine muffin mix, ⅓ cup (65 g) sugar, cinnamon and butter in bowl and mix until crumbly. Add pecans and set aside.

Pour blueberry pie filling into sprayed 7 x 11-inch (18 x 28 cm) glass baking dish. Drain can of blueberries from muffin mix and pour berries over top of pie filling.

Sprinkle remaining ¼ cup (50 g) sugar and cinnamon over top, then with your hands, crumble muffin mixture over top of pie filling.

Bake for 35 minutes. Serve hot or room temperature and top with a dip of vanilla ice cream. Serves 8.

 # Blueberry Crunch

1 (20 ounce) can crushed pineapple with juice	565 g
1 (18 ounce) box yellow cake mix	510 g
3 cups fresh or frozen blueberries	445 g/465 g
⅔ cup sugar	135 g
½ cup (1 stick) butter, melted	115 g

 Preheat oven to 350° (175° C).

 Spread pineapple in sprayed 9 x 13-inch (23 x 33 cm) baking dish and sprinkle with cake mix, blueberries and sugar. (It is even better if you sprinkle 1 cup (110 g) chopped pecans.) Do not stir.

 Drizzle with butter and bake for 45 minutes or until bubbly. Serves 15.

While some historians tell us cobblers are probably a derivation of English pies, it is reasonable to assume their origin started in the northeastern colonies with the settlers. Pioneers used whatever they could get to make all their food creations.

The place of origin is less important than the imagination of the people who settled America. They used only ingredients they could carry or find in the general area where they lived. They adapted the recipes from their home countries and came up with purely American originals.

Cherry-Cinnamon Bake

1 (20 ounce) can cherry pie filling   *565 g*
1 (12 ounce) can refrigerated
    cinnamon rolls   *340 g*

Preheat oven to 400° (205° C).

Spread pie filling in sprayed 8-inch (20 cm) baking dish. Set aside icing from cinnamon rolls and arrange rolls around edge of baking dish.

Bake uncovered for 15 minutes. Cover and bake for additional 10 minutes. Spread icing over rolls and serve warm. Serves 8 to 10.

More statistical studies are finding that family meals play a significant role in childhood development. Children who eat with their families four or more nights per week are healthier, make better grades in school, score higher on aptitude tests and are less likely to have problems with drugs.

Lickety-Split Apple Crisp

This apple dish could not be easier. It is a great standby dessert if you keep the pie filling and oatmeal on hand. It can be put together in minutes, and there is little clean-up.

2 (20 ounce) cans apple pie filling	*2 (565 g)*
3 (1.6 ounce) packets cinnamon-spice	
* instant oatmeal*	*3 (45 g)*
½ cup flour	*60 g*
¾ cup firmly packed brown sugar	*55 g*
½ cup (1 stick) butter, melted	*115 g*

Preheat oven to 350° (175° C).

Pour apple pie filling in sprayed 9 x 13-inch (23 x 33 cm) baking dish.

Combine oatmeal, flour and brown sugar in bowl. Stir in melted butter and mix well.

Crumble mixture over pie filling. Bake for 45 minutes or until top is golden brown. Serves 12 to 16.

TIP: *For additional flavor, sprinkle 1 teaspoon (5 ml) apple pie spice over apple pie filling before the topping. You may also add ½ cup (55 g) chopped pecans to the topping mixture. And last but not least, serve it warm with a scoop of vanilla ice cream for the ultimate taste treat.*

Peach Crisp

4¾ cups peeled, sliced peaches	730 g
3 tablespoons lemon juice	45 ml
1 cup flour	120 g
1¾ cups sugar	350 g
1 egg, beaten	
Butter	

 Preheat oven to 375° (190° C).

 Place peaches in sprayed 9-inch (23 cm) square baking dish and sprinkle lemon juice over top.

 Mix flour, sugar, egg and dash of salt in bowl. Spread mixture over top of peaches and dot with a little butter.

 Bake until golden brown. Serves 8 to 12.

A shortcut for homemade cookies is to double the recipe to make an extra batch of dough and freeze the extra dough. Roll dough in logs, wrap in plastic wrap or wax paper and seal in a plastic bag. When you're ready to bake, just slice into ¼-inch (6 mm) cookies and bake. It's a great idea to label your package with the name of the cookies, the date frozen, and the cooking temperature and time.

Peach Crumb

1 (20 ounce) can peach pie filling	565 g
½ cup quick-cooking oats	40 g
½ cup flour	60 g
½ cup firmly packed brown sugar	110 g
½ cup (1 stick) butter, melted	115 g

Preheat oven to 350° (175°).

Pour peach pie filling in 8-inch (20 cm) square baking dish.

In medium bowl, combine oats, flour and brown sugar. Stir in butter until mixture blends thoroughly.

Sprinkle mixture evenly over peach pie filling. Bake for 40 to 45 minutes or until topping is brown. Serves 4 to 6.

A group of chess players were checking into a hotel and talked to each other in the lobby about a tournament victory. After some time, the hotel manager asked them to leave the lobby.

"Why?" asked one of the players. "Because I don't like a bunch of chess nuts boasting in an open foyer.

 # Peachy Amaretto Crunch

2 (20 ounce) cans peach pie filling	2 (565 g)
½ cup amaretto liqueur	125 ml
1 (18 ounce) box white cake mix	510 g
1 cup slivered almonds, toasted	170 g
½ cup (1 stick) butter	115 g

Preheat oven to 350° (175° C). Spread pie filling evenly in bottom of sprayed 9 x 13-inch (23 x 33 cm) baking dish and pour amaretto over filling.

Sprinkle cake mix evenly over top of filling and sprinkle with almonds. Cut butter into ⅛-inch (3 mm) slices and place over surface of cake mixture.

Bake for 40 to 45 minutes or until top is brown. Serves 12 to 16.

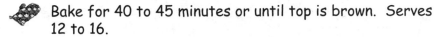

When I was a boy of 14, my father was so ignorant I could hardly stand to have the old man around. But when I got to be 21, I was astonished at how much the old man had learned in seven years. —Mark Twain

Strawberry Crumble

2¼ cups biscuit mix	270 g
1 cup oats	80 g
1 cup packed brown sugar	220 g
½ cup (1 stick) butter, softened	115 g
1 cup strawberry preserves	320 g

 Preheat oven to 375° (190° C). Combine biscuit mix, oats and brown sugar. Cut in butter with pastry blender until mixture is crumbly.

Press half mixture in sprayed 9-inch (23 cm) square baking pan. Spread strawberry preserves over mixture to within ¼-inch (6 mm) of edges.

Sprinkle remaining mixture over top and gently press into preserves.

Bake for 30 minutes or until light brown. Cool and cut into bars to serve. Serves 6.

We are always the same age inside.
—Gertrude Stein

When you need a dessert in a hurry, buy a cheesecake and pour cherry pie filling over the top.

Easy Cheesecake

2 (8 ounce) packages cream cheese, softened	2 (225 g)
½ cup sugar	100 g
½ teaspoon vanilla	2 ml
2 eggs	
1 (9 ounce) ready graham cracker piecrust	255 g

Preheat oven to 350° (175° C).

Beat cream cheese, sugar, vanilla and eggs in bowl. Pour into piecrust.

Bake for 40 minutes. Cool and serve with any pie filling. Serves 6 to 8.

No one really knows the origin of cheese, but there is archaeological evidence of cheese molds as early as 2000 BC. Basic cheese pies or cakes were thought to be a source of energy. There are some accounts that cheesecake may have been served to the athletes of the First Olympiad in Greece in 776 BC.

Very Blueberry Cheesecake

34 vanilla wafers, crushed	
6 tablespoons (¾ stick) butter, melted	85 g
1 (.3 ounce) packet unflavored gelatin	10 g
2 (8 ounce) packages cream cheese, softened	2 (225 g)
1 tablespoon lemon juice	15 ml
1 (7 ounce) jar marshmallow creme	200 g
¼ cup powdered sugar	30 g
1 (16 ounce) can blueberries, drained	455 g
1 (8 ounce) carton frozen whipped topping, thawed	225 g

Place crumbs in sprayed 9-inch (23 cm) springform pan. Pour melted butter in pan, mix well and pat down.

Soften gelatin in ¼ cup (60 ml) cold water in saucepan. Place over low heat just until it dissolves.

Combine cream cheese, lemon juice, marshmallow creme, powdered sugar and gelatin in bowl and beat until smooth.

Puree blueberries in blender. Fold whipped topping and pureed blueberries into cream cheese mixture and pour into springform pan. Refrigerate for several hours before serving. Serves 12 to 14.

Praline Cheesecake

1 ¼ cups graham cracker crumbs	130 g
¼ cup sugar	50 g
¼ cup (½ stick) butter, melted	55 g
3 (8 ounce) packages cream cheese, softened	3 (225 g)
1 ¼ cups packed dark brown sugar	275 g
2 tablespoons flour	15 g
3 eggs	
2 teaspoons vanilla	10 ml
½ cup finely chopped pecans	55 g
Pecan halves	
Maple syrup	

 Preheat oven to 350° (175° C).

 Combine crumbs, sugar and butter in bowl and press into 9-inch (23 cm) springform pan. Bake for 10 minutes.

 Beat cream cheese, brown sugar and flour in bowl on medium speed with until it blends well. Add eggs, one at a time, and mix well after each addition. Blend in vanilla, stir in pecans and pour over crust. Bake for 50 to 55 minutes.

 Loosen cake from rim of pan, but cool before removing rim of pan. Refrigerate.

 Place pecan halves around edge of cake (1 inch/2.5 cm from edge) 1 inch (2.5 cm) apart. Pour syrup over cheesecake. When you slice cheesecake, you might want to pour another teaspoon of syrup over each slice so some will run down sides. Serves 10 to 12.

Wind-in-the-Sails Cheesecake

1¼ cups graham cracker crumbs	130 g
½ cup flaked coconut	45 g
½ cup chopped pecans	55 g
2 tablespoons light brown sugar	30 g
¼ cup (½ stick) butter, melted	55 g
2 (8 ounce) packages cream cheese, softened	2 (225 g)
1 (14 ounce) can sweetened condensed milk	425 g
3 eggs	
¼ cup frozen orange juice concentrate, thawed	60 ml
1 teaspoon pineapple extract	5 ml
1 (20 ounce) can pineapple pie filling, divided	565 g
1 cup sour cream	240 g

 Preheat oven to 300° (150° C).

 Mix graham cracker crumbs, coconut, pecans, brown sugar and butter in bowl. Press firmly into 9-inch (23 cm) springform pan and set aside.

 Beat cream cheese in large bowl until fluffy. Gradually beat in sweetened condensed milk.

Continued next page...

Continued from previous page...

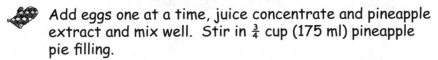

Add eggs one at a time, juice concentrate and pineapple extract and mix well. Stir in ¾ cup (175 ml) pineapple pie filling.

Pour into sprayed springform pan. Bake for 1 hour or until center sets.

Spread top with sour cream and bake for additional 5 minutes. Cool, spread remaining pineapple pie filling over cheesecake and refrigerate. Serves 10 to 12.

In 1872 a dairy farmer was trying to make Neufchatel cheese when he stumbled on cream cheese. In 1875 he packaged his cream cheese in small foil packages and sold them as Philadelphia Cream Cheese. By 1928 after the Kraft Company bought the company that owned the trademark, Philadelphia Cream Cheese continued in its foil package and was then sold nationwide.

White Chocolate Cheesecake

2 cups graham cracker crumbs	210 g
1 cup slivered almonds, finely chopped	170 g
¼ cup (½ stick) butter, softened	55 g
8 ounces white chocolate	225 g
4 (8 ounce) packages cream cheese, softened	4 (225 g)
¾ cup sugar	150 g
5 eggs	
2 tablespoons flour	15 g
1 teaspoon vanilla	5 ml
Strawberries or raspberries	
Sugar	

 Preheat oven to 275° (135° C).

Combine graham cracker crumbs, almonds and butter in bowl and mix well. Press into 10-inch springform pan. Melt white chocolate in double boiler, stir until smooth and remove from heat.

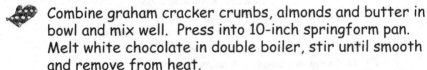 Beat cream cheese in bowl until smooth and fluffy and add sugar. Beat in eggs, one at a time, and add flour and vanilla. Mix until smooth and fold in melted white chocolate.

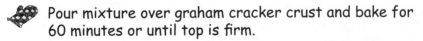 Pour mixture over graham cracker crust and bake for 60 minutes or until top is firm.

Continued next page...

Continued from previous page...

 Cool completely, cover and refrigerate overnight.

 Slice strawberries (leave raspberries whole), sprinkle on a little sugar and refrigerate overnight. To serve, remove sides of springform pan. Spoon ¼ cup (60 ml) fruit over each slice of cheesecake. You should get about 16 slices of cheesecake. Serves 12 to 16.

TIP: *The best way to slice cheesecake is to use a sharp knife, clean after each slice, then dip it in water before slicing the next piece.*

Cream cheese is an American invention that changed the way cheesecake was made and simplified the process. Today, almost all cheesecakes are made with cream cheese.

New York is known for its rich, thick cheesecake and it is famous worldwide. The secret ingredient is in the extra egg yokes added to the cream cheese.

This gives it a much richer, creamier taste than similar cheesecakes. The authentic New York cheesecake is served plain without fruit or toppings of any kind.

In addition to New York style cheesecake, Chicago is known for its version which includes sour cream. Philadelphia boasts of a creamier, lighter version than New York cheesecake. And, St. Louis is known for its rich gooey butter cake with lots of flavors and varieties.

Caramel Sauce for Cheesecake

2 cups sugar	400 g
1 ½ tablespoons light corn syrup	22 ml
2 tablespoons butter	30 g
⅔ cup whipping cream	150 ml

 Combine sugar, corn syrup, ½ cup (125 ml) water and butter in saucepan over medium heat; stir almost constantly until mixture turns light brown. Pour in whipping cream a little at a time and continue stirring until mixture gets to right consistency to pour over cheesecake.

Butter Pecan Sauce

¾ cup pecan pieces	85 g
1 - 2 tablespoons butter	15 - 30 ml
¾ cup packed brown sugar	165 g
¼ cup cornstarch	30 g
¾ cup whipping cream	175 ml

 Preheat oven to 300° (150° C). Lay pecan pieces out on baking pan and toast in oven for about 15 minutes. Remove, cool and process into small pieces, but not ground.

 Melt butter in saucepan and add brown sugar and cornstarch. Stir constantly over medium heat and cook until mixture starts to thicken.

 Add whipping cream and continue to cook until it almost boils, reduce heat and add pecan pieces. Stir until it reaches sauce consistency. Remove from heat, cool slightly and pour over cheesecake or ice cream. Makes 1 cup (250 ml).

Desserts

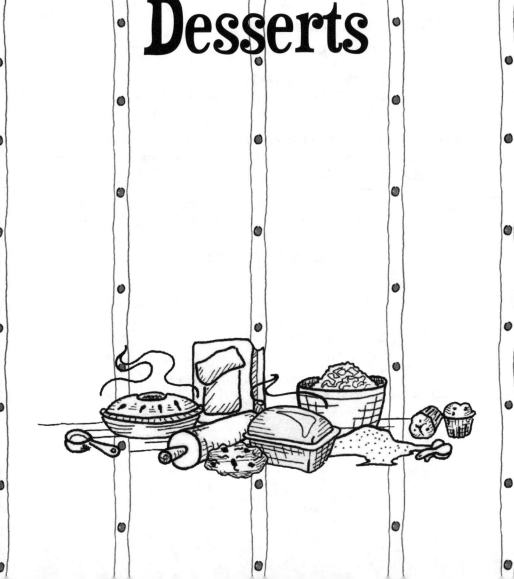

Cinnamon Souffle

1 loaf cinnamon raisin bread	455 g
1 (20 ounce) can crushed pineapple	
with juice	565 g
1 cup (2 sticks) butter, melted	225 g
½ cup sugar	100 g
5 eggs, slightly beaten	
½ cup chopped pecans	55 g

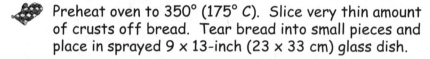 Preheat oven to 350° (175° C). Slice very thin amount of crusts off bread. Tear bread into small pieces and place in sprayed 9 x 13-inch (23 x 33 cm) glass dish.

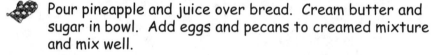 Pour pineapple and juice over bread. Cream butter and sugar in bowl. Add eggs and pecans to creamed mixture and mix well.

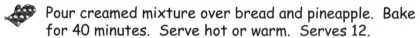 Pour creamed mixture over bread and pineapple. Bake for 40 minutes. Serve hot or warm. Serves 12.

No matter how old a mother is, she watches her middle-aged children for signs of improvement.

—Florida Scott-Maxwell

Oma's Bread Pudding

1½ cups fresh breadcrumbs	90 g
3 cups hot milk	750 ml
2 eggs, beaten	
⅔ cup sugar	135 g
1 tablespoon butter	15 ml
½ teaspoon vanilla	2 ml
½ cup chopped nuts	85 g
Whipped cream	

 Preheat oven to 350° (175° C). Combine breadcrumbs, milk, eggs, sugar, butter and ¼ teaspoon (1 ml) salt in bowl. Mix well.

 Add vanilla and nuts. Turn mixture into sprayed baking dish.

 Bake for 35 to 40 minutes or until firm. Serve with whipped cream. Serves 6.

 You do not really understand something unless you can explain it to your grandmother.

—Albert Einstein

Strawberry-Fruit Pizza

1 (18 ounce) package sugar cookie dough	510 g
1 (8 ounce) package cream cheese, softened	225 g
½ cup sugar	100 g
1 pint strawberries or raspberries	715 g/490 g
⅓ cup strawberry jelly for glaze	105 g

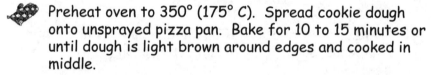

Preheat oven to 350° (175° C). Spread cookie dough onto unsprayed pizza pan. Bake for 10 to 15 minutes or until dough is light brown around edges and cooked in middle.

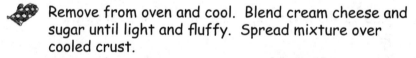

Remove from oven and cool. Blend cream cheese and sugar until light and fluffy. Spread mixture over cooled crust.

Arrange strawberries on top. Warm strawberry jelly and brush over strawberries with pastry brush. Refrigerate before serving. Makes about 2 dozen pieces.

It's better to find the whole worm in your apple than it is to find half a worm.

Baked Custard

3 cups milk	750 ml
3 eggs	
¾ cup sugar	150 g
1 teaspoon vanilla	5 ml
Ground cinnamon	

 Preheat oven to 350° (175° C). Scald milk in saucepan. Beat eggs in bowl and add sugar, ¼ teaspoon (1 ml) salt and vanilla.

Pour scalded milk slowly into egg mixture. Pour into 2-quart (2 L) baking dish and sprinkle a little cinnamon on top.

Bake in hot water bath for 45 minutes. Serves 6.

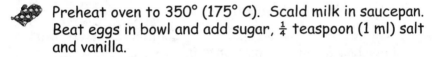

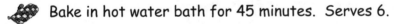

Anger is one letter short of danger.
—Eleanor Roosevelt

Crispy-Topped Pudding

2 cups flaked coconut	170 g
1 cup (2 sticks) butter, melted	230 g
2 cups flour	240 g
½ cup sugar	100 g
2 (22 ounce) containers chocolate	
or vanilla pudding	2 (625 g)

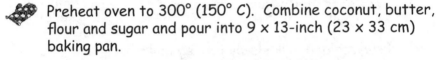

Preheat oven to 300° (150° C). Combine coconut, butter, flour and sugar and pour into 9 x 13-inch (23 x 33 cm) baking pan.

Bake for 45 minutes, stirring every 10 minutes. (Mixture will be crumbly.) Remove from oven and set aside half mixture for topping.

Spread pudding over crumbs and smooth; sprinkle remaining crumb mixture on top. Refrigerate before serving. Serves about 6 to 8.

It is incumbent upon every generation to pay its own debts as it goes. A principle which if acted on would save one-half the wars of the world.

—Thomas Jefferson

Pavlova

3 large egg whites
1 cup sugar   200 g
1 teaspoon vanilla   5 ml
2 teaspoons white vinegar   10 ml
3 tablespoons cornstarch   45 ml
Whipped cream
Fresh fruit

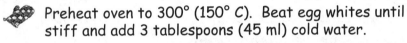 Preheat oven to 300° (150° C). Beat egg whites until stiff and add 3 tablespoons (45 ml) cold water.

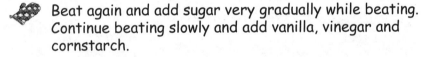 Beat again and add sugar very gradually while beating. Continue beating slowly and add vanilla, vinegar and cornstarch.

On parchment-covered baking sheet, draw 9-inch (23 cm) circle (use a pie pan to draw circle) and mound mixture within circle. Bake for 45 minutes. Leave in oven to cool.

To serve, peel paper from bottom while sliding pavlova onto serving plate. Cover with whipped cream and top with assortment of fresh fruit such as kiwi, strawberries, blueberries, etc. Serves 6 to 8.

Let us have faith that right makes might; and in that faith let us to the end dare to do our duty as we understand it. —*Abraham Lincoln*

Chocolate-Cherry Pavlova

You can alter the flavor of basic Pavlova with liqueur and fruit to create a dessert that is just as delicious and with a personality all its own. In this version, chocolate and cherries are the featured ingredients, set off with a chocolate liqueur and whipping cream.

5 egg whites	
2 cups sugar, divided	400 g
1 teaspoon vinegar	5 ml
1½ cups whipping cream	375 ml
¼ cup creme de cacao liqueur	60 ml
1 (15 ounce) can cherries, well drained	425 g
1 (3.5 ounce) chocolate bar, grated	100 g

Preheat oven to 250° (120° C). Prepare baking sheet by lining with foil or parchment paper.

Use bowl or round baking dish as template and draw 10-inch (25 cm) circle on foil or paper. Set aside. Beat egg whites at high speed until soft peaks form.

Gradually add 1¼ cups (300 g) sugar and continue to beat until mixture is white and glossy with soft peaks, about 10 minutes.

Add vinegar and beat at high speed for additional 5 minutes.

Continued next page...

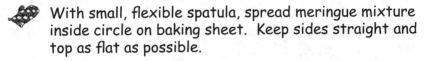

Continued from previous page...

With small, flexible spatula, spread meringue mixture inside circle on baking sheet. Keep sides straight and top as flat as possible.

Draw spatula up sides of meringue circle to form "ribs". (This will give a finished look and add strength once meringue is baked.)

Bake for 1 hour. Turn oven off and leave pavlova in oven for additional 2 hours.

When ready to assemble, carefully remove meringue base from foil or paper and place on serving plate.

Beat whipping cream with remaining $\frac{1}{4}$ cup (50 g) sugar and creme de cacao until soft peaks form. Spread whipped cream mixture over surface of meringue base.

Arrange cherries attractively on top and garnish with grated chocolate. Serves 6 to 8.

I would rather try to carry 10 plastic grocery bags in each hand than make two trips to bring in my groceries.

Fruit Fajitas

1 (20 ounce) can fruit pie filling	565 g
10 flour tortillas	
1½ cups sugar	300 g
¾ cup (1½ sticks) butter	170 g
1 teaspoon almond flavoring	5 ml

 Divide pie filling equally on tortillas, roll and place in 9 x 13-inch (23 x 33 cm) baking dish.

Combine 2 cups (500 ml) water, sugar and butter in saucepan and bring to a boil.

Add almond flavoring and pour mixture over flour tortillas. Place in refrigerator and let soak for 1 to 24 hours.

When ready to bake, preheat oven to 350° (175° C).

Bake for 20 to 25 minutes until brown and bubbly. Serves 6 to 8.

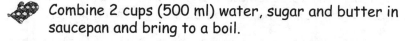

When you go on a diet, are you a poor loser?

Treasure-Filled Apples

6 medium, tart apples
½ cup sugar   100 g
¼ cup Red Hots® candies   55 g
¼ teaspoon ground cinnamon   1 ml

 Preheat oven to 350° (175° C). Cut tops off apples
and set aside. Core apples to within ½ inch (1.2 cm) of
bottom. Place in sprayed 8-inch (20 cm) baking dish.

Combine sugar, candies and cinnamon in bowl and spoon
2 tablespoons (30 ml) into each apple. Replace the tops.
Spoon any remaining sugar mixture over apples.

Bake for 30 to 35 minutes or until apples are tender.
Baste occasionally. Serves 6.

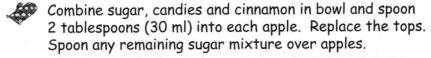

*A hard thing about business is minding
your own.*
                              —Anonymous

Common Baking Pans

Round Baking Pans

Size	Volume
Muffin Cup:	
2¾ x 1½-inch (7 x 4 cm)	scant ½ cup (125 ml)
Pie Pan:	
9 x 1½-inch (23 x 4 cm)	5 cups (1.2 L)
Cake:	
8 x 1½-inch (20 x 4 cm)	4 cups (950 ml)
8 x 2-inch (20 x 5 cm)	6 cups (1.4 L)
9 x 1½-inch (23 x 4 cm)	6 cups (1.4 L)
10 x 2-inch (25 x 5 cm)	11 cups (2.6 L)
Bundt:	
9 x 3-inch (23 x 8 cm)	9 cups (2.1 L)
10 x 3½-inch (25 x 9 cm)	12 cups (2.8 L)
Tube:	
9 x 3-inch (23 x 8 cm)	12 cups (2.8 L)
10 x 4-inch (25 x 10 cm)	16 cups (3.8 L)
Springform:	
9 x 2½-inch (23 x 6 cm)	12 cups (2.8 L)

Common Baking Pans

Square and Rectangular Baking Pans

Size	Volume
Square:	
8 x 8 x 1½-inch (20 x 20 x 4 cm)	6 cups (1.4 L)
8 x 8 x 2-inch (20 x 20 x 5 cm)	8 cups (1.9 L)
9 x 9 x 1½-inch (23 x 23 x 4 cm)	8 cups (1.9 L)
9 x 9 x 2-inch (23 x 23 x 5 cm)	10 cups (2.4 L)
Rectangular:	
7 x 11 x 2-inch (18 x 28 x 5 cm)	6 cups (1.4 L)
9 x 13 x 2-inch (23 x 33 x 5 cm)	14 cups (3.3 L)
Loaf:	
8 x 4 x 2½-inch (20 x 10 x 6 cm)	4 cups (950 ml)
9 x 5 x 3-inch (23 x 13 x 8 cm)	8 cups (1.9 L)

Bibliography

A Texas Hill Country Cookbook. Blue-Lake-Deerhaven Cookbook Committee.
    Marble Falls, Texas. 1976.

Agriculture in Pennsylvania. Charles Meck. Countryman Press; 1999.

Backroads of Pennsylvania. Marcus Schneck. Voyageur Press. 2003.

Brilliant Food Tips and Cooking Tricks, USA. Joachim, David. Rodale, Inc., 2001.

Century in Food: American Fads and Favorites. Beverly Bundy; Collector Press: Portland; 2002.

Classical Southern Cooking. Damon Lee Fowler. Gibbs Smith. Layton, Utah. 2008.

Easy Cooking with 5 Ingredients. Barbara C. Jones. Cookbook Resources.
    Highland Village, Texas 2002.

Fashionable Foods: Seven Decades of Food Fads. Sylvia Lovegren. McMillan. New York. 1999.

Good Housekeeping Woman's Home Companion. Curtis. 1909.

Leaving Home. Louise P. Grace, R.D. Cookbook Resources. Highland Village, Texas. 2000.

Louisiana, The Pelican State. Gildart, Leslie S. World Almanac Library, 2002.

Michigan Spirit of the Land. Kathy Jo and Ed Wargin. Voyageur Press. 2005.

Michigan: A History of The Wolverine State. Willis Dunbar. William B. Eerdman's Publishing
    Company. 1995.

Miss Sadie's Southern Cooking. Cookbook Resources, LLC, Highland Village, Texas. 2005.

Mother's Recipes. Jones, Sheryn and Barbara. Cookbook Resources.
    Highland Village, Texas 2000.

Oxford Companion to Food. Alan Davidson. Oxford University Press. Oxford.

Oxford Encyclopedia of Food and Drink in America. Volume 2.

Pennsylvania Dutch Designs. Rebecca McKillip. Stemmer House Publishers. 1983

Pennsylvania: A History of the Commonwealth. Randall Miller. Pennsylvania State University
    Press. 2002.

Roadside Attractions: Cool Cafes, Souvenir Stands, Route 66. Brian Butko.
    Stackpole Books. 2002.

Soul Food: Classic Cuisine from the Deep South. Sheila Ferguson. Grove Press. New York, New
    York. 1989.

Southern Food: At Home, on the Road, in History. John Egerton, Ann Bleidt Egerton.
    Alfred A. Knopf, Inc. 1947. University of North Carolina Press. 1993.

The Dictionary of American Food and Drink. Mariani, John F. New York, New York. Hearst Books,
    1994.

The Encyclopedia of Herbs, Spices and Flavorings. Ortiz, Elisabeth Lambert.
    New York, New York: BK Publishing Inc. 1992.

The Ethnic Food Lover's Companion. Eve Zibart, Menasha Ridge Press.
    Birmingham, Alabama. 2001.

The Glory of Southern Cooking. James Villas. John Wiley & Sons. Hoboken, New Jersey. 2007.

*The Heritage of Southern Cooking: An Inspired Tour of Southern Cuisine Including Regional
    Specialties, Heirloom Favorites and Original Dishes.* Camille Glenn. Black Dog Leventhal.
    New York, New York, 2007

The Joy of Cooking. Rombauer, Irma S. and Becker, Marion Rombauer. New York, New York.
    Bobbs-Merrill Co., Inc. 1975.

The New Basics Cookbook. Rossos, Julie and Lukins, Sheila. New York. Workman
    Publishing Co., Inc. 1989.

The New Food Lovers Companion. Herbst, Sharon Tyler. Hauppauge, New York.
    Barron's Educational Series, Inc. 2001.

Index

C

D

E

Pineapple

Pies, Tarts, Cobblers and Cheesecakes

Q

R

S

T

V

W

Y

Z

Cookbooks Published by Cookbook Resources, LLC
Bringing Family and Friends to the Table

The Best 1001 Short, Easy Recipes
1001 Slow Cooker Recipes
1001 Short, Easy, Inexpensive Recipes
1001 Fast Easy Recipes
1001 America's Favorite Recipes
Easy Slow Cooker Cookbook
Busy Woman's Slow Cooker Recipes
Busy Woman's Quick & Easy Recipes
365 Easy Soups and Stews
365 Easy Chicken Recipes
365 Easy One-Dish Recipes
365 Easy Soup Recipes
365 Easy Vegetarian Recipes
365 Easy Casserole Recipes
365 Easy Pasta Recipes
365 Easy Slow Cooker Recipes
Super Simple Cupcake Recipes
Leaving Home Cookbook and Survival Guide
Essential 3-4-5 Ingredient Recipes
Ultimate 4 Ingredient Cookbook
Easy Cooking with 5 Ingredients
The Best of Cooking with 3 Ingredients
Easy Diabetic Recipes
Ultimate 4 Ingredient Diabetic Cookbook
4-Ingredient Recipes for 30-Minute Meals
Cooking with Beer
The Washington Cookbook
The Pennsylvania Cookbook
The California Cookbook
Best-Loved New England Recipes
Best-Loved Canadian Recipes
Best-Loved Recipes from the Pacific Northwest
Easy Homemade Preserves (Handbook with Photos)
Garden Fresh Recipes (Handbook with Photos)
Chocolate Explosion! Cookbook (Handbook with Photos)
Milkshakes and Coffee Concoctions (Handbook with Photos)
Easy Slow Cooker Recipes (Handbook with Photos)

Cool Smoothies (Handbook with Photos)
Easy Cupcake Recipes (Handbook with Photos)
Easy Soup Recipes (Handbook with Photos)
Classic Tex-Mex and Texas Cooking
Best-Loved Southern Recipes
Classic Southwest Cooking
Miss Sadie's Southern Cooking
Classic Pennsylvania Dutch Cooking
The Quilters' Cookbook
Healthy Cooking with 4 Ingredients
Trophy Hunter's Wild Game Cookbook
Recipe Keeper
Simple Old-Fashioned Baking
Quick Fixes with Cake Mixes
Kitchen Keepsakes & More Kitchen Keepsakes
Cookbook 25 Years
Texas Longhorn Cookbook
Gifts for the Cookie Jar
All New Gifts for the Cookie Jar
The Big Bake Sale Cookbook
Quick and Easy Family Baking
Easy One-Dish Meals
Easy Potluck Recipes
Easy Casseroles Cookbook
Easy Desserts
Sunday Night Suppers
Easy Church Suppers
365 Easy Meals
Gourmet Cooking with 5 Ingredients
Muffins In A Jar
A Little Taste of Texas
A Little Taste of Texas II
Ultimate Gifts for the Cookie Jar

cookbook
resources LLC

www.cookbookresources.com
Toll-Free 866-229-2665
Your Ultimate Source for Easy Cookbooks

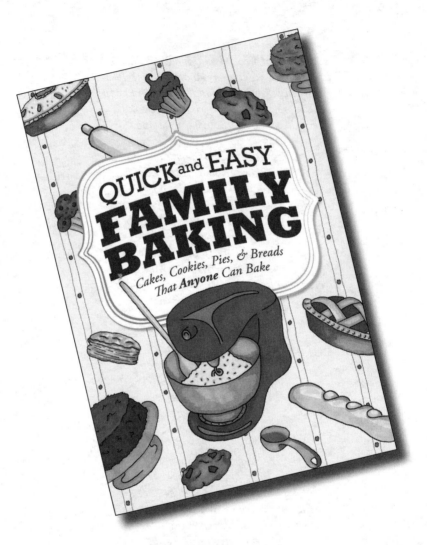

QUICK and **EASY**
FAMILY
BAKING
Cakes, Cookies, Pies, & Breads
*That **Anyone** Can Bake*

cookbook
resources LLC
www.cookbookresources.com
Toll-Free 866-229-2665
Your Ultimate Source for Easy Cookbooks